THE BIG BOOK OF
Jewish
CONSPIRACIES

THE BIG BOOK OF
JeWISH
CONSPIRACIES

David Deutsch and
Joshua Neuman

Editors of **Heeb: THE NEW JEW REVIEW**

 ST. MARTIN'S GRIFFIN ᴍ NEW YORK

www.stmartins.com

Images page xvi, 8, 19, 39, 56, 65, 69, 100, 113, 124, 144, 154, 181, 188, 202, 207, 218, 227, 235, 250, 254 by Allan Mietla.

Images page 26, 34, 50, 93, 107, 127, 139, 191 by Jesse Brown.

Images page 84, 158, 240 by Cliff Mott.

Image page 166 by Seth Olenick.

Library of Congress Cataloging-in-Publication Data

Deutsch, David.
    The big book of Jewish conspiracies / David Deutsch and Joshua Neuman.—1st St. Martin's Griffin ed.
        p. cm.
    ISBN 0-312-33439-7
    EAN 978-0312-33439-0
        1. Antisemitism—Fiction. 2. Jews—Persecutions—Fiction. 3. Conspiracies—Fiction. 4. Satire. I. Neuman, Joshua. II. Title.

PJ5055.19.E77B54 2005
892.4'37—dc22

2004051468

First Edition: April 2005

10 9 8 7 6 5 4 3 2 1

David Deutsch:

To my parents, Zvi and Sue, for making me believe I could be a writer, and to my wife, Aliza, for helping me prove it

Joshua Neuman:

To my eternal coconspirator, Jonathan Neuman

CONTENTS

INTRODUCTION

In 2001, a pack of bipedal monsters crashed planes full of human beings into the World Trade Center. And throughout much of the world, the response wasn't to denounce the murderers or mourn the dead—it was to blame the Jews. When we read the delusional pronouncements coming from such diverse sources as our esteemed allies in the Saudi royal family to the poet laureate of New Jersey,[1] we felt it would have been absurd if it weren't so vile. And then we thought that we were right the first time. It's just absurd.

We decided to write a book, one that would chronicle Jewish conspiracy theories throughout the ages and try to capture the utter ridiculousness of their logic. Some of the conspiracy theories that follow will no doubt sound familiar. They are the greatest hits of Jew hatred, which have become part of the vernacular of anti-Jewish thought. Others will not sound familiar, as they are merely the product of our imaginations. Though we shiver at the thought that some idiot somewhere will come across a copy of this book and think he has unearthed a piece of serious scholarship, we take comfort in the notion that throughout our years in grade school, high school, college, and grad school, very few have confused our writings with anything remotely resembling serious scholarship. Although this book is satire, completely made up and in no way intended to be taken as truth, we would like to take this occasion to acknowledge that the subjects satirized in this book are indeed serious ones.

There, we've acknowledged it.

---

1. We always felt that they should have extended Joe Piscopo's term for life.

* * *

If you're expecting a scholarly account of the history of Jewish persecution in Western civilization, then you should probably stop reading right now because this book treats even the most unfathomable horrors of history with the earnestness that Mel Brooks treats the Third Reich in *The Producers*.[2] If you believe that such subjects should always be dealt with in a sensitive and serious manner, this book will leave you horrified, or at least somewhat nauseated. We might not endorse this point of view, but we can respect it. But just think about this. We don't know what goes on in the minds of the people who really believe in Jewish conspiracies, but we feel pretty sure of one thing: They don't like to have those beliefs laughed at. So if you believe that living well is the best revenge, then read on and enjoy as we take you on a trip through Western civilization like you've never been taken before.

In this book, you will learn how the Jews poisoned the wells of Europe during medieval times to bring about the beginning of the bottled water industry; how a Berlin pharmacist engineered the First World War; that Reuven Krochmal changed his name to Ray Kroc as part of his plan to make gentile men as doughy as himself. You will learn about the invisible hand[3] that has secretly steered thousands of years of history. Among our conspirators we will find the usual suspects (arms merchants, moneylenders, media moguls) but also the unexpected (hobos, divorce lawyers, and fraternity brothers). Our conspiracies are a proverbial celebration of Jewish diversity, featuring, among others, a urologist from upstate New York, an ancient Ethiopian stand-up comic, and the wife of Imperial China's premier kosher restaurateur. Most will be people, like wrestling coach Sheldon the Maccabee, adman Herman

---

2. And we don't even offer any snappy musical numbers.
3. Adam Smith knew about the invisible hand; he just didn't know that it belonged to an invisible Jew.

LeWine, or Dallas hatmaker Isaac Grunboim, who were left out of history, while others, like Leonardo Da Vinci, Ben Franklin, and *The Love Boat*'s Bernie Kopell, you might already be acquainted with from other contexts. You will learn that Jewish conspiracies are conceived in the most diverse of settings: from the predictable (a meeting among Hollywood's major players), to the unexpected (over coffee and strudel in a living room in Frankfurt), to the downright surreal (a bar mitzvah at the Mombassa Marriott in Kenya). Finally, you will find that Jewish conspiracies are fueled by a mosaic of motives both great and small—greed, of course (the Crusades), as well as jealousy (the Crucifixion) and sexual frustration (1492), but also by the desires for freedom (Hanukkah), justice (Chinese Revolution), and love (homosexuality).

As for the methods that Jewish conspirators employ, well, why spoil the fun and tell you?

We would love it if this book helped stem the flow of anti-Semitic conspiracy theories. Alas, we can make no such promise. But while we may not be able to stop them from spreading, maybe, just maybe, with this book, we can at least get our own small share of the profits.

Two gentiles talk to one another, it's a conversation;
two Jews, it's a conspiracy.
—The Authors

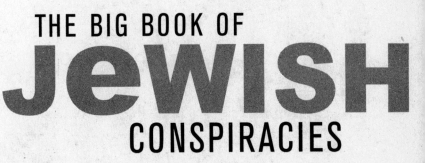

THE BIG BOOK OF
JeWISH
CONSPIRACIES

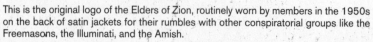

This is the original logo of the Elders of Zion, routinely worn by members in the 1950s on the back of satin jackets for their rumbles with other conspiratorial groups like the Freemasons, the Illuminati, and the Amish.

CHAPTER ONE

IN THE BEGINNING

The fall 2003 meeting of the Elders of Zion[1] was taking place, and the members were not happy. Ever since 9/11, the rumor mill had been working overtime, cranking out Jewish conspiracies. You had seemingly the whole Arab world claiming that the Jews were responsible for the attack on the World Trade Center.[2] You had the prime minister of Malaysia saying that the Jews controlled the world. And in Egypt you had an extremely successful soap opera about the elders themselves taking the number-one spot in the ratings from *Sheikh Ishaq Fulminates Against the Zionist Entity*, the popular Saudi cooking show.

> **In Egypt you had an extremely successful soap opera about the elders themselves taking the number-one spot in the ratings from *Sheikh Ishaq Fulminates Against the Zionist Entity*, the popular Saudi cooking show.**

"I don't understand it," grumbled Abe Foxman from the Anti-Defamation League. "All this stuff is so defamatory, and we keep being anti it, and it just isn't working. How many high school students do we have to run through our sensitivity training courses before the scourge of defamation is finally defeated?"

"We could set up a new museum on the Mall dedicated to countering conspiracy theories," offered Paul Wolfowitz, the Washington, D.C., rep, who had taken time from planning the proliferation of

---

1. The Elders of Zion began as a synagogue bowling team in nineteenth-century Prague. It soon came to dominate the Bohemian Division, then the whole Austro-Hungarian League, and then...well, you know.
2. And Amiri Baraka, the poet laureate of New Jersey, working out his issues with his Jewish ex-wife by doing the same.

soft-serve ice cream stands in Iraq. "You know, throw in a few anti-Catholic or antigay conspiracy theories to make it seem multiculti, and call it something like 'The Museum of Conspiratorial Intoler-ance'?"

"No," said Noam Chomsky for higher education, talking around the Big Mac he was eating. "The shvartzers would still complain that the Jews got another museum, and it's not like the one we have is working so good. I think we should create a new discipline, called 'Conspiracy Studies', endow a few chairs at the major universities, and eventually it will become a graduation requirement at most schools."

"That takes too long," interjected Thomas Friedman, there for print journalism. "We've got to do something *now*. I suggest a se-ries of investigative pieces—"

He was interrupted by Dr. Jay Zitzfleysch, the eminent proctolo-gist (as eminent as a proctologist gets) representing the concerns of the medical profession. "Look, we need to think out of the box. We've got the know-how; why don't we just put special transmitters in people's rectums that cause them to defecate uncontrollably whenever they say anything about Jewish conspiracies? We'll do it to every man who gets a colonoscopy."

"But that's only going to get the men over fifty, we've got to think of the *kids*," said Abe, wringing his hands.

Alan Dershowitz, the legal field's solon-in-residence spoke up. "Everybody relax. Why are we coming up with all this fancy nonsense, when all we have to do is make it against the law, and sue the hell out of anybody who so much as thinks about the Elders of Zion. As my predecessor as the legal representa-tive to this body might have put it, 'If you ban the lie, they will not try.'"

"Excuse me for being presumptuous, but I've been learning the laws of slander, and it's given me an idea," said Jerry Springer for broadcast journalism, adjusting his yarmulke as he lifted his head from the volume of Talmud he had been studying. "Why don't we have some reality-TV shows like *When Anti-Semites Attack!* We'll give them the whole treatment—ominous music, slow motion, dramatic reenactments with really sinister-looking actors playing guys like Farrakhan—you don't mind, do you, Louis?"

"Not at all, my brother," said the former Louis F. Kahn, there for the purpose of making sure the black man was kept down and the white man distracted.[3]

"That's just stupid," objected Thomas, who resented both having to endure a professional association with Jerry, as well as the way that the latter always managed to get the last cherry Danish, leaving him with the prune.

"Ah, maybe you understand the camel jockeys, Friedman," sneered Noam, slamming down the two-liter bottle of Coke he was drinking. "But Jerry knows the American people. I like what he's saying."

The group began squabbling among themselves, ignoring Jerry's pleas that they stop. Finally, a loud belch echoed through the room.

"Noam, please have some sense of decorum," chided Jerry.

"It wasn't him this time, it was me."

All eyes turned to the man sitting in the seat held by the entertainment industry.

"I know I'm not a regular," apologized Soupy Sales. "But Sandler asked me to fill in while he's sick, so I guess I've got as much right to speak as anybody. Don't you think it's time we moved in a completely new direction?"

"That's what I was saying," sniffed Jay.

"No, you're still talking about fighting conspiracy theories—I think we should embrace them."

"What do you mean 'embrace them'?" queried Barbra Streisand for the music industry.

"If you can't beat 'em, join 'em. Look, you're some schmuck who

---

3. And in a pinch, the former calypso singer oversaw the interests of the music business.

lives in your parents' basement. You've got no job, no girlfriend, no life," said Soupy. "You don't want to admit you're a schmuck, so you blame the Jews. 'It's their fault people think I'm a schmuck!' And when you paint a swastika, or rant about the Elders of Zion, what happens? I'll tell you what happens: All of you have a conniption and act like you're about to be shoved in an oven. So how does the schmuck feel? Like a million bucks, because maybe he has no job and lives in a basement, but he can make the most powerful men in the country dance anytime he misspells some graffiti on a synagogue wall. So let's not play the part they've written for us. Instead of playing Ophelia—'Methinks the lady doth protest too much'— every time some schmuck says the Jews control the world, let's make a joke out of it."

"And what's that going to do?" said Thomas.

"It's going to take away their weapon. Look, next time some schmuck says, 'The Jews are behind 9/11,' we say, 'Sure, *and* let's not forget about the JFK assassination.' Schmuck says, 'The Jews control Hollywood,' and we say, 'Sure, and the Republican Party.'"

"But how does that help us? We *are* responsible for all those things," said Barbra.

"Of course...but not the way we're going to tell them we are. By the time we're done, the idea of a Jewish conspiracy is going to be a joke, and so will these schmucks."

"Intriguing," mused Jerry. "How do you propose to do this? A TV special featuring you, I suppose?"

"Look, if somebody offers, I won't say no. But I was thinking that a book would work. A book about Jewish conspiracies."

The men from the various sectors of the financial world had, up to this point, kept their counsel. Now, however, their point man, Alan Greenspan, spoke up.

"Soupy, I like it. And you know what's great about it? Unlike most of the lame schemes you guys always come up with—and honestly, how many Holocaust museums do we need?—this one may actually make money. I mean, look at the sales for the *Protocols of the Elders of Zion* in the Arab world alone—and that's only one conspiracy! If we can hit half those numbers, it'll be a killing."

Most of those gathered muttered their consent. Only Abe continued to object. "I'm a little concerned about what was just suggested. What about those who read this book and take it seriously? Have we thought about what this will do to the kids?"

"No, this is perfect," rejoined Paul. "It's like a Trojan Horse. Let somebody quote this book as authoritative, and you can immediately dismiss everything else he says. But," he cautioned, "we need to keep our distance, like we did with *Gentleman's Agreement*. What's our most goyish publishing house?"

They turned to Elizabeth Wurtzel from the publishing world. She thought for a minute.

"St. Martin's," she finally offered. With no objection, she continued. "We also need the right person to write it, somebody who *nobody* could take seriously, so that there's no chance that there'll be any real blowback."

"Don't worry," replied Soupy. "I know just the guys…"

CHAPTER TWO

LET MY PEOPLE GO . . .
ON LONGER LUNCH BREAKS

The royal gift bearer presented Pharaoh with the can of assorted nuts sent by Moses, bowed low, and began to drag himself out backward, licking the ground so as to leave no trace of his presence that may pollute the ambience surrounding the god-king. Pharaoh lifted the gift and smiled. The previous day's negotiations had gone late into the night, but it seemed like some real progress had been made, and that the labor dispute with the Hebrews could be resolved without a strike. Surely, this gift from Moses—who knew well how his erstwhile brother loved nuts—boded well for the next round of negotiations. Pharaoh opened the can—and nearly had a heart attack, as the asps that had been tightly coiled in the can popped out. Although the royal exterminator confirmed that the asps were duds—their fangs had been removed—Pharaoh, who had a fear of snakes (of which Moses was equally well aware), was not placated. To make matters worse, since no one was permitted to witness the fear of the god-king and live, Pharaoh's favorite royal gift bearer had to be killed by the royal exterminator, who was in turn slain by the mummified corpse of the royal gift bearer brought back to life by the mystical power of the tanna leaves. The leaves were then withheld, leaving the mummy as immobile as the exterminator, and both were fed to the royal scarabs, which were then fed to the royal asps, which gave Pharaoh the willies all over again.

As they had for several days, Moses and Aaron appeared for the discussions, and Moses boomed out in his stentorian voice, "Pharaoh, let my people go . . . on longer lunch breaks!" Today, however, Pharaoh was hardly conciliatory, and, without explanation (he could hardly admit the affair with the snakes), ordered Moses and Aaron from his presence. Stunned by this reaction, Moses said nothing as they left the palace. Aaron turned to him. "Hate to say I told you so...but are you ready for Plan B?" Moses set his powerful jaw, slowly nodded his head, and, steely gaze staring off into the distance, didn't notice the barest hint of a smile that crossed Aaron's lips.

The story really begins several decades earlier, a time when the Hebrew population of Goshen was booming. They'd arrived a few hundred years earlier, a mere seventy heads, and now numbered several million. Things had gotten out of hand, and something had to be done.[1] Thus, Pharaoh ordered Jewish male infants to be removed from the population. In theory, they were to be killed, but as hieroglyphics testify, the Egyptian elite had considerable difficulty moving their limbs at anything other than right angles—probably as a result of a vitamin D deficiency—and thus their efforts at copulation were often painful failures. Jewish boys increasingly came to be viewed the way that Chinese girls are today—by this we mean, as prospective adoptees for yuppie couples, not as prospective mail-order brides for creepy singles. Thus, when a boy, Morris, was born into the home of Amram the Levite, it was with a heavy heart that they had to send him away, but at least they

Jewish boys increasingly came to be viewed the way that Chinese girls are today—by this we mean, as prospective adoptees for yuppie couples, not as prospective mail-order brides for creepy singles.

had the satisfaction of knowing he would be well cared for. They had no idea *how* well cared for—Morris was actually taken in by the princess, and renamed Moses, after her grandfather.[2]

---

1. The phrase "letting things get out of hand" actually stems from this period, and specifically referred to the problem of Hebrew overpopulation. Judah's son Onan, in order to limit family size, had kept his "thing" in his hand, thereby keeping his wife barren. It was only when things got out of hand (and into other body parts) that the population boomed beyond control.
2. His name was actually Thutmoses, but let's face it, even during his reign, it was sort of a sissy name.

Moses' upbringing was like any other child's in the royal family, and he gave little thought to his Hebrew lineage. His grades weren't good enough to get in, but when his father made a big donation to the Osiris Center for Student Afterlife, Moses went off to Luxor University. It was his second semester, and to fulfill his tribal studies requirement, he took a course in Hebrew history. For the first time, he started to see himself as a Hebrew, and as he took a new look at himself, he began looking at Egyptian society in a

Discovered in 1997 in a Hyksos archive that preserved papyri whose derogatory account of native Egyptian royalty makes them virtually priceless, this papyrus features the bright colors and realistic style indicative of the Neo-Senephrin school. Senepher II was the most skilled artist of the Old Kingdom, who achieved great success drawing sex manuals that illustrated complex geometric designs that would allow stiff-limbed Egyptians to achieve coitus.

whole new light as well. Newly militant, he saw a group of Hebrew workers on campus striking against their overseers, and he felt that his place was with them, not the other students. He dropped out of school and began a personal quest to discover his roots.[3] He eventually discovered his birth family, including his brother, Aaron, who was a leader of the United Hebrew Trades, the largest Hebrew labor union in Goshen.

Aaron's goal, as he saw it, was to work Hebrew and Egyptian alike for as much grain as his storehouses could hold, and he saw Moses as the key to the silo. With his brain behind Moses' regal bearing and inspirational passion to pursue justice, Aaron felt that there was no limit to how far he could work this shakedown. He just had to stir up the slaves to the point where they would go on strike, crippling the Egyptian economy. Aaron would also engage in some industrial sabotage, the idea being to so threaten the Egyptian economy that Pharaoh would be willing to pay anything to end the chaos. The key was making the sabotage seem like divine acts, allowing Pharaoh—who had previously refused concessions since it was unseemly for the god-king to give in to commoners—to save face by claiming it was the will of the gods. And Moses was so righteous and high-minded that he would never suspect his brother of duplicity. When they first began making demands on Pharaoh, they immediately attracted the sort of press that Aaron could never have hoped to achieve on his own; the problem was that it was too successful, and Pharaoh—who could rationalize conceding to Moses since he had been a member of the royal family—immediately seemed on the verge of making unprecedented concessions, which might have been great for the slaves, but wouldn't have done much for Aaron's bottom line. Something had to be done to sabotage the negotiations, without making it look like he was behind it; hence, the can of snakes.

---

3. Like many Jewish college kids searching for identity, he dabbled in black culture, which explains his Kushite wife.

The strike was on, and Aaron was free to move to the next phase. For months, the Hebrew Butchers' Guild, which normally shipped the forbidden blood they drained to a Sarmatian blood cult, had been stockpiling it. In the middle of the night, a group from the Hebrew Carters and Drawers of Water dumped the stockpile into the Nile, just south of the palace. The next morning at dawn, Pharaoh and his retinue went out to make offerings to the god of the river, and Moses and Aaron were waiting. Moses demanded that Pharaoh give in, or he would smite the river god. Pharaoh sneered, Moses smote, and then Pharaoh laughed, for nothing happened. All the Egyptians were chuckling over Moses' failure, when the current began to bring in the blood poured the previous night, and the laughter died in their throats. That, in and of itself, was not too bad, but it was pretty painful when the little pyramids were built in their throats to mark their chuckles' graves. It looked like a big win for the Hebrew negotiating team, and Aaron led Moses away to let their awesome display of power sink in.

> **All the Egyptians were chuckling over Moses' failure, when the current began to bring in the blood poured the previous night, and the laughter died in their throats. That, in and of itself, was not too bad, but it was pretty painful when the little pyramids were built in their throats to mark their chuckles' graves.**

In the weeks to come, the country ground to a halt as workers throughout the land walked off the job. Moreover, the acts of sabotage, exacerbated both by the strike and by Pharaoh's earlier slaying of the royal exterminator, continued. Nobody was cleaning the streets, or manning the laundries, or keeping an eye on the heavens for the arrival of locusts, so it wasn't difficult to make the "miraculous" appearance of frogs, fleas, and other vermin into major crises. Given the poor sanitation conditions, disease began to spread among both man and animal, leading to the death of most of

Egypt's cattle, including their sacred bulls.[4] Moses continued to beseech Pharaoh, but as long as the divine sabotage continued, his advisors warned him not to give in to pressure, and to refuse negotiations until the Hebrews called off their God. Just in case, they instructed him to seek foreign laborers who could replace the Hebrews.

Things soon reached their denouement. The royal astrologers had been distracted by their fleas and festering boils, and hadn't noticed that the signs in the heavens pointed to a great blackening of the sky. Just a few hours before the eclipse was set to begin, Aaron got a report that it was about to start, and he rushed Moses down to warn Pharaoh that if their demands weren't met, darkness would descend upon the land. Pharaoh threw Moses out, and the darkness came. By a fortuitous happenstance, it didn't afflict Goshen. That night, the Hebrews sat down to enjoy a festive meal to thank God for allowing the disasters of the recent weeks to pass over them. While they were doing so, a wondrous thing happened—all throughout Egypt, those Hebrew children who had been raised as Egyptians, and who had followed the rise of Moses with such interest, rose as in a mass and went to rejoin their brethren and sistren up in Goshen, which due to the blackout was the only place in Egypt where the bars were still open.

Presuming that Pharaoh was suitably softened up by all that had happened, and being pushed by his own people to end the strike, Aaron went privately to meet with Pharaoh and offered to settle, at terms not unfavorable to the Egyptians, for a considerable donation to the Aaron ben Amram retirement fund. Here, however, is where Aaron was a victim of his own success. The Mayans had responded favorably to Pharoah's request for migrant workers, so

---

4. It was actually after this episode that *bullshit* took on its negative connotations. Originally, the feces of the Apis, or sacred bull, was highly esteemed, and "bullshit" was thus something of great merit or value. With the Apis powerless to protect themselves, however, wags started to use the phrase sarcastically, and eventually the original meaning was completely lost.

Pharaoh, deciding that he no longer needed the Hebrews, ordered them out immediately.

And so they packed up and headed out, all in eighteen minutes. The masses, freed from bondage[5] but with their future uncertain, were terrified and angry, and Aaron was the target of their rage. It might have gone badly for him had Moses not stepped forward and, his voice ringing out with all the passion, intensity, and clear diction that had made him a leader to begin with, reminded them of something he'd learned back in college: That the Hebrews did have land, that their forebear Abraham had made a number of real estate deals back in Canaan, and surely the Hebrews would be welcome there. The crowd murmured its assent, and they were off.[6] The general consensus among the Egyptians was "good riddance to bad rubbish," until many began noticing their valuables missing, and it dawned on them that the "bad rubbish" had helped itself to reparations. Pharaoh assembled his chariots and began to pursue them. This was much harder than it sounds, since the last Pharaoh to use the chariots hadn't bothered to put all the pieces where they belonged, nobody could find the Allen wrench, and the assembly instructions were half in cuneiform. It took a few weeks to put them together, and even then, he couldn't get rid of this annoying *squeeeeak* in the left wheels whenever they turned.

The Hebrews, meanwhile, were making their way through the "Sea of Reeds," a term being used by real estate developers for what had been known as "The Swamp of Desolation." Pharaoh, having already built Pe-Ithom and Pe-Rameses, was planning on building a third city, Casa del Boca Horus, on the spot, and was having it drained. As the Hebrews passed by, organizers for the United Hebrew Trades convinced the Nubian slaves working the

---

5. Except, of course, those whose sexual predilections led them to take their assorted slings and harnesses with them.

6. According to Maimonides. According to Nachmanides, they muttered their consent, and according to Gersonides, most of the crowd didn't really hear what he said, but just wanted to get going in case there was traffic.

buckets to join them. In a last act of defiance, they broke open the Reed Sea Dam, and the swamp began to fill in again, just as the Egyptian army arrived.[7] Trapped in the rapidly filling swamp, the army soon became the navy, and a very unsuccessful navy, what with the drowning, poor navigation skills, and discomfort with the whole situational homosexuality thing.

Their old lives gone, their pursuers drowned, and their bridges burned, the Hebrews turned toward Canaan and began to head north, to freedom, figuring it couldn't take more than a couple of months, and they'd be home free. As for Aaron, he didn't get quite what he'd hoped for, but after working out a deal to gain the even more lucrative priesthood for himself and his descendants, he was more than satisfied. And if you think that *this* account is implausible, well, you should hear the *other* version of what happened.

---

7. The soldiers' angry and desperate cries of "Dam! Dam!" later evolved into the modern homonymous epithet.

CHAPTER THREE

THE BOOK OF **PROFITS**

David, son of Jesse, walked past the Israelites on his way to meet the giant in battle. His long, silken hair was flowing down to his shoulders, his cheeks as hairless as on his bar mitzvah and still wet with the tears of his mother, his feet bare, and the only things he carried were a sling with five stones, and a lyre. He strummed this while he walked, singing sweet hymns of praise to God. The Israelites' King Saul offered the shepherd boy his armor and weapons.

"No, Your Majesty," he demurred humbly. "For God will protect me, and I need go into battle with no shield but this"—he pointed to the six-pointed star emblazoned on his tunic—"His sign that He goes before me to war."

The women in the crowd had been murmuring about his physical beauty, and they were now joined by the men muttering about his spiritual strength and courage, and the hermaphrodites muttering about both. A voice called out: "David, don't go, he'll kill you!"

The crowd fell silent, horrified that somebody would say what they were all thinking. But David turned calmly.

"No, my fellow Israelites, fear not for me, for mighty is the Lord, for though you see but these small stones, I bear with me my rock and my redeemer, and it shall not be me, but He, that smiteth yon giant."

With that, he strode off to the field of battle, where Goliath of Gath stood, all six and one-half cubits of him,[1] and the whole

---

1. It's difficult to estimate how much exactly that is, since a cubit was the length of a forearm, and since people back then were much smaller, scholars agree that Goliath was between three and a half and six feet tall.

Philistine army behind him. It looked like another big win for the big Philistine.

"David's so beautiful, so pure," sighed an Israelite woman.

You should have seen him three years ago, thought Samuel the Prophet, as he nodded to one of his runners to go and lay another bet on David.

When Samuel—who was known as "the Prophet" because of his seemingly uncanny ability to predict the outcome of sporting events—had first seen David, the shepherd "boy" was a hirsute, powerfully built twenty-seven-year-old who was snapping the neck of a wolf with his bare hands. Samuel was always on the lookout for new talent, but still, Samuel might have just tucked him away with all the other tough guys he saw on a regular basis had David not begun to sing. He was untrained, to be sure, and a little off-key, but he had the voice of an angel. In a flash, Samuel knew that this shepherd was going to make him a fortune. It would take a lot of work to get him ready, but it was going to be worth it.

It didn't take much to convince David's parents to let him go tend Samuel's flocks for a little while. It was a little strange that nobody could recall Samuel having any flocks, but David was, after all, a twenty-seven-year-old who was still tending his father's flocks, so his parents didn't ask too many questions. Samuel's people shaved his body bare, leaving only the hair on his head, which they untangled, conditioned, and dyed a warm auburn from its natural fiery red. He was given singing lessons and trained to play the lyre.[2] He was trained in various martial skills and did a lot of cardio to lose bulk but maintain his strength. To keep his skin young and supple, he was given frequent mud baths from the Dead Sea, which at the time was actually known as the Dying Sea. And, of course, they gave him etiquette and locution lessons to

---

2. Although he was never very good, he was competent, and it is untrue, as later critics alleged, that David would just pretend to play while a more skilled musician was performing behind a curtain.

help lose that thick Yehuda accent and learn to speak like a Levite. After two years of this, David looked like a teenager and was allowed to return home, where he resumed the life of a simple, if dreamy, shepherd.

Meanwhile, the Israelites' neighbors, the Philistines (who had been known as the "Sea Peoples" until everyone became so damn PC!) had been on a roll, smiting the Amorites, Moabites, Ammonites, and Hittites. Nobody was quite sure of where the Philistines had come from originally. Some believed that they were refugees from fabled Atlantis. Others thought that they were the survivors of the great volcanic eruption that brought low mighty Knossos. Still others thought that they'd seen them hanging in the parking lot behind the old 7-Eleven that got torn down to build Route 17. Whatever the case, they had arrived in Canaan by the thirteenth century B.C.E. or so, and whether it was raiding the Israelites' flocks, pillaging their villages, or simply playing their music too loud, they had been a neighborhood nuisance ever since.[3] Philistine-Israelite relations had calmed down a little since the lawsuits had been settled between them and Samson Contracting Co. over the shoddy material used in building the Great Temple of Dagon.[4] But the arrival on the scene of Goliath of Gath changed all that. It was said of him that he was so big that it took the seed of two men to create him, the wombs of two women

---

3. Some suggest they were angry over the fact that all the other tribal names ended in *ite* while theirs ended in *ine*.

4. Since renamed the Great Rubble Pile of Dagon.

to carry him, and the breasts of three wet nurses to feed him (which explains why he turned out to be a breast man). By the time he was seven, he was as big as a grown man; by the time he was ten he was the size of a grown man with an overactive pituitary gland; by the time he was fourteen he was just a freak. In our more sophisticated and understanding era, young Goliath would have been cared for and nurtured, given a basketball, a free ride through school, and lots of sympathy when his knee blew out junior year. Alas, the Philistines were not so wise, and they gave him a spear, a lot of military training, and stuck him in the front of the army when they went to "war."

We put war in quotation marks, because there actually wasn't a whole lot of fighting involved. Although the constant invasions that plagued the Holy Land in the ancient world are usually cast as resulting from its location between Asia and Africa, the truth is that most of the tribes there had no particular interest or skill at warfare, and were thus used for practice by the neighboring empires. In fact, the greatest victory won by the invading Israelites themselves had been achieved solely by the fearsome tactic of blowing a trumpet. Like a modern army firing bullets over the heads of trainees to give them the feel of danger without actually experiencing any, Assyrians, Egyptians, Babylonians, and so forth used to send their recruits into Canaan to train. Thus, when locals would fight among themselves, they weren't particularly bloody affairs. Often, the champion of one army would challenge his opposite number, bets would be laid, and, based on the outcome, the appropriate lands and possessions would change hands. Goliath had been winning big, even by handicapping himself by fighting three or four opponents at a time. By the time Goliath got around to the Israelites, he had an undefeated record, all but one by first-round decapitations, and that one was by technical decapitation, since he squeezed the Jebussite warrior so hard that his head popped off. It was not surprising then that when the Philistines turned their attention to the Israelites, nobody was willing to take Goliath up on

> **By the time Goliath got around to the Israelites, he had an undefeated record, all but one by first-round decapitations, and that one was by technical decapitation, since he squeezed the Jebussite warrior so hard that his head popped off.**

the challenge, and it looked like the Philistines might have just been able to take whatever they wanted. Then David stepped up.

Up to that point, of course, David had been a complete unknown. Soon after he accepted Goliath's challenge, however, people began to speak of his grace, his good looks, his voice, and so on. Still, given that Goliath was accustomed to fighting several opponents at a time, it didn't seem like too many Israelites were going to be willing to bet on the outcome. Then rumors started spreading that Samuel the Prophet was backing him. Now, some people simply thought Samuel had lost it. "Maybe he did correctly predict that Saul would become king, but this is just crazy." Still, enough people—especially in David's tribe of Yehuda—believed in him that they started to lay bets.[5] As for David, he exuded the cool confidence of a man who knew a secret: Samuel had told him that he'd been watching Goliath fight for years, and that he saw a weakness. Goliath had what was known in the fight game as a glass temple. It wasn't uncommon in giants, who, after all, didn't usually have to worry about getting hit in the head. According to Samuel, all you had to do was hit him a good *zetz* with a rock, and he'd go down like a cedar of Lebanon. By the time the day of the big fight came, most of the land of the Philistines, and a good portion of the tribal lands of Yehuda, were up for grabs.

And so David handed his lyre to a comely young woman, promising he'd get it back when he had slain Goliath, and, with nothing but his sling and his six-pointed star,[6] he strode forth to meet

---

5. There were at least enough legitimate bettors to cover up the fact that most of the bets were being laid by shills for Samuel.

6. Underneath which was an iron plate—after all, God helps those who help themselves.

This parchment fight announcement represents the most significant find in the Dead Sea Schwarma Shop Scrolls. These scrolls—which contain sports, gossip, adult services ads, and other material not considered significant enough to have been included in the Qumran archive—were discovered in 1957 when an archaeologist working on the Dead Sea scrolls stopped by for a schwarma and noticed writing on his napkin. It turned out that the schwarma stand had been using the scrolls as napkins and wrappers for years, unaware of their historical import. Unfortunately, despite the efforts of restoration experts, most of the scrolls remain horribly tehina stained.

Goliath, who stood there, taunting him with cruel words about his mother's personal hygiene and shaking his spear in a menacing manner. This was often enough to unman even the manliest of men, but David calmly placed a stone in his sling, swung it around his head, and let it go. Had slow-motion battle been more developed by that point, the crowd doubtlessly would have seen exactly how the stone flew. As it was they simply saw Goliath stagger, then recover himself, then smile, and then topple over. A cheer went up from the Israelite camp, as loud as the groan that arose from the Philistines, and, after the hourglass ran out on Goliath, the Israelites surged across the field to claim their prizes. Nobody paid much attention to the funerary detail that loaded Goliath's body into a wagon and hauled it away. Samuel watched them drive off, then turned his attentions back to the Israelites, who were celebrating their win and their winnings, a good portion of which would ultimately end up in his pocket. The crowd—thrilled that they could now lay claim to the coveted Philistine land of Gaza—took up a chant: "Saul has won us thousands, but David has won us tens of thousands!" Saul didn't look too happy, but then, Samuel thought, with another glance at David, that might not matter, after all. As for Goliath, the body was hurried to the coast, where Samuel had a ship waiting to transport the giant to one of the trendy new Greek colonies in the Crimea. Forced to fight because of his size, Goliath's faked death—and the generous bribe he received for throwing the fight—finally allowed him to fulfill his dream of opening a small bistro specializing in Meso-Mediterranean fusion.

CHAPTER FOUR

HANUKKAH UNCUT

Sheldon the Maccabee watched Simon the Lithe grapple with his Greek foe, the fruits of victory dangling just before him; all Simon had to do was reach out, and triumph would at long last be his. He reached his hand out, and stopped. He couldn't bring himself to clutch the fruits and twist. He had no time to mourn his failure of will, however, since his opponent was not so reticent. Unable to bear the pain in his groin, Simon tapped out. It was another humiliating defeat for the Jerusalem Jewish wrestling team, another stunning victory for their Syrian Greek rivals. That might not have been so bad a few years earlier, when Israel was gaga for all things Greek. Jewish men underwent costly and painful cosmetic surgery to make it look like their foreskins were still attached.[1] Greek names were popular, and at Jewish playgrounds you could hear mothers calling out "Shlomocles!" and "Herschelarchus!" And Hebrew/Hellenic fusion was all the culinary rage.[2]

But in 168 everything changed, when the Seleucid emperor, Antiochus IV, suffered one of the worst humiliations a sitting monarch has ever had to endure. The history books record that his attempted invasion of Egypt was thwarted when he was met by a Roman envoy who drew a circle in the sand around the startled Seleucid and forbade him to leave until he'd signed a treaty promising not to invade Egypt. Fearful of Roman intervention, he signed. Less well known is that afterward, the envoy made him put on his best party dress and sing "I'm a Little Teapot." Since Antiochus was

---

[1]. And some Jewish women, eager to woo Greek men, even wore artificial uncircumcised penises. This will make more sense shortly, but not much.

[2]. Some of this was pretty bad, like the moussaka and matzo brei, but the Greek salad with herring wasn't too awful (if you left off the herring).

thwarted in his efforts to pick on someone his own size, he decided to pick on somebody considerably smaller: the Jews. He launched a campaign to de-Judaize them, banning circumcision, Sabbath, and kosher dietary observance. Perhaps the most offensive policies, however, involved the desecration of the Temple. It was an extreme and harsh program. First, they had to sacrifice pigs in the Temple. Then they had to eat pigs in the Temple. Then they had to attend weekend spirituality retreats with pigs in the Temple. To add insult to injury, after it was desecrated, the Greeks converted it into a Greek-style center of worship, complete with full day spa and salad bar.

While the more Hellenized members of the community may have welcomed the changes, the majority of the Jews bridled under the oppression. These changes particularly angered the Maccabee family. Cohanim, they were due to begin serving a term as high priests, as well as operating a one-year lease on the Temple court's lucrative goat concession. Now, the jobs of the priestly caste had been outsourced to Brahmins imported from the Indus River Valley. The Maccabees began to plan an armed uprising, with each Maccabee given a task. It was the job of Sheldon (who, besides being the Jerusalem Jewish wrestling coach, was, by nature, an exceptionally critical person) to evaluate the strengths and weaknesses of the Greeks, and what he saw on the wrestling mat disturbed him. It was not merely that the Greeks were in peak physical condition. As Sheldon saw it, that in itself was merely a result of the true cause of Greek power, the world-beating secret weapon of the Greeks that the Jews would have to overcome: the Greek adulation of man-on-man love.

To be sure, many in the ancient world practiced sodomy,[3] but only the Greeks got really, really good at it. To appreciate just how good they were, it should be recalled that their civilization managed

---

3. Or "stevery," as it was known in those parts of the ancient world more familiar with Steve's licentiousness than with Sodom's.

to attain an extraordinarily high degree of homosexual arousal without all the technological innovations—elaborate harnesses, recreational drugs, Don Johnson and Mickey Rourke's cinematic tribute to gay love, *Harley Davidson and the Marlboro Man*—that are considered an essential part of the gay lifestyle today. Among the men of Hellas, not only could the love speak its name, it could write an epic poem about it. As a result, Greek men were obsessed with achieving physical perfection. This, in turn, led them to want to flaunt their physical perfection in athletic competition.

> **It was not merely that the Greeks were in peak physical condition. As Sheldon saw it, that in itself was merely a result of the true cause of Greek power, the world-beating secret weapon of the Greeks that the Jews would have to overcome: the Greek adulation of man-on-man love.**

Moreover, the nature of Greek sporting events made it difficult for less sexually liberated Mediterraneans to compete. In wrestling it was pretty obvious, since very few non-Greeks were willing to go all the way, which is basically what nude wrestling entailed. But other sports also had their pitfalls. Javelins were in the form of giant phalluses.[4] Poles for pole vaults were in the shape of gianter phalluses. Nude footraces often left non-Greek runners feeling both disoriented and icky—especially the relays, since you didn't exactly hand off the baton; you inserted it. So it was hardly surprising that many non-Greek athletes felt inferior in comparison to their buff Hellenistic rivals. More important, however, this ethos was carried into the military field. Greek militaries were made up of pairs of lovers, the idea being that first of all, you'd fight harder to protect your boyfriend, and second, you'd fight harder so that your boyfriend wouldn't look at you like you're a big sissy-pants. Whatever the motivations, it definitely

---

4. And the more traditional Jews used circumcised javelins, which, while more aesthetically pleasing, weren't quite as aerodynamic.

gave the Greeks a morale that was hard to beat. But after giving it careful examination, Sheldon thought he'd figured it out.

"We could put up incorrect road signs so the Greek soldiers get lost," offered Judah the Maccabee at the Maccabee family war council and pancake jamboree.

"You said that one two hours ago," fumed Simeon the Maccabee.

"Well, I haven't heard any great ideas coming from you—'Oh, let's cover the battlefield in olive oil and olive pits, so that when they charge, they'll fall down.'"

The Maccabees began to fight among themselves when Sheldon, just entering the room, cleared his throat.

"Maccabees, please, let's save it for the Greeks. Besides, I've got the solution to our problems—all we have to do is make the Greeks ashamed of their man-on-man-ophilia."

He explained his rationale to them.

"Well that's great," responded Judah when he was done. "But how do we do that? Whoever heard of a Greek man who didn't like to shtup other men?"

"Aha," rejoined Sheldon. "They like to shtup other men, but they don't like people to know that they get shtupped themselves."

In his own inimitable[5] way, Sheldon had hit upon the fundamental weakness of the Greeks' sexual ethos. While it was considered perfectly acceptable for teenagers to shtup one another, or for an adult to shtup a teenager, for an adult male, getting shtupped was seen as being completely emasculating, on a par with putting your hair in curlers, which Greek men also did, but were also embarrassed by. The question was how to exploit that embarrassment. For the answer, Sheldon took a trip to Alexandria, the greatest metropolis of the Middle East. There, he met with Menelik the Aethiop. Captured in a campaign against Kush, Menelik had been brought back to Alexandria, where he soon impressed all those around him

---

5. *Inimitable,* in this case, should be viewed as *inflammable,* and actually means highly imitable.

with his sense of humor. In the years since he'd purchased his freedom, he had become the most popular entertainer in the city, and had recently been given the most highly coveted performance spot in Alexandria, the Agora in front of the Apollo Temple. There, every Saturday night he led a troupe of performers—mostly Kushites and Nubians—who sang, danced, and amused sell-out crowds. The next morning, Alexandrians of all types would be repeating Menelik's jokes, anecdotes, and observations, and within a matter of weeks, all the Middle East, be it Ptolemaic or Seleucid, would be laughing along. What few people realized was that Menelik was actually an Ethiopian Jew. It wasn't something he was public about, but as both a Jew and a comic Menelik was touched by Sheldon's appeal, and he agreed to help.

While it was considered perfectly acceptable for teenagers to shtup one another, or for an adult to shtup a teenager, for an adult male, getting shtupped was seen as being completely emasculating, on a par with putting your hair in curlers, which Greek men also did, but were also embarrassed by.

The next Saturday night, Menelik got up to deliver his monologue. For ten minutes, the crowd heard him rip into Greek sex practices.

"How do you tell the men from the women in Greece? When have you ever heard of a Greek woman giving a blow job?

"Greek men never lie…but they do bend over a lot.

"Why can't Greek men raise chickens? Because they only care for the cocks."

Within a few weeks, the eastern Mediterranean was awash with jokes about how Greek men put out. At first, many Greek men just laughed it off, but soon the jokes started getting to them. Men who had previously been inseparable began to spend time apart. In Judea, the Maccabee underground took it to the next level, by specifically targeting those soldier/lover pairs they had identified.

"Hey, Patroclus, you're riding that chariot as hard as I hear Ajax rode your ass last night."

"Nice work with that javelin; if you're as skilled with Menelaus's 'javelin,' I can see why he always has a smile on his face."

Before long, the Greek forces in Judea began to lose their unit cohesion. The pairs began to spend less time training with one another, and even quit working out as much. When Jerusalem Jewish track and field took first place in the regional championship in December, the Maccabees knew it was time to strike. Out of shape, out of practice, and unwilling to take a spear point for their exes, the Greeks soldiers didn't stand a chance. The Jews recaptured the Temple, and in the wreckage of the day spa, found a container of pure olive massage oil. Miraculously, the oil lasted eight days, by

When archaeologists first unearthed this vase on Cyprus in 1936, they thought that, like images of Perseus with the head of Medusa, it depicted some lost myth—a Greek hero bearing the severed member of a beast they dubbed "The Phallotaur." For years it was on display in the Monsterology Wing of the British Museum, until recent discoveries by Israeli archaeologists of the same image on vases, frescoes, and cereal boxes from the Second Temple Period led them to conclude that it commemorated the victory of the Jerusalem Jewish Track-and-Field team over their Seleucid archrivals.

which point they had found a new supply. In honor of the event, Maccabees—who were now not just the priests, but the rulers— threw a huge rededication gala for the Temple,[6] and the Jews have been celebrating the occasion ever since.

---

6. One guess as to who the headliner was—and who had joined his entourage as a "spiritual advisor."

CHAPTER FIVE

FRATRICIDE

"Jeeeeesuuuuuuuus!" Caiaphas screamed, and the rest of the Sadducee fraternity came running. What had made Caiaphas scream stunned them into silence. Their wine cellar was completely empty, and there was a big hole in the wall leading to a passage on the other side. This was bad enough, but what made it even worse was that their frat house was full of guests who had come for the wine and hummus party they were throwing to drum up support for Caiaphas's candidacy for the school's "King of Harvest Fest" election that was coming up.

"What happened?" asked Yirmiyahu.

"What do you mean 'what happened?'" fumed Caiaphas. "Jesus happened."

"How do you know?"

"Trust me. I know."

And he did. Ever since Joshua "Jesus" Nazarethsky had arrived at Aramaic University, he had been the bane of Caiaphas's existence. The popular freshman[1] could have joined any frat (and indeed, Caiaphas had courted him as a pledge), but he instead petitioned Dean Pilate for the right to form his own. Although Galilee House was small (twelve members other than Jesus), it

Ever since Joshua "Jesus" Nazarethsky had arrived at Aramaic University, he had been the bane of Caiaphas's existence.

---

1. Those familiar with the New Testament might wonder why Jesus was a thirty-two-year-old freshman. It should be recalled that in biblical times, people lived much longer than they do today, and so the benchmarks of their life cycle were considerably different from what they are today. Bar mitzvahs took place at twenty-five, college began at thirty, and men didn't start to wear their pants really, really high until they were at least one hundred.

soon took on a reputation as the biggest party frat on campus, a title formerly held by the Sammies, as the members of the Samari-
tan frat were then called. Not only were their parties by far the
most popular, Jesus himself had become a larger-than-life character. He was known for his smooth tongue, a skill that translated to
great success with the ladies, as an epidemic of "virgin births" during his two years on campus would confirm. He was equally known
for his ability to extricate himself from trouble with the school administration. Granted, this wasn't necessarily the most difficult
thing in the world.

Dean Pilate had a reputation as a softie, which is why he'd been
assigned to the position in the first place. With his family connections, he had become a vice-proconsul of Judea, but after his
efforts to mediate an intertribal conflict by having the feuding
Bedouin clans "sit down and talk about their feelings" resulted in a
war that lasted five years, it was decided that he should be given a
less critical assignment. Although officially still a vice-proconsul,
his job as dean kept him occupied and out of trouble. His tenure at
Aramaic University had been a fairly uneventful one, and Dean Pilate, a rotund, myopic fellow with a slight obsessive-compulsive
disorder, made a point to avoid confrontation.

Jesus was certainly well known to him. On a number of occasions, Caiaphas had brought Jesus before him on charges of violating either school policy or the by-laws of the Pan Anti-Hellenic
Fraternity Council. There had been the time that a bakers' strike
broke out on a Friday, and it seemed like without any loaves, it
would be a dull Saturday night on fraternity row. But that Saturday morning, Jesus and his frat brothers picked grain, and that
night, Galilee House "miraculously" had enough loaves for anyone who wanted to come and partake. Jesus was charged with
breaking the school rules on harvesting on the Sabbath, but his
response that "Sabbath is made for man, not man for the Sabbath"
convinced the dean that while the letter of the regulation might
have been violated, Jesus had obeyed the spirit of the regulation.

Then there was the time that Jesus had been caught burning incense from the Temple. Without question, that was grounds for expulsion, and Caiaphas was savoring his victory. But at his hearing, Jesus produced a note from a doctor prescribing the incense for medical treatment of someone named Lazarus, who he claimed was one of Galilee's pledges. After Jesus' heartrending account of how the incense had virtually brought Lazarus back from the dead, not only did the dean acquit him, he even set up something called "The Lazarus Fund" to help people with Lazarus's condition. What that condition was, and indeed, whether or not Lazarus actually existed, the dean never really ascertained, nor that the administrator of the fund was Jesus himself. Then there was the time that he was caught in Flagrante Delicto[2] with Cindy Magdalene, Mary's sluttier younger sister.[3] Although it wasn't grounds for expulsion, it could have resulted in Galilee House losing its charter, but when Jesus defended himself by asking the council, "Let he who has been without Cindy cast the first stone," even Dean Pilate had to look away shamefacedly.

Thus, as Jesus' frat brothers hoisted the barrels of wine out of the cistern, while the guests cheered, he felt a certain confidence that this was just one more success to burnish his already sterling reputation.

"Man, it's like turning water into wine," observed one guest. "You *definitely* have my vote."

"Jesus, dude," said Judas, Jesus' roommate and closest friend in the frat. "This is totally awesome. I wish I could see the faces of those Sadducees. Dude, when word of this gets around, your election as king is guaranteed."

"Yeah," seconded Peter. "From now on, when people want to party, they're going to ask themselves 'What would Jesus do?'"

Despite his feelings that he would get nowhere with his com-

---

2. An intimate little bistro located just off campus.
3. Cindy gave it away; at least with Mary, you had to pay for it.

plaints, Caiaphas felt that the proper procedures had to be followed. The dean welcomed him into his office.

"I know what you're here about, but don't you think that expulsion is a little harsh? After all, isn't this sort of merry rivalry the sort of thing that fraternity life is all about?"

"Dean, I understand your unwillingness to…"

Something on the dean's desk caught Caiaphas's attention.

"…I understand your unwillingness to expel Jesus, but some punishment must be meted out. How about you ban Galilee House from throwing any parties for the next month. Parties aren't even allowed from now until after the election in three weeks, anyway."

"No expulsion proceedings?"

"No, sir, just a simple proclamation. Here, I can write it out for you right now."

He took a sheet of vellum from the desk and wrote the order out.

Pilate looked it over. "Well, that's seems very reasonable. I'm glad to see that you're not getting so obsessed over Jesus anymore. Now, let me just affix my seal."

"Here it is." Caiaphas put it in Pilate's hand, making sure to clasp his hand in the process. "Oh, sir, I'm so sorry, I forgot."

"No, don't worry, it was an accident. Let me just clean up."

He went off to an alcove where he kept a basin for just such circumstances. While he was there, Caiaphas put the vellum in his pouch, took a sheet from a different pile, and wrote the order on it. After ten minutes, the dean came out.

"Here it is, sir."

Pilate put his stamp on it.

"There you go, now just give that to my secretarium on the way out."

"Thank you, sir, you have a good day."

The month passed uneventfully. The elections came, and as expected, Jesus won handily. That Sunday, he appeared before students amassed for the school's big harvest festival and they hailed him with palm fronds, which may not sound like much, but it sure beat what the king of the Fertilizing Fest got hailed with.

"Boys," Jesus said to his frat brothers. "We need to celebrate. Party, Thursday night."

"Are you sure you should do that?" asked Judas nervously. "I mean, you're still banned for another week."

"Don't worry, Judas. We'll keep it small, off campus. Even if he finds out, and even if he has any authority over it, what's the worst he could do to me? This is Dean Pilate we're talking about."

That Thursday night, they booked a banquet room at Rahab's, a popular inn. The wine was flowing pretty freely, but Judas seemed stressed out.

"Judas, dude, lighten up," said Jesus, clapping his arm around Judas's shoulders. "You know...I love you, man."

Just then, Roman soldiers burst in and seized Jesus. Although partygoers were horrified, and his frat brothers afraid, Jesus told them not to worry.

"I'll be back at the house in time to light the Sabbath candles."

Early the next morning, while most of the campus was still sleeping off the previous night's reveries, Jesus was led into the dean's office.

"Good morning, Dean Pi—"

"Well, well, well." Caiaphas, sitting in the dean's chair, spun to face Jesus.[4] "If it isn't 'The King of the Jews.'"

"Where's Dean Pilate?"

"He's occupied."

"I'll wait."

"I'm afraid that's not really an option. You violated his order, and you know what the punishment for that is."

"Oh, what's he going to do, lecture me?"

"That might have been the punishment if you'd violated *Dean* Pi-

---

4. The chair was strapped to the back of a slave on hands and knees who rotated as dictated.

late's orders. Unfortunately for you, you violated an order from *Vice-Proconsul* Pilate." He held up the original copy of the order. Written by Caiaphas, signed by the dean, it was on a sheet of official vice-proconsul stationery that had been lying on the dean's desk at the time. "That's a crime against the state. And the punishment for that is crucifixion. Now, if you'll forgive me, I have to draw up plans for the immediate dissolution

Though crucifixion may sound kind of harsh, it was actually considered a humane alternative to the older punishment of Star-of-Davidization.

of Galilee House." Though crucifixion may sound kind of harsh, it was actually considered a humane alternative to the older punishment of Star-of-Davidization.

"Forgive you? You don't know what you're doing." Jesus raised his fist menacingly, but the soldiers grabbed him and hauled him away. Caiaphas could hear his scream as they dragged him down the hall. "Dean Pilate, my lord, why have you forsaken me!"

The dean came back into the room from his alcove, drying his hands. "Did you call me?"

"No, sir, you must just be hearing things."

"What was it you wanted to talk about?"

"Oh nothing, sir. I had a problem, but I think it's been taken care of."

Caiaphas joined the rest of the Sadducees, who were waiting outside the dean's building, taunting Jesus as he was led away. Judas came running up to him.

"What's going on, Caiaphas?"

"What do you mean, Judas? We had a deal. You fulfilled your part of the bargain, now I'm fulfilling mine."

"What are you talking about? You promised to fix my grade point average if I told you if Jesus threw any parties."

"That's right. And now that your roommate is going to be executed, you get an automatic 4.0 GPA."

The horror of what he had done dawned on him. Judas walked

עֲדֹוּﬠﬥש ARAﬦAIC UﬥiﬠERSiﬢ

SPRING SEMESTER

Name: Judas Iscariot

	GPA:4.0
Course	Grade
Samaritan Studies	A
Intro to Art Appreciation: Looking Beyond Idolatry	A
Studies in Future Archaeology	A
Leprosy as a Metaphor	A

The discovery of Judas's actual report card—uncovered in the 1920s while digging the foundations for Hebrew University on Mount Scopus—is one of archaeology's most significant finds, but also produced one of its most enduring mysteries: Why was this document written in English when it's well established that Aramaic University didn't start keeping records in that language for a full five years after he dropped out?

off in a daze, Caiaphas's laughter following him. That night, Judas's parents found out the worst news a Jewish parent could expect to hear about a child—he had dropped out of college. After years of therapy, he would get over his guilt and set up a small business providing scapegoats for the Temple's sin offerings. After the destruction of the Temple, he was ruined financially, however, and took his own life.

The rest of the story is much as the world knows it. Jesus carries the cross, is put on it, is pierced on it, and dies on it. As was custom, he was taken down and buried by nightfall. The next night, things were pretty dismal at the Galilee House. What they really wanted to do was find some fitting way to memorialize their friend and leader. Nobody could remember whose idea it was, but the eleven remaining frat brothers broke into the crypt, took out Jesus' body, and propped it up in the dean's chair.

Standing outside the dean's window, they heard his high-pitched scream as he entered the office, followed by the sound of his unconscious body falling to the floor.[5]

"Man," said Peter. "They'll be talking about this one forever."

---

5. They then carried him around in the chair and had him wave to people in a scene reminiscent of *Weekend at Bernie's*. They, did not, however, staple anything to his head.

CHAPTER SIX

WEAPONS OF MASS DELUSION

Rosh Hashanah in the year 1094 was not a happy day for Chaim Deathmacher. As the itinerant arms merchant picked sullenly at his kugel, a familiar voice rang out to him across the reception hall of the Great Synagogue of Constantinople: "Deathmacher, why so despondent?" Deathmacher looked up and found himself face to face with Reuven Blades, a local sword dealer with whom he'd done frequent business.

"You wouldn't believe the trouble I've had back west, Reuven. Between the Truce of God and the Peace of God, people have gotten the notion that war is un-Christian. It's getting so that lately, all I'm selling is dubbing-swords, and those things last forever. 'I dub thee Sir Loin of Beef!' a tap on the shoulder, and then it's back in the box for another year."

"Tell me about it. For a while it looked like the Seljuk Turks and Byzantines might go at it, but lately, it's all about the diplomacy. What is it with Byzantines and diplomacy?"

"You know, we really need a good war."

"Yes, well, it looks like the only way we're going to have a war is if we start it ourselves."

It was as if torches had been lit over their heads. They looked at one another, and smiled.

Reuven traveled down to Jerusalem, where he hired some character types from the Hebrew Actors Guild to impersonate Seljuk soldiers and harass some Christian pilgrims en route to the Holy Land.[1] Back in Europe, Chaim spoke with some acquaintances of

---

1. In response, the pilgrims developed a ritual of ceremonially killing and consuming their foe—in the form of an animal they called a turkey in memory of the land of their trauma.

his at Europe's major broadsheets, who took the story of the harassed pilgrims and turned it into a major media event. Soon it was the talk of Europe, with everybody wondering what could be done to prevent this sort of travesty again. The crowned heads of Europe made the usual protests, but despite the pressure from the editorialists, the matter might have stopped there, had not Deathmacher upped the ante by taking out ads in all the major European broadsheets in the name of "The Institute for Seljuk Expansion," declaring to all Christians that "Our God, praise be unto Him, could kick your God's ass," getting it past the censors by having it accompanied by a woodcut print of a giant foot descending upon a donkey being led by someone bearing a passing resemblance to Jesus.

This was more than Pope Urban II could bear, and he decided to call upon the French, recognizing the need for Europe's bravest warriors. Of course, this occurred some eight hundred years before the doctrine of papal infallibility was adopted. At the Council of Clermont, the Holy Father proposed a great crusade in order to liberate the Holy Land, a request received with unanimous approval by the assembled warriors. According to legend, however, their enthusiasm in part stemmed from linguistic confusion. After the pope said, "I want you to go on a crusade," the Norman representative, who had grown up in England, responded irately, "We—" Before he could continue, however, the French knights, misinterpreting him and eager to agree with one of the most powerful French states, roared their approving "Oui! Oui!"

Blades and Deathmacher had planned well for this occasion. They offered a whole line of weapons to be used specifically for the Crusades, such as the Port-O-Wall, a 250-pound stone wall with shoulder straps that was marketed with the slogan "Turn *Every* Battle into a Siege with Port-O-Wall!" and the Military Censer, which, unlike the censer commonly used during Mass, was filled with Greek fire and swung around, spraying the incendiary like a primitive flamethrower. Moreover, along the crusaders' marching routes, their subcontractors hawked such things as Saracen Repellent and Armor De-Glarer (the advertisement for which featured two French knights impaling one another on their swords, so blinded by the glare of their armor in the sun that they couldn't tell that they weren't Turks).[2]

And, of course, they were not the only tribesmen to take advantage of the opportunities presented by the war. Perhaps the most ingenious Jewish invention of the time, and one that had the most impact on French history, was the chastity belt. Playing on the fears of the knights that their wives might not be so faithful in their absence, a Jewish locksmith in Troyes, Kalonymous the Portal-Opener, began to sell a "wundrose garmynte, to keep thine lady-love as pure and chaste as when thou fyrste chased hyr." After explaining his device, and offering a not-inconsiderable honorarium, Kalonymous received an endorsement from the archbishop of Paris, and the chastity belts sold like gruel, which was the medieval equivalent of "sold like hotcakes," and Kalonymous graciously allowed his fellow Jewish locksmiths to share in his patent. The French armies trudged off happily, confident that they held the one key to their wives' vaults. What they neglected to consider, of course, was that for every key, there was a mold. While no records are left as to what use, if any, may have been made of those molds,

---

2. Saracen Repellent was actually lard, which, though it may have kept some Muslims at bay, left many knights literally frying in the hot desert sun. This may also help to explain the account of Friar Jacques D'ormevous of the siege of Antioch. According to the good monk, the beleaguered men became so hungry that they began imagining the aroma of the largest and most delicious pork roast the world had ever seen, leading to at least seven documented cases of cannibalism, one of which actually involved a knight entirely consuming himself.

The "Flaming Eye of Death" was designed to act as a primitive laser, burning a hole through the torso of a foe. If anything, it worked too well, and was banned after killing all but the last man of a troop of knights who wore the helmets while following one after another through a narrow mountain pass on a particularly sunny day.

historians have long puzzled over the fact that, despite the absence of so many men during the First Crusade, the French population actually increased.[3] Some returning knights may have been skeptical of their wives' protestations of innocence, particularly in light of the evidence, but the declaration by the archbishop of Paris that it was all a great miracle seemed to allay their suspicions. Moreover, according to the few accounts we have on the subject, the returning knights found that in their absence, their wives had somehow acquired a wide array of erotic skills that may have made their suspected indiscretions more forgivable, and that would give the French the reputation as great lovers, which they have enjoyed ever since.

To be sure, the First Crusade was not all a picnic for the Jews. In the Rhineland, the Jews suffered two waves of violence during 1096. In the first, Peter the Hermit, who seemed to have a tenuous grasp of the whole "hermit" concept, led an army of peasants in an assault against the Jews in the large cities. Since their simple peasant armament consisted largely of their dung shovels and hardened dung, this proved fairly ineffective, although it did leave the Jews feeling unclean and a little nauseated. Peter and his men never quite made it to the Holy Land; in Hungary, they were captured and sold as slaves to the Romanians, who then sold them back to the Hungarians, and so on. This went on for several years, until the Romanians and Hungarians realized how stupid it was and decided that their time would be better spent in continuous warfare over the ownership and pronunciation of Transylvania.

Much more serious was the arrival in the late spring of Count Emicho and his knights, who proceeded to launch assaults against the Jewish populations of all the major cities, usually with the assistance of the local populations. In city after city—Worms,

---

3. This also might answer the question as to why, although they are descended from the Germanic Franks, so many French have dark hair and prominent noses.

Mainz, and Cologne, to name but a few—the Jewish population was given the choice of conversion or death—overwhelmingly, they chose the latter. The primary exception to this was the city of Speyer. There, the attack took place on Saturday, and the Jewish community, as willing to die for their faith as their fellows in other cities, but unwilling to violate the sanctity of the holy day by being slaughtered, hired their Shabbes Goys to die in their place. Even in the wake of this tragedy, however, the Jews managed to salvage a small taste of vengeance as well as profit. In Mainz, one Jew, a prosperous merchant named Ezra the Prosperous Merchant, having seen his entire community butchered mercilessly, offered himself as a convert. The conversion of such a prosperous figure was considered a great victory, and he was welcomed with open arms. As a mark of his new faith, Ezra offered to design and provide uniforms for not just Emicho and his men, but for all the crusading armies.

> **In city after city— Worms, Mainz, and Cologne, to name but a few—the Jewish population was given the choice of conversion or death—overwhelmingly, they chose the latter. The primary exception to this was the city of Speyer. There, the attack took place on Saturday, and the Jewish community, as willing to die for their faith as their fellows in other cities, but unwilling to violate the sanctity of the holy day by being slaughtered, hired their Shabbes Goys to die in their place.**

The offering of this new Christian was gratefully accepted as a sign of his heartfelt devotion to the true faith, and soon, all crusaders were proudly wearing the outfit: a white tunic with a bold red cross emblazoned on the chest, perfectly marking the heart and lungs. Although it was noted by some crusaders that the Muslim archers were amazingly lethal, nobody seemed to make the connection between the archers' accuracy and the huge targets worn by the crusaders. To be more correct, nobody on the Christian side made the connection. When Salaam ibn Bolon, a captain of archers in the Seljuk army, was asked what his orders were for his men, he reportedly replied, "Orders, schmorders, just shoot the targets these schmucks have on their chests!" As for Ezra, while he had provided the uniforms for free, he had asked the pope if, in all humility, he could be given the sole right to transport the corpses of dead knights back to France for burial. Touched by Ezra's simple piety, the pope granted him this holy—and lucrative—monopoly.

Of course, the crusade of 1096 was only the first of many. Through the Middle Ages, crusades would be launched against the Muslims, the Byzantines, the Albigensians, and others. And wherever the crusaders fought, the firm of Deathmacher and Blades (incorporated 1097 as a limited liability company) was there to supply them with their killing needs.

CHAPTER SEVEN

BLOOD BROTHERS

It was the last day before Passover 1128, and Laibel of York was desperately trying to get his last matzos baked before the midday rush, when one of his gentile bakers, Pepin Breadsmith, cut himself on a large mixing spoon. This may seem strange to us, but due to the primitive technology available at the time, almost everything in the Middle Ages was jagged, and items—spoons, chairs, pillows, etc.—that pose little or no threat today often resulted in serious injury. Before leeches could be applied, which was at the time the normally prescribed treatment for blood loss, copious amounts of blood had poured into the dough.

At that point, Laibel's brother, Laibish, walked in. Laibish was the mashgiach, whose job it was to oversee the baking process to make sure it was done properly.

"Laibish, where have you been? You're supposed to be making sure this sort of thing doesn't happen!" Laibel was practically shouting at his somewhat shiftless younger brother.

"Oh, well, you see," Laibish responded, shamefacedly, "Nechemia the brewer was trying to empty out his last keg before the holiday and I thought I would help him. Why, what happened?"

Laibel clued him in as to what had taken place.

"But that's terrible, Laibel. If the matzo's ruined, so are you!"

"Oh, it's not just me, Laibish. Do you think that your reputation as mashgiach can suffer another disaster like last year's bar mitzvah fiasco?"

"That's not my fault," whined Laibish. "How was I supposed to know that bacon comes from a pig? I mean honestly: pork, ham, and bacon? You want cow, you ask for beef. You want chicken, you ask for chicken. You want pig, you ask for a thesaurus."

"The point is, you need to come up with a solution, or we're both finished."

Ah, the Middle Ages—what a glorious time. Barbarian rampages were down, dragon slaying was up, and the latest advances in leech technology promised a future free of disease. Although the Jewish population was small, it was industrious and ingenious. Indeed, life for the medieval Jew was a constant intellectual obstacle course. Every day brought new challenges, as the Jew interested in survival had to ask himself numerous questions to ensure that survival: Should I hide? Where should I hide? Should I flee? To where should I flee? If anything, the reputation the Jews have for intellectual acumen dates from this period, when Jews had to become out of the box thinkers, or die. Indeed, the phrase "out of the box" actually dates from anti-Jewish persecutions in the Holy Roman Empire during the thirteenth century, in which Jews were placed in boxes and thrown in the Danube, and only the truly clever ones could find ways to think themselves "out of the box." Thus, on at least one level, this crisis was a welcome relief to the two brothers, involving as it did some Christian's blood as opposed to their own.

> **The phrase "out of the box" actually dates from anti-Jewish persecutions in the Holy Roman Empire during the thirteenth century, in which Jews were placed in boxes and thrown in the Danube, and only the truly clever ones could find ways to think themselves "out of the box."**

"I've got it," exclaimed Laibish. "The rule of one-sixtieth. Let us say some milk were to inadvertently spill into a meat broth, that would normally render the broth unkosher—unless the amount of milk was less than *one-sixtieth* that of the broth. So while blood is unkosher, Pepin is sixty years old..." He let the end of the sentence dangle in the air.

"So," said Laibel, picking it up. "We go by the law of one sixty-year-old and hope that's close enough." There was no time to ask anybody else and so Laibel made the decision: The matzo was baked, and sold, eaten by Jews at seders throughout York. On the third day of Passover, Laibel was astounded to find huge lines waiting in front of his bakery. The Jews of York couldn't get enough of his matzo, and everybody wanted to know what his secret recipe was.

The brothers recognized that they had a gold mine on their hands. They also recognized that there was no way they were going to be able to keep this a secret, particularly from the town's Jewish council. The council wasn't too sure about the theological justification, but there was little they could do—for the first time, Passover had passed over without any of the Jews of York suffering from extreme gastrointestinal discomfort. It was decided that blood could be used for matzo, and Laibel—or "Blood Laibel," as he was called behind his back—was given a monopoly on matzo baking in England. Business was booming, but of course, how much money can you make selling matzos? Sure, during Passover things were great, and it being the Middle Ages, there were still a few ogres around who ate them like crackers, but still, you weren't going to get rich. That's when the brothers got to thinking: "If gentile blood can make even matzo taste good," they reasoned, "imagine what it could do to food that already tasted good!" And so what had been restricted to Passover started spreading to other holidays. They set up a bakery and began putting gentile blood in the hamentashen at Purim, the blintzes at Shavuos, and the rugelach all year round. In order to keep up with the demand, Laibel and Laibish stepped up collections. Thankfully for the Jews of England, the people of the Middle Ages were accustomed from a young age to the idea of giving blood. Medical theory since ancient times had suggested that the body was governed by four fluids, or humors, as they were known: blood, phlegm, yellow bile, and black bile.

An imbalance in any of these humors caused illness—fever, for example, could be caused by overheated blood. Consequently, Laibel hit upon the idea of having agents travel around England on wagons, offering to relieve people of their ailments by relieving them of the offending bodily fluids. To raise the stakes for prospective donors, they even invented a new malady—hemogoblins, wee beasties that inhabited blood and wreaked all kinds of havoc on the unsuspecting. The distinctive wagons of the "Evylle Humour Man" became a common sight in England.[1] Nobody thought to wonder what happened to all that blood after it was drawn, and even after the Jews' expulsion from England, others, not making the connection, took up the role of "Evylle Humour" men. Eventually, some enterprising competitors realized that a possible alternative to removing overheated blood might be cooling it, and with frozen confections, the "Goode Humour" men appeared, soon driving their rivals out of business and memory.

As news of the unparalleled quality of the brothers' baked goods spread to the Continent, the brothers set up facilities all over Europe, although not Romania, since, after a brief visit, Laibel reasoned that it was one of the few places where the gentiles might consume *their* blood. As demand increased, so did the need for blood. Instead of merely drawing a pint or two from each victim—it was actually during this time that the pint became the standard serving size for beer in England, since Laibish got Jewish-run public-houses to offer a pint of beer for each pint of blood you gave—they started taking all of it. There was always a crusade or monster that could explain why somebody suddenly disappeared, and the *York Times*—owned by a family of dyspeptic Jews most grateful for the brothers' culinary innovations—certainly did its utmost to convince the masses that that's what was happening.

Jealous of the brothers' success, however, the gentile English Bakers' Guild launched its own investigation. After their efforts to experiment with their own secret ingredients failed (not even the

---

1. In the event that people suspected what they were doing, the wagon was designed to break apart, the heavy sides falling away, allowing the driver to escape in a small surrey. Similarly, the large dray-horse that pulled the wagon would split in half, freeing a small, fast pony that would pull the smaller vehicle.

English would eat the black bile biscuits), they decided to press the case against Laibel and Laibish and began to accuse them of killing Christian children. The brothers could honestly deny this, since, contrary to popular misconception, they didn't kill children. First of all, it wasn't economical, since they have much less blood than adults. Second, child-stealing was almost wholly a monopoly of the Gypsies, who sold them to the casts of long-running morality plays that were losing popularity and felt that cute children would draw larger audiences. One of the most popular means by which Gypsies acquired children was to dress like giant, large-eyed animals and lead them to their Gypsy wagons. The animals had to be nonthreatening (giant wolves, foxes, and bears wouldn't do), so rabbits were an obvious choice. Since snow would make it easy to be tracked, child-stealing season didn't begin in earnest until spring, right around Easter/Passover, a development that ultimately led the Jews to be blamed, and the Easter Bunny to be revered. While the brothers may have been interested in the lucrative child trade, they weren't going to cross the Gypsies, since, after all, they'd steal your children. Impressed as much by the brothers' apparent innocence as by the sizable bribe they gave him, the local lord refused to intervene on the Guild's behalf.

The charges of child-killing would build up and eventually lead to the Jews' expulsion from England, but at the time they had little impact either there or on the Continent. Although the bakers' guild warned its French counterparts, it insisted on doing so in English, and the French insisted on pretending that they didn't understand them. They did, however, pass the warnings on to the Germans, where dislike for the French led to dismissal of the charges against the Jews. "After all," as Count Hochmuth IV of Schmutzdorf is reported to have said, "you can't really blame someone for cutting up the French." In Spain, the local Sephardic population argued that the Spanish had nothing to worry about, since they couldn't stand heavy Ashkenazi cuisine no matter what they put in it. In Italy, things were more serious. There, a bakery employee was con-

vinced to convert and presented to the authorities a cookbook—
"To Serve Christian Man"—used by the bakery. The brothers hired
Rabbi Jacobo Yardi, a respected Jewish legal authority and gour-
mand, to defend them. Confronted with concrete evidence that the
Jews were using Christian blood with their matzo, Rabbi Jacobo
was given one chance to defend the practice against the Curia of
Pope Artifice VII. Failure would result in his torture, the forcible
conversion of the Jewish community, and the bakery being
dropped from Zagat's. The learned rabbi responded to the pope
thusly:

"Since you believe that when you consume wine and a cracker,
it becomes the blood and body of Jesus, you must also accept
that when you consume blood and a body, it becomes wine
and a cracker. And since there's no crime in drinking
wine and eating crackers, we have done nothing wrong."

> **"Since you believe that when you consume wine and a cracker, it becomes the blood and body of Jesus, you must also accept that when you consume blood and a body, it becomes wine and a cracker. And since there's no crime in drinking wine and eating crackers, we have done nothing wrong."**

A stunned silence fell upon the crowd, but though the collected cardinals searched and searched, they could find no
law prohibiting the consump-
tion of wine and crackers. The pope applauded the rabbi for his
wisdom, and for as long as he was pope, the Jews of Italy were allowed to eat blood with their matzos.[2] Indeed, they became so
brazen as to spread the blood on top of the matzo, not even both-
ering to mix it in. Given the fairly high level of interaction between
Jews and Christians in Italy at this time, it should not be surprising

---

2. In 1589, a rabbi in Wittenberg tried to employ the same argument as Rabbi Jacobo.
Unfortunately for him, the Reformation had taken place, and the court, not believing in
transubstantiation, had the rabbi executed and the rest of the city's Jews converted into
condominiums.

that many Italian Catholics adopted the practice as well, although being good Christians, they substituted the blood of Muslim prisoners of war. Eventually, the church cracked down (it wasn't the blood it objected to so much as the matzo, which it felt was Judaizing the youth), but in the sixteenth century, the introduction of tomatoes from the New World led to efforts to duplicate the appearance, if not the taste, of this forbidden delicacy, with the final result eventually evolving into today's pizza.

This points to the changing conditions that ultimately led the Jews to end the practice of using Christian blood in cooking. During the Middle Ages, people were constantly on the lookout for ways to supplement their meager food supply. The French, for example, made an art out of consuming things—like snails and frogs—that most people found nauseating. The Germans perfected the sausage, a way of making every part of an animal (plus assorted odds and ends—one medieval bratwurst recipe calls for adding "three pages from the Book of Proverbs, diced") palatable by grinding it beyond recognition and stuffing it into an organ. The English simply lost their sense of taste entirely. The Jews, for their part, used Christian blood—as a popular Medieval Jewish saying went: "Matzo tastes better with Christian blood in the batter."

With the Age of Exploration, spices from the Indies became cheaper and more readily available, and exotic new foods that had never been seen before began arriving from the Americas—like tomatoes, potatoes, sugar, and chocolate. The potato in particular revolutionized European—and hence European Jewish—dietary patterns. Historians have long credited the potato with Europe's population boom. While the improved diet certainly played a part in reducing the mortality rate, part of that reduction can also be attributed to the drastic decline in Christian-killing on the part of Europe's Jews in the same time period. Jews could eat potatoes on Passover, and even use potato flour for baked goods. Suddenly, blood for matzo, or for anything else, no longer seemed so important. Why sweeten your pastries with blood when you have sugar?

Beef Bourguignon

INGREDIENTS: GRUEL
SALT
COW

DIRECTIONS: SPREAD GRUEL LIBERALLY OVER COW AFTER THE EARLY MORNING DEW HAS DRIED, MAKING SURE NOT TO GET IT ON THE NAUGHTY BITS. ALLOW GRUEL TO BAKE IN SUN ON COW ALL DAY LONG. AS SUN SETS, SCRAPE HARDENED GRUEL OFF OF COW, MAKING SURE TO GET ENOUGH COW FOR FLAVOR, BUT NOT SO MUCH THAT THE LORD HAS YOU FLOGGED FOR DAMAGING HIS CATTLE. CUT GRUEL INTO BRICKS. ADD SALT. IF SALT IS UNAVAILABLE, USE DANDRUFF.

Coq au Vin

INGREDIENTS: GRUEL
WATER
CHICKEN FEED

DIRECTIONS: CAST LARGE QUANTITIES OF CHICKEN FEED BEFORE THE LORD'S POULTRY. AT THE END OF THE DAY, COLLECT WHAT REMAINS OF THE FEED. GRIND WITH MORTAR AND PESTLE INTO FINE POWDER. MIX WITH GRUEL. FORM INTO CHICKEN PIECES. ADD WATER (EITHER WELL OR RIVER, PER TASTE AND DESIRE FOR CHOLERA), AND BOIL UNTIL CHICKEN DROPPINGS RISE TO SURFACE OF POT. SCRAPE SURFACE, DISCARDING DROPPINGS, AND ENJOY.

Gateau de Framboise

INGREDIENTS: GRUEL
DIRT
CHALK DUST

DIRECTIONS: COLLECT BERRY-INFUSED DIRT FROM LORD'S RASPBERRY PATCH. MIX WITH GRUEL, TWO PARTS GRUEL TO ONE PART DIRT. FORM INTO CAKE, AND BAKE IN FIRE UNTIL HARDENED. DUST WITH SPRINKLING OF CHALK DUST.

Gruel

INGREDIENTS: MILLL-FLOOR GLEANINGS
SAWDUST
WATER

DIRECTIONS: COLLECT WHAT YOU CAN FROM THE LORD'S MILL-FLOOR. MIX WITH EQUAL PARTS SAWDUST, AND WATER TO DESIRED CONSISTENCY. BOIL UNTIL SAWDUST DOESN'T CUT THE INSIDE OF YOUR MOUTH WHEN YOU CHEW.

This cookbook—part of the James Beard Collection at the Institute of Fine Dining in New York—illustrates the meager diets available to most Medieval Europeans. The fact that this book offered recipes for festive holiday meals only emphasizes how abysmal things were.

Why have blood candies when you can have chocolate? Why drink hot, buttered blood when you can have tea or coffee? These new products tasted better, and they brought far fewer anti-Jewish massacres in their wake. Of course, Laibel and Laibish were long since gone from the scene by that point. Their business, however, was still around and changed with the times. It still exists as one of the leaders in the kosher food industry; discretion, litigation, and the nagging suspicion that some of their "old-fashioned" recipes may be *very* old-fashioned, however, prevent us from naming it.

CHAPTER EIGHT

DON'T DRINK THE WATER

Throughout the continent, mobs of angry men, and the occasional premenstrual woman, were massacring the Jews, believing the latter to be responsible for the plague that had befallen them. Israel of Ancona, a prosperous merchant—he had an exclusive contract to sell zucettos[1] to the Catholic Church—and one of the great leaders of medieval Jewry, did all that he could to stop the killing. He petitioned whatever authorities he could find—the Holy Roman Emperor, the pope, the duke of Earl—but to no avail. Desperate to find a solution, Israel met with Italy's other great Jewish leaders, Salomone de Soncino, who owned northern Italy's largest town-crier service, "Sonci-News," and the moneylender Judah the Leg-Breaker. The latter was actually just very accident prone, but the name was good for business nonetheless.

"What are we to do?" wailed Judah. "It seems as if the Master of the Universe has abandoned us."

"We must not give up hope," said Israel. "Just because the Lord has not shown Himself, it doesn't mean He will not help. Perhaps He will guide us, if we just take the first step. Salomone, perhaps you can do a special investigative report on the origins of the plague to cast blame away from the Jews?"

"It will do no good," replied Salomone. "Since this began, the gentiles refuse to believe what my criers say. We'd probably be better off having my criers say we *are* to blame."

Israel got that sort of faraway look in his eyes that people in

---

1. Zucetto: Italian for yarmulke. Yarmulke: Yiddish for kippah. Kippah: Hebrew for skullcap. Skullcap: goyish for beanie.

soap operas get so that the viewers know that they're deep in thought, and a faint smile crossed his lips.

"Perhaps you're right," he said. "Perhaps we can't get our enemies to stop killing Jews. But at least we can make them pay for the privilege."

Thus was born an audacious plot to change Europe's drinking habits, net the three a sizable profit, and rack up a considerable body count in the process.

It all began in 1347, when a ship left Caffa, a Genoese colony on the Black Sea. The city had been under siege by the Mongol Hordes, who thought that people kept referring to them as the "Mongol Whores," which put them in an almost permanent bad mood. Their siege was having little effect, however, since Caffa had walls, which rendered fairly ineffective the usual Mongol tactics of charging and whooping. To top it off, the Mongol army was struck by a plague—and not just any plague, but a bubonic plague. While their military tactics may have been of little use, their funerary rituals—which consisted of loading corpses into catapults and hurling them great distances—would have dramatic repercussions both for Caffa and for Europe.[2]

As the plague ravaged Caffa, a group of Genoese merchants came up with a desperate plan to escape, not just with their own lives, but with what they saw as a valuable commodity: rats, which at the time were viewed by many Europeans as harbingers of good health and good fortune. The theory was that just as rats would leave a sinking ship, so too would they abandon a doomed town. Consequently, a large rat population was seen as a surefire sign that a city had a rosy future. These merchants felt that not only would they be able to guarantee their own survival by fleeing with

---

2. When it was suggested to the Mongol commander that the catapults might be put to better use as siege weapons, he reportedly replied that humans, no matter how forcefully hurled, could never knock down walls, and had the offender summarily catapulted into the Caffan fortifications to prove his point.

large numbers of rats, they might also be able to sell them for a tidy profit back in Genoa.

The ship docked in 1348, by which point most of the crew was dead or dying. As customs officials inspected the doomed ship with horror, they could at least be thankful that the rats had made it safely to shore. The port's chief medical officer felt that too much clean ocean air might have been the cause of the mysterious malady that afflicted the crew, and arranged for the few survivors to be rushed to the crowded town square, where it was hoped that the robust smells of the city might restore them to good health. Alas, it was not to be, and soon not only was the crew dead, but the illness was spreading throughout Genoa and beyond, as the many travelers who regularly passed through that cosmopolitan port city carried the disease far and wide.

Europe at the time was enjoying perfect plague conditions. Cities were cramped and overcrowded, and with no sewer or sanitation systems, garbage and waste were thrown into the streets, which, when it rained, became teeming swamps of filth. To be sure, the streets of the larger cities were paved, but since they were paved with blocks of dried human feces—the phrase "shitting bricks" was not originally metaphoric—it did little to improve the overall atmosphere. Disease was common, but the Black Death, as the plague came to be known (much to the consternation of blackamoor-rights advocates) was like nothing that Europe had ever seen before. Desperate for salvation, Europeans tried a bewildering array of cures. Many believed the plague was a divine punishment, and some, known as Flagellants, wandered around Europe torturing themselves in the hopes of purging themselves of sin.[3] Others, rejecting this approach as foolish superstition, tried a more rational approach. Rats were healthy. Therefore, cats were not. Some Jews were named "Katz." Therefore, killing Jews would

---

3. A less well-known approach was taken by the Flatulents, who though equally concerned with purging themselves, ended up torturing others.

prevent the plague. Granted, it wasn't *very* rational, but considering that the finest minds of Christian Europe spent most of their time trying to turn lead into gold, it wasn't bad. In town after town, Jewish communities were completely wiped out. In some towns without Jews, mobs were so desperate for the life-saving properties of Jew-killing that they forcibly converted Christians to Judaism just so that they could kill them. It was at this point that Israel and the others stepped in.

Rats were healthy. Therefore, cats were not. Some Jews were named "Katz." Therefore, killing Jews would prevent the plague. Granted, it wasn't *very* rational, but considering that the finest minds of Christian Europe spent most of their time trying to turn lead into gold, it wasn't bad.

Israel laid out the plan, and they put it into action. Salomono sent his criers out to announce that special additives that help protect against the plague were being placed in all the wells, a message that was soon picked up by town criers throughout Europe. Then Israel approached the Holy Father with a simple request. He understood that the pope couldn't intervene to stop the Jewish massacres, but perhaps he could issue a statement to the effect that the Jews absolutely were not engaged in poisoning the wells. The pope saw this as a fairly harmless gesture on his part, since nobody had accused the Jews of doing so, and announced that the proclamation should be read in churches across the Continent. The effect on the Christian population was electrifying, as it became convinced that the Jews were, in fact, poisoning the wells. Still, they needed water to drink, and began casting about for alternatives. For several months, Judah and a consortium of other Jewish money-lenders and merchants had been

In some towns without Jews, mobs were so desperate for the lifesaving properties of Jew-killing that they forcibly converted Christians to Judaism just so that they could kill them.

quietly buying up natural springs all across Europe—Bath, England; Evian and Vichy in France; Bad Selz, Bad Tolz, and Baden-Baden in Germany; and so on. Using agents who could pass as non-Jews—many, in fact, were the survivors of those Christians forcibly converted by the mobs in the previous year, who took to their new religion with a literal vengeance—they began bottling and selling this water all over the place as a healthy alternative.

Soon most of Europe was drinking this water. After a few years, the consortium dropped the hammer. They sold their interests in most of the springs, bought up breweries and distilleries all over

Judenrein [Jew-Free] was only one of numerous brands of bottled waters which were highly regulated by the *Judenreinheitsgeboten* of 1348, which set strict rules for what defined waters as "Jew-free" or "Jew-lite." The motto of Judenrein was "Trinken Sie Nicht Rhein; Trinken Sie Judenrein!" [Don't drink from the Rhine; Drink Judenrein!]

Europe, and *then* poisoned the springs.[4] Between the fears of the wells, and the actual deaths from the springs, most Christians were more than happy to abandon water for beer, whiskey, vodka, and so on. It would take centuries before the bottled water industry would recover, and before non-Jews figured out that they'd be much better at avoiding Jewish conspiracies if they weren't drunk all the time.

---

4. The one spring they continued to own was Bad Selz, which explains the long-standing Jewish affinity for selzer water.

CHAPTER NINE

RENAISSANCE MEN

Watch where you're going, Jew." The words stung Carmine Rabinovitch even though he had heard the religious epithet many times during his life in fifteenth-century Florence. At the age of forty-five, Carmine had become perhaps the most respected man in Florence's Jewish ghetto,[1] where he was an impresario, a tastemaker, and the ultimate arbiter on what was hot and what was not. Indeed, he had, in fact, coined the distinction "hot" or "not" during a summer job he had as a teenager waiting tables at Mamelle Bella's when describing the difference between the restaurant's soup du jour and that of Mamelle Mia's, the restaurant across the street. Although the owner of the latter tried desperately to argue that gazpacho was not supposed to be hot, the damage had already been done, and Carmine's reputation had been made.

It was a reputation that would only improve over the years. When the Education Committee at Temple Emmanuelo came under fire for signing off on curriculum materials that included a candid discussion of sex education by a social worker named Niccolo Mandelbaum, he spun it to the PTA as part of a discussion on Jewish continuity. When the spoiled cholent of Giuseppe Morgenstern, the ghetto's butcher, caused twelve cases of food poisoning on the first night of Passover, it was Carmine who deftly initiated a publicity campaign, framing the cholent as "so rich and hearty you'll eat until you puke." And when Rabbi Franco Weiner was caught having

---

1. And fairly well liked in Florence's barrio and Little Saigon as well. Most historians date the term *ghetto*—the exact meaning of which remains unclear—from Venice's decision in 1516 to force the Jews into an enclosed area of the city. In fact, the Venetians simply adopted the term used for Florence's Jewish neighborhood since at least 1437, when the Jews there began to move in large numbers into the old black neighborhood of that name.

an affair with the wife of the head of the men's club, it was Carmine who shifted public attention to the rabbi's impressive record increasing synagogue membership with the motto: "Rabbi Weiner will do just about anything to keep our numbers up." It was because of the respect he commanded inside the ghetto that made the disrespect he experienced outside it so painful, especially since that disrespect so often took the form of beatings.

Things had not always been that way. Jews had originally been made welcome in Florence, but the city fathers were forced to give in to papal injunctions against them when the Florentine public school system began winning all the math and science awards, and the pope, upset by Roman Biblical Science's poor showing, threatened to invoke a little-known rule that authorized him to strip the republic's leaders of all their comfortable shoes. Thus, Carmine was a big fish in a small pond, and the abuses and disabilities he faced every day as a Jew in Florence were a cruel reminder that in the scheme of things, he was a nobody.

Distraught, Carmine pondered his plight as he walked along the Ponte Vecchio, the bridge which connected the Palazzo Vecchio with the Pitti Palace. The merchants and artisans selling this and that who routinely clogged the walkways of the bridge were packing up for the day. Carmine leaned against the stone rail and watched the moon reflect on the waters of the Arno. Suddenly, there was a commotion on the other side of the bridge followed by a large splash and then the sound of screaming. Someone was drowning.

Carmine—who taught swim instruction at Camp Zurka Veshengo[2] the summer after graduating college—dove into the Arno to save the drowning man. It wasn't easy, considering the man's considerable girth, but using the cross-chest carry—which, by itself, would have been enough to get him in trouble with the religious

---

2. While in North America it has become a custom for Jews to give Native American names to their summer camps, Gypsy names have been used in Europe since time immemorial.

authorities—he was able to guide him to shore. Still coughing and struggling to regain his breath, the man looked at his rescuer and his eyes lit up.

"Aren't you Carmine Rabinovitch?"

"I am indeed," replied Carmine.

"Oh, how whimsical is Lady Fortune! From the evil clutches of my most scorned to the benevolent hands of my most revered! Carmine Rabinovitch, I have always wanted to meet you. Allow me to introduce myself: Lenny Davinski, at your service."

Lenny Davinski was another Jew trying to make it outside of the ghetto, and wanted Carmine's help in selling himself. As a young strange boy, his one friend was Schmendroclus, an elderly refugee from the recently collapsed Byzantine Empire. As Schmendroclus lay dying—a process that actually took ten absurdly melodramatic years—he gave Lenny a great gift: a library of Byzantine reprints of classical works, including a copy of Suetonius's *Lives of the First Twelve Caesars*, which, horrible title notwithstanding, was pretty racy stuff. Thus inspired by what he'd read and seen, Lenny devoted himself to becoming an artist and managed to apprentice himself to Verrochio, the most gifted artist in Florence. He put the youth in charge of mixing his colors, but when the Holy Virgin's lips came out as Passion Pink instead of Maidenly Mauve, Lenny was let go.

On his own, Lenny had but one problem—lack of talent. Europe was still dominated by the Gothic aesthetic—everything improperly dimensioned, without perspective, and wearing too much black eyeshadow. But under the influence of the classics, Lenny's style was archaic, boring, and hopelessly realistic. When Lenny painted an apple, it looked good enough to eat. When he painted a book, it looked good enough to read. And when he painted a person—well, let's just say that his obsession with anatomical realism allowed him to earn a meager living selling his pornographic post-cards on the Ponte Vecchio, where his one steady client was a gay Venetian who had developed a fetish for men with multiple arms while trading in India. But ever since Fra Savonarola of

Bologna[3] had started taking after-dinner strolls across the bridge, Lenny had been getting spit upon. This was not as bad as being upon a spit, which is where Savonarola threatened to put him, but was still pretty unpleasant. The abuse came to a climax that evening when Fra Savonarola ordered two particularly strapping monks to throw Lenny and all of his pornographic postcards into the river.

Though Carmine was not a big fan of pornography, having been traumatized as a youth when his mother found his stash of smutty canvases under his bed, his heart went out to Lenny, for the latter's aspirations reminded him of his own. As the soggy pair walked back to the Jewish quarter that evening, Lenny told him not only of his own life, but of what he'd learned of the classical world. It was an eye-opening experience for Carmine.

"I was born during the wrong age," opined Lenny. "If I had been born in Greek and Roman times, I would have been a star; in this age, I'm a filthy vagrant. If only I could be reborn in another era."

Reborn. Someone much less savvy wouldn't have paid much attention to the word. But for Carmine Rabinovitch, the word triggered an epiphany, one that could help his newfound friend, but more important, confirm the superiority of his public relations skills in the secular world. The idea was simple: Turn Davinski into the icon of a new aesthetic, one borrowing liberally from the ancients, yet relevant to the fifteenth century. The idea may have been simple, but the means were anything but. Carmine got to work the next morning.

A thousand years earlier, the church fathers had been terrified that if given the choice between pagan licentiousness and Christian rigor, people would go with the beautiful slave girls peeling grapes. Thus, for a millennium the church had maintained the lie

---

3. At the height of Savonarola's fame, his birthplace stood for truth and wisdom. After his fall from grace, however, *Bologna* became synonymous with nonsense. A similar rise and decline in status befell the birthplace of the sixteenth-century English ladies' man Jerome of Limpdick after his dissipation robbed him of his virility.

that the Romans were not more morally lax than the church, but more strict. From a young age, the faithful had it instilled in them that they had it a lot easier than their forebears did. The church made them tithe 10 percent of their income; the ancient Romans would charge 48 percent. The church forbade them from eating meat on Fridays during Lent; the ancient Romans forbade them from doing so on Mondays, Wednesdays, and Fridays. The church held infants under water for three seconds during baptism; the ancient Romans held them down for three minutes. This complex edifice of lies made the typical European feel thankful for the excessive social norms of the church, and in Spain and Portugal, special hymns of gratitude for those excessive norms were actually sung in church. In order to maintain the façade, works like Suetonius's had been pushed aside by the church, in favor of Stoic philosophy and harsh legal rulings that were hardly likely to encourage further interest in Roman culture. For example, as a reminder to newly minted Catholics of how much better things were under the church's beneficence, Pliny's classic admonition to suffer stoically, *The Barbarians Have Moved My Cheese*, was often given as a Confirmation present along with the standard quill set. So Carmine's first step was to produce a translation of Suetonius into Italian, making sure to spice up that already *caliente* tome with a few additional lurid tales designed to appeal to the rumored fetishes of Florence's high and mighty, including stories of Nero's sex life,[4] Caligula's depravity,[5] and Tiberius's enormous collection of comfortable footwear.

The timing was perfect. The printing press made the book inexpensive enough for the literate masses, and they read the book to the other 98 percent of the population. Moreover, the upper classes of Lombardy and Tuscany had considerable discretionary

---

4. With a particularly graphic chapter, titled "Nero Does Pallas," detailing Nero's real-life acting out of his fantasy involving the Greek goddess of wisdom.
5. With an extremely realistic, anonymously drawn image of Caligula's horse in a miniskirt.

wealth and were always on the lookout for new ways to spend it. Coming decades before the basilica craze of the early sixteenth century, and at a time when most people just wanted to forget the whole "hammer pants" fiasco of the early 1470s, Carmine's idea for a rebirth of classical culture was set to become the hottest trend in centuries. With people beginning to view the Greeks and Romans in a more positive light, Carmine moved to the next step: undermining the moral authority of the church. At morning Mass at the Church of San Nicola Al Ceppo, Carmine se-

> Coming decades before the basilica craze of the early sixteenth century, and at a time when most people just wanted to forget the whole "hammer pants" fiasco of the early 1470s, Carmine's idea for a rebirth of classical culture was set to become the hottest trend in centuries.

cretly inserted an additional note card into the priest's stack so that in the midst of his sermon that day he launched a vicious diatribe against those who used porcelain vases as paperweights. While perplexing most listeners, this enraged the Medici family, which felt that they'd come to an understanding with the church on the matter. At the Church of Sal Mineo, he disguised himself as a monk and stood in the central nave handing out pamphlets urging the laity to abstain from using all definite articles on Thursdays unless their feet were bare; in that case they could sing them in falsetto, but would have to first become castrati. And one evening at the Church of Santa Croce, he had the Borowitz Brothers Ghetto Contractors add a Star of David made of polychrome marble to the façade. The church's efforts to explain it away as a "six-pointed Jesus wheel" didn't do much to stem the confusion of the congregation. Of course, it should be noted that the people had already been growing sick and tired of Scholasticism, the church's main intellectual movement, for half a century, ever since it became obsessed with "How many __ can dance on the head of a pin?" jokes. Carmine's manipulations were simply the last straw for the people of Florence. Clearly, the church had gone mad.

With popular sentiment among the Greeks and Romans shifting and the church's authority wavering, it was time for the final step of Carmine's public relations campaign: the creation of his own broadsheet, which he called *Renaissance Man*. Published under the Catholic pseudonym Angelo Smith, the broadsheet celebrated the hip, swinging lifestyle of the Greco-Roman world and satirized the pieties and hypocrisies of the church. *Renaissance Man* wasn't just a broadsheet[6]: As an editorial in the first issue stated, it was a lifestyle—and the symbol of that lifestyle was Lenny Davinski, whom Carmine called Leonardo da Vinci and listed as creative director in the masthead. The cover of the first issue featured the Mona Lisa. It was revealed in the accompanying interview that in order to achieve the level of anatomical accuracy for which he became famous, Da Vinci painted all his women naked, and only then painted clothes on them. Florentine men swore they could detect a little nipple action going on, and as Lenny's art became all the rage, stories of his notorious nightlife exploits made the Florentine artist famous throughout the Continent. Thousands of artists emulated his aesthetic, and tens of thousands of men emulated his playboy lifestyle including the silk pajamas and pipe, which would become his trademark.

Though Lenny's fame was firmly enshrined in the history of

---

6. The presence of paintings of beautiful women on the covers did lead to the actual coining of the term *broadsheets*, which was used in England in much the same way that *lad mags* is used today.

With features like "Mandolins: What's Hot, What's Not?", "Do You Have What It Takes to Be a 'Prince?'", and of course, "Find Out What Makes Our Covergirl, Lisa, Moan," the first issue of *Renaissance Man* was like nothing medieval man had ever seen before. Although the commercial run featured clothed illustrations, there was a very small limited edition that was run off before Leonardo painted clothes on, made available to a select group of influential collectors. An even more limited edition featured Mona Lisa fully clothed, but with an afro.

Western art, Carmine continued to promote the Renaissance, and the writers he promoted would go on to have a tremendous impact on Western civilization. He recruited the Borowitz brothers to write a column on architecture and interior decorating under the name Bramante. On the strength of that, they won the bid on the Tempietto in Rome. This beautiful church at the center of the city revolutionized architectural thought, which since the time when Viking raids were a common occurrence maintained that churches should ideally be isolated and ugly. Carmine convinced Niccolo Mandelbaum, who had developed a reputation as the most notorious Casanova in the ghetto,[7] to write a metaphoric guide to being a player. To get past the church censors, who demanded that all manifestations of eroticism be sublimated in homoerotic paintings of naked cherubs, it ran as a regular column on political power entitled "The Prince", under the pseudonym Machiavelli.

All of this may seem unlikely today, but it should be recalled that under the influence of the church, people had become accustomed to the allegorical, and even the most simple instructions were often presented as allegories without any apparent loss in comprehension. For example, "The Abstemiouse Shepherde goeth not before his Flokk, but bydeth and herdeth from the Syde" was what passed for a speed limit sign on the road to Canterbury in 1348. Readers were well enough aware of what Machiavelli was really talking about that to this day, the term *mack* is synonymous with *player.* Years later, Carmine made a similar coup with the book written by the butcher Giusseppe Morgenstern's precocious nephew Tomasso, who had recently moved to England. Since Jews were not allowed in England at the time, he anglicized his first name to Thomas and shortened his last name. At Carmine's suggestion, he then changed it again, from Genstern to More. As Thomas More, he quilled a lurid tale about being stranded on an

---

7. We recognize the anachronism and would like to call attention to the fact that Giacomo Casanova used to refer to himself as "a real Mandelbaum" some three centuries later.

island in the Caribbean with a bunch of hot natives. Carmine, who had long since gone into book publishing, brought it out under the guise of a critique of medieval society entitled *Utopia*.[8]

Of course, as the movement became more popular, others got into the game as well. As is often the case with art, dealers began to "discover" artists who had died years earlier and connect them to the movement. Thus, Giotto, another pornographer who, it was said, once painted a fly so realistically people thought they could touch it (unspoken was the belief that they could also unbutton it) is seen as part of the Renaissance despite having painted a century earlier. Other broadsheets, like *Classical Education* and *Swingin' Humanist* competed with *Renaissance Man*, but they never came close to Carmine's circulation numbers.

Most think the Renaissance was brought upon by the corruption of the Church, the horrors of the Inquisition, and the beginning of Rationalism, but it could not have happened without Carmine Rabinovitch. Carmine ended up retiring to the countryside in Tuscany, where he married a twenty-one-year-old peasant girl and lived off the earnings from his broadsheet. Leonardo is, of course, recognized as one of the great men of history, but nobody realizes that his curious habit of writing backward was really just because he never quite got over the switch from writing from right to left in Hebrew to writing from left to right in Italian.

---

8. More got a little too cozy with his new identity and ultimately switched both religions and publishers. His second book, *Utopian Beach Bunnies*, was considered a commercial flop, leading his new publishers to behead him.

CHAPTER TEN

1491

Guillermo de la Nussbaum nearly fell out of his hammock: The entire Arawak village was rushing to the beach.[1] Brushing aside two of his fifteen wives, he sped past the two bamboo synagogues he'd built, one that he attended and one he wouldn't be caught dead in. (Some readers may think that this is an old joke, but it wasn't in 1492.) Reaching the beach, he saw three ships at sea and encountered a group of men whose disturbingly tight pants and castanets marked them as fellow Spaniards. The native children were welcoming the sailors with bananas, mangoes, and coconut milk. There were not, however, any coconut telephones. You're thinking of *Gilligan's Island*, many episodes of which also featured the island's discovery, but with far less ensuing genocide. Guillermo brushed aside the Arawak chief, who was greeting Christopher Columbus, and embraced the startled Italian.

"Welcome, my friends," he said. "Welcome to paradise!"

Now Columbus hadn't imagined that he'd be greeted in Spanish upon reaching his final destination, especially in a Spanish that sounded so very much like English. But he presumed that this was some Spanish merchant who had made his way overland to Asia, one who would doubtlessly be impressed by his own illustrious feat. That comfortable illusion was soon shattered, however, as was the notion that Guillermo didn't mean paradise in the metaphorical sense. Guillermo *actually* believed that he was in heaven.

---

1. *Arawak* is actually a name that the Spanish gave to the natives who had previously referred to themselves as "the primitive savages." In 1991, individuals claiming that they were the offspring of this tribe launched an unsuccessful effort to be formally recognized by their original name.

For nearly five centuries, this painting by the Pinta's shipboard artist was known as "Columbus Is Down with the Arawaks," and was meant to show how hip the Admiral of the Oceans was. It was only when it was being restored for the 500-year anniversary of Columbus's voyage that they took off the frame and found the original title: "The Jew Who Got There First."

"I don't know how you met your untimely ends, but let me tell you my story," he said.

"We are in heaven, and all are considered equal in the eyes of God." It should be noted that it was still some two decades before the Spanish became aware of the Filipinos, who, if truth be told, kind of get on God's nerves.

"Thus, I am free to state proudly that I am a Jew, from Malaga, Spain. I was born in 1452, the same year that the church sanctioned the enslavement of infidels. Not surprisingly, I had a miserable childhood—even by pagan standards. I had but one friend, a Moorish lad named Rasheed, who came from a home with a single mother, which in the Moorish context meant that his father could only afford one wife. Since the Moors had just launched their most devastating assault—the insertion of algebra into the Western curriculum—my friendship with Rasheed earned me nothing but even more scorn. As we all know, children are cruel. But when it came to me, the kids sunk to new depths. They routinely stole my gruel money, put thumbscrews in my mittens, and placed 'stone-me' signs on my back. My father was a skilled carpenter who manufactured and sold—at cost—prosthetic foreskins to the Marranos."

After clearing up some confusion among those sailors who mistook Marranos—Jews forced by pressure from the authorities to adopt Christianity but who secretly practiced Judaism—with Morronos, those Jews who secretly think Tom Arnold is a comic genius, Guillermo continued with his account.

"Although he was a Jew devoted to the faith of his forefathers, he was also quite a ladies' man, and his time was pretty much divided equally between his two passions.[2] And, oh, how I idolized the man. Unfortunately, his time in this world was cut short. Even right now I can hear him uttering the last words from his deathbed. 'Guillermo,' he told me. 'The thing that comforts me, the thing that

---

2. Sometimes quite literally, as those who looked beneath the bima and spotted Gabriella Suarez performing fellatio upon him as he recited the maftir aliyah on Shabbat Shuva in 1463 can attest.

will let me to drift peacefully into the next world, is the knowledge that you have a circumcision, and you know how to use it.' Now these words were even more poignant considering that my father's deathbed was, in fact, a bed of nails. While this may sound pretty painful, you wouldn't believe the closeout the Inquisition was having, and with the box spring and delivery thrown in, it was too good a deal to pass up.

"Now you probably wouldn't believe it when you see me frolicking among the angels here in Paradise, but I was the farthest thing from Don Juan back in Spain. Well, to be honest, Jose Delgado of 4520 Calle del Cid lived two blocks farther from Don, but I lived uphill. I was thirty-nine years old and had never consummated the sexual act with a woman. Yes, there had been a brief encounter with the Iron Maiden during one of my visits to my father at the Interrogarium (as the dungeon was then known), but the Inquisitor walked in before I could finish. Yet, to allay my loving and reprobate father's fears about my loneliness, throughout his life I had concocted a series of half-baked lies that cast me as a womanizer. I stuffed my codpiece, boasted of the expert skills I acquired under the sexual tutelage of an Ottoman wench,[3] and even claimed to have had a ménage à trois with two women in Lisbon, knowing how impressed he'd be that I'd fulfilled every man's fantasy of doing it with two Lisbians. When my father passed, in addition to the normal grieving process, I had to deal with the realization that my life was one giant lie, a lie covering up for the unbearable self-hatred that lay at the center of my being. I endeavored to take my life.

> **My father's deathbed was, in fact, a bed of nails. While this may sound pretty painful, you wouldn't believe the closeout the Inquisition was having, and with the box spring and delivery thrown in, it was too good a deal to pass up.**

---

3. "Ottoman wenches" were particularly big-assed slaves used as human footstools. The term *Ottoman* then became applied more generally to the Turks, the size of whose posteriors was legendary, depending on how you understand that word.

"Remember this was 1491—the revolver hadn't been invented so I couldn't shoot myself. The gas oven hadn't been invented so I couldn't asphyxiate myself. And I haven't even heard of Ben Franklin—so forget about the old radio in the tub routine. No, I had to be creative. I walked into a bar in a Moorish neighborhood and requested that the house band play a Gregorian chant. Yes, I was beaten to a pulp, but unfortunately was not killed.

"Next, I informed the parents of the altar boys what organ Fra Felipi was actually practicing on. When word got out about what I had done, the monks took me to their torture chamber, where I was bound and lashed, but not killed. This, of course, was in large part because much of the lashing was done with the monks' tongues.

"My failures at suicide only increased my self-loathing. My extraordinary pain demanded an extraordinary solution. I decided to sail off the edge of the earth! It was a stormy night and all of the sailors were carousing at the Salty Seaman tavern so I had little problem getting a vessel. I unfolded the main sail and wedged the canon[4] against the tiller directing the ship due west directly into the eye of the storm. The rest is blurry: I remember the winds knocking me off my feet. I must've banged my head on the steerage. I missed the actual sailing off the edge of the earth part, but when I woke up I was here—in heaven. Kinda funny: I couldn't even get a date on earth, but here in Paradise I can't get a wink of sleep."

Columbus and his crew, not having seen a woman in months, were much more interested in the scantily clad dancing girls than in Guillermo's story. And the Arawaks were much more interested in the wine that the Spanish had brought ashore, which bad as it was, beat the hell out of their traditional ways of getting wasted such as smoking banana peels, licking tree frogs, and huffing Freon. Two men, however, were mesmerized by the sheer improbability of Guillermo's story: ship doctor Maestro Alonso and planker

---

4. That's not a typo; the ship was actually transporting a collection of the Great Works to be burned in Rome.

Enrique Canción. The doctor had changed his name from Morrie Abramson for professional reasons. As Alonso, he had achieved a certain degree of fame in the European medical world by inventing a concoction of herbs known as "Spanish Flyagra," which awakened the sexual desire in whomever consumed it. Canción, also a Jew, was responsible for making insubordinate crew members walk the plank when they acted up. His formal education was in comparative religion at the University of Salamanca, but as un-Christian views came to be labeled heretical by the church, his parents urged him to pick up something a bit more practical.

Maestro Alonso pulled Guillermo aside. "You are a very lucky man, indeed," he said. "But not for the reasons you suspect. You're not in heaven, my friend. You did not sail off the edge of the world. The world is round. We are no closer to the Elysian Fields than we are to Spain."

Guillermo was shocked. But it was not the kind of shock experienced by a man who wakes up with a woman who is not, in fact, a real woman, but rather, the shock of a man waking up with a woman who is not, in fact, a real blonde.[5] "But with the guy/girl ratio, I thought for sure..." Incredulous, his eyes drifted to the chief's lovely Virgin Daughter. She licked her lips seductively and shifted her weight back and forth from hip to hip, a motion that caused even those experienced seafarers to get dizzy. "So you're telling me that that isn't an angel?"

Guillermo looked around. Sailors and native girls were pairing off and heading into huts. Seven of Guillermo's fifteen wives were not in sight. And then the most startling of thoughts crept into his

---

5. 'Cause, after all, who needs heaven when you're getting hot Arawak action 24–7?

head: "I'm no longer the only guy around with pale skin, a hairy back, and a bad case of scurvy. Now I have competition."

Guillermo's two new friends couldn't help but notice his morose visage, and they also couldn't help but feel that as long as the strapping Spanish conquistadors were around, they'd also be denied an ample share of ample Arawak booty.[6] Then, all of a sudden Maestro Alonso's eyes lit up: "Columbus set out to find Asia," he said. "Let's convince him that's where he is."

"Convince him he's in Asia?" asked Guillermo.

Canción caught on: "More than anything in the world Columbus wants *fame*. It is his dream to someday be mentioned in the same breath as Marco Polo. He wants cities named after him, parades thrown in his honor, and sales of electronics to occur just because of his navigational skills. If he thinks he discovered a new route to the East, he will want to rush back to Europe to reap the rewards of fame."

Guillermo was starting to come around, but couldn't help but wonder aloud: "How in the world are we going to convince him that this place is China?"

"I didn't say it would be easy," replied Maestro Alonso.

But the three went to work. Though their efforts to train the Arawaks to tug at the sides of their eyes to make themselves look Asian proved to be unsuccessful, they did convince them to act in ways that would make Columbus and his crew believe they were closer to mainland China than they would have otherwise thought. Guillermo taught the Arawak women to cook lo mein and encouraged them to serve it in tiny, cardboard boxes. Canción got the men to stop wearing their *"¡Yo soy 100% Boricua!"* T-shirts. Maestro Alonso surreptitiously made peepee in the Spaniards' Coke and then attributed it to an inscrutable "Chinese joke."

The conspiracy worked...almost too well. Contrary to what politically correct revisionist historians would have you believe,

---

6. And now you know how those words became homonyms.

Columbus and his crew did not start raping and pillaging as soon as they arrived. In fact, it was nearly four full days before they began to do so. But after more and more evidence piled up that he had landed somewhere off the coast of mainland China, Columbus immediately began planning his return to Europe, a plan that would involve the transfer of Chinese slaves to be sold in the markets of Seville. Doing so, he reasoned, would enable him to pay off the considerable debts he tallied putting together his expedition. The story that Queen Isabella had pawned her crown jewels to pay for Columbus's trip is apocryphal. She pawned them in order to change all the street signs in Granada from Arabic to Spanish after her army's victory there.[7] So Columbus started rounding up the most marketable Arawaks, which generally meant able-bodied women between the ages of eighteen and twenty-five. He also insisted that the chief's Virgin Daughter come, as he put it, "to represent the royal house of the Arawaks." He then leered and twirled his mustache, which he had grown specifically for the occasion.

When the three conspirators realized what had happened they had to think fast. They came up with an idea. Guillermo met with the Arawak chief and argued that even if the Arawaks could fight off Columbus and his crew, more Europeans would subsequently come to enslave them, armies that could not be fought off. The chief, claimed Guillermo, needed to adopt a more pragmatic strategy, one that would guarantee the safety of the Arawaks headed back to Europe—especially considering that one of them would be his most beloved Virgin Daughter. What these slaves needed was a chaperone, someone who spoke Spanish and could advocate on their behalf upon their arrival in Europe, a chaperone like Guillermo.

---

7. The pawnshop, owned by Jose Gonzalez Hernandez de Soto Lipschitz, was a favorite among the locals in Seville. During 1492, he held a year-long "Being Expulsed: Everything Must Go" sale. Thinking that his prices had to be rock-bottom, people flocked from miles around to take advantage of his misfortune. The last laugh was his, though, since he ended up converting and staying in business.

Meanwhile, Canción and Maestro Alonso informed Columbus that Guillermo de la Nussbaum was planning to catch a free trip back to Europe, where he would claim credit for discovering a new route to the East.

Columbus saw the fame, the glory, the cushy endorsement deals for breakfast cereal, all going down the drain.

"I can't refuse him passage," he moaned. "Without him, the deal is off with the chief, and with his Virgin Daughter. What can I do?"

"Well..." said Alonso. "There is one possibility..." He described a hellish place to the northwest where legend held that cannibals lived, a place of no uncertain return.

The wheels were in motion: The chief reluctantly agreed to hand over his daughter and the other slaves under the condition that Guillermo chaperone. Columbus agreed to this condition, loaded up his slaves, and set sail—northwest. Columbus then proceeded to force Guillermo into a lifeboat and sent him off toward the coast. Canción and Alonso approached Columbus with a concern: that Guillermo's fifteen wives might act as advocates for him back in Spain. Columbus wasn't happy with the loss of valuable slaves, but he saw their point, and they agreed to row the wives to the mainland. After the last batch of wives had landed, Columbus and his men waited...and waited. Concerned about his crew, Columbus led a party to the beach, finding it empty but for Alonso's blood-stained vest, and Canción's planking hat, with a huge man-sized bite taken out of it.

"*¡Madre de Dios!*" cursed Columbus, forgetting momentarily that he was Italian and not Spanish. "Cannibals! Quickly men, set sail from this cursed place!"

Back at the "cursed place," which Guillermo named "Miami Beach,"[8] the three Spanish Jews divided Guillermo's wives among themselves and watched the ships sail away. They would build the

---

8. The word *Miami* derives from the two Arawak roots "mi" (*my*) and "ami" (*place of comfortable Jewish retirement*).

first Miami condominium, where all eighteen of them would happily grow old together.

The log, which Columbus presented to Ferdinand and Isabella, of course, made no mention of Guillermo de la Nussbaum, whose voyage across the Atlantic in 1491 was summarily, and not surprisingly, omitted from the historical record. That same historical record, it should be added, left out the name of the virgin daughter who Columbus brought back to Europe: Syphilis.

CHAPTER ELEVEN

NOTHING GETS BETWEEN ME AND MY CALVIN

Eliezer Fein sighed ponderously.

"My fellow Jews," he said. "Things don't look good. We might own half of the Rhineland between us, but let's face it—it was one thing when the Christians were so bad with money they had to borrow it, and even when they were so bad they couldn't pay it back, but it's reached the point where there isn't even any money for us—and we're the moneylenders!"

When Eliezer spoke, the other moneylenders listened. His family had been lending money in the city of Strasbourg for two hundred years since 1348, when the founder of the family firm heard about new business opportunities opened up by the recent massacre of the city's Jews during the Black Death. He had originally tried to lend burial shrouds, but found the return rate was pretty low, and so switched to money, which was a pretty rare commodity in medieval Europe. As some readers are doubtlessly aware, collecting interest was considered a sin by the Catholic Church, and thus forbidden. Since Jews were damned anyway, however, they were allowed to do so. From the Jews' perspective, while you weren't allowed to collect interest from your fellow Jews, it had been a long time since Christians could lay any claim to being members of the tribe, and thus were considered fair game. For a few centuries, all was well. Jewish moneylenders like the Feins lent money, the gentiles put up their possessions as security, and either they repaid the money or the Jews collected on their possessions. The problem was that by the 1530s, the gentiles had no money left, and the Jews pretty much owned all their possessions, which may sound enviable, but who were they going to sell them to?

To understand how things reached such a revolting state of affairs, one needs to know a little something about Christianity and
money. Due to a faulty translation from the Old Testament, the
church fathers believed that, rather than being wary of "false
prophets," they should beware "false profits."[1] Thus, the church developed a deep antipathy to the notion of making money. Not only
was earning money looked down on, but even having too much
money was viewed as a despicable and lowly thing. Indeed, it was
during this time that the church started holding bingo tournaments,
with the goal being to *lose* money—if your numbers were called,
you got to double your losses. In its infinite goodness, it seems, the
church was willing to accept the sinful money of its congregants
unto its own heavenly bosom.

The problem, of course, was that while money might have been
viewed with suspicion, it did come in handy when you needed to
buy something. In the early Middle Ages, this wasn't such a problem, since nobody had anything that anybody wanted, and if they
did, somebody invariably killed them and took it. As more things
were acquired, grown, looted, pillaged, and so forth, and as the so-
cieties became safer, the old means of acquiring goods no longer
worked. There had been a barter system, but as the more upwardly
mobile abysmal serfs moved up into the ranks of the miserable
peasantry, there was a much greater demand for the creature
comforts that could no longer be met simply by trade. It was easy
when you wanted wheat in exchange for your carrots, but what if
you wanted luxuries, like shredded wheat? What if you were a
noble who wanted to build an extension on your summer torture
chamber? What if you were a king who had to pay for the dowry
of your hideously mutated inbred daughter? What then? Then
you needed money, and for that, you needed Jews, who, increasingly prohibited from doing much else in medieval Germany,

---

1. This was hardly the most glaring mistranslation the church fathers made. The worst
was reading that the Messiah would have a virgin birth, instead of what Isaiah actually
said, which was that the Messiah would have "an aversion to birds."

It was easy when you wanted wheat in exchange for your carrots, but what if you wanted luxuries, like shredded wheat? What if you were a noble who wanted to build an extension on your summer torture chamber? What if you were a king who had to pay for the dowry of your hideously mutated inbred daughter? What then?

became experts at the golden stuff. This was great for a couple of hundred years, but as noted above, by the sixteenth century, the well had run dry, which led the moneylenders of the various cities to discuss what could be done. Eliezer continued his speech:

"On paper, we are all rich men.[2] But what use is it to hold the deed on the inn, when all I can collect are leftovers—and unkosher leftovers at that? And what use is it to hold the title to the church, when all I can be paid is confessional gossip, and that's anonymous? Granted, the deed to the brothel isn't a bad deal, but still—"

"Face it, Eliezer, it's over," interjected Simon the Usurious, from the Swiss Cantons. "The only way these goyim are going to make any money is if their priests tell them they can. And that's not going to happen anytime soon."

The meeting ended without resolution, but Eliezer couldn't get what Simon had said out of his head. What if there could be a new religious ethic for the Christians, one that viewed making money in a positive light? Some might question the wisdom of encouraging gentiles to make money. But from the Jews' perspective, you wanted them to make money, you just didn't want them to keep it. The church hadn't had a monopoly on German Christianity for nearly two decades, ever since Martin Luther began to chip away at the church's authority. It all started in 1519 when Martin Luther, the father of the Reformation, met Johann

---

2. In fact, in the sixteenth century, if you had paper on which to be, you were by definition rich.

Stenzel, who had been sent by the pope to raise money for the construction of St. Peter's basilica and had built a huge bingo hall across from Luther's apartment. When Luther complained about the noise and lights, Stenzel ignored his pleas, telling him, "What are you going to do? Start your own church?" He didn't seem interested in money matters, but maybe Eliezer could find somebody else. A few weeks later, Eliezer went to collect the month's gossip from the local priest, only to find him in a dark mood. When asked, the priest replied that John Calvin had come to Strasbourg. Intrigued, Eliezer looked into this Calvin fellow, and he liked what he heard.

John Calvin had been born in Noyon, France, in 1509. The money his parents would have spent on giving him a real last name went into his college fund, and as a young man, he attended the University of Paris where he wrote and published his *Institutes of the Christian Religion*, in which he laid out his arguments for the Protestant reform that was beginning to take root in France. Although he was not excommunicated, he did have to leave the school, much to the delight of his roommate, Ignatius of Loyola, who was always kept awake by Calvin's snoring.

Calvin kicked around France for a while, then spent some time in Geneva, where, due to allegations of sexual impropriety with a congregant, he was again asked to leave.[3] By 1538, he was beginning a three-year sojourn in Strasbourg, which is where he was when Eliezer heard about him. He was young, passionate, and popular, and if Eliezer had anything to say about it, he was going to transform the European economy.

For several months, Eliezer immersed himself in the New Testament. Even though Calvin was a respected authority on Christian theology, Eliezer couldn't help but feel that a lifetime of talmudic casuistry[4] had prepared him well for the argument to come. On

---

3. Swearing to never give herself to another man, the Swiss Miss, as she came to be known, devoted the rest of her life to providing warm beverages to those lost in the Alps.

the appointed night, he invited the young scholar to meet him in a private room at the inn to discuss matters of theology.[5] Feeling that Calvin would be suspicious of a Jew, he had disguised himself as a gentile, or at least how he pictured a gentile should look, meaning that he flecked his beard with pieces of bacon, spilled beer on his tunic, and was reading a copy of *Field and Stream*. Calvin was a little suspicious when the stranger greeted him by pointing to the chair and saying, "Please sit, my fellow goy," but the conversation soon turned to the Holy Scripture, and he was impressed by his host's erudition. Soon Eliezer got to the heart of the matter: the sorry state of the economy. After expounding on the matter, Eliezer asked Calvin the sixty-four thousand guilder question:

"Could it not be, young Christian rabbi, that the church has been as wrong about this as about everything else, and that, in fact, making gelt is not only allowed, but even, nu, maybe a good thing?"

"Ah, but does it not say, my friend, that the love of money is the root of all evil?"

"Of course, but who's talking about loving money? If you love money, you keep it. I'm talking about spending it. Would you give away something you love?"

"Hmmm, no, that's true. But wealth brings haughtiness, and is it not said that the meek shall inherit the Earth?"

"Yes, but may it not be presumed that they are merely the heirs of their wealthy relatives, who had it first?"

"Well said, but is it not easier for a camel to pass through the eye of a needle, than for a rich man to enter into the kingdom of heaven?"

"A camel through the eye of a needle? Well, how hard is that?

---

4. Unfortunately, there is no English translation for the phrase *talmudic casuistry*.

5. There are those who believe that dim memories of this meeting formed the legends that would eventually inspire both *Faust* and that episode of *The White Shadow* where Jackson was lured into betting on Carver games.

With enough money, the rich man can simply buy an enormous needle, or an exceptionally small camel."

And so it went into the night, the two men trading parables, passages, and comic books, these last to illustrate a point by Calvin on the uses of a barter system. Eliezer countered by pointing out that it only worked when the comics were of equal value, but how could you decide how many issues of *The Transubstantiator* #5 in very fair condition were worth one mint-condition *Heavenly Mysteries* #1?

> **"A camel through the eye of a needle? Well, how hard is that? With enough money, the rich man can simply buy an enormous needle, or an exceptionally small camel."**

They argued back and forth, well into the wee hours of the morning, and Eliezer felt he was no closer to convincing the man. Eliezer sighed and pushed himself back from the table. He hadn't wanted it to come to this, but now he had no choice. The French clergyman was a man of conviction, to be sure. But he was still a *French* clergyman, and Eliezer knew what his weakness was.

"Hans, Fritz..."

The door burst open and two enormous German peasants who did repo work for Eliezer stormed in, grabbing Calvin and thrusting him out the window by his ankles.

"I'm sorry it's come to this, but you wouldn't listen to reason. So here's what you're going to do, or these Germans are going to do what they do best to the French..."

The plan was laid out to him. Eliezer had explained his plan to the other moneylenders, and they had agreed to pool their resources to buy the deeds to much of Geneva from Simon the Usurious, who let them have it at cost. It would take a few years, but they were giving it to Calvin. All he had to do was espouse a new theology, one in which economic success was a sign of God's grace.

"Other than that, it's yours to do with what you want."

"You mean, I can pass whatever laws I want?"

This woodcut engraving of the Sermon on the Mount is originally from a 1637 Geneva edition of the Bible, but was reprinted frequently throughout the Calvinist world. The pimpin' style of Jesus contrasted starkly with the fashion aesthetic of the Puritans, who favored somber black panther skins and velvets over the more ostentatious leopard and satin ensemble depicted here.

"Whatever you want. Ban drinking, ban gambling...ban Jews, for all I care. Just push the earning money."

"I'll do it."

Hans and Fritz hauled him back in. Eliezer gave him the specifics of the plan and told him to start working on his new theology.

"And remember," he cautioned as he left, "if we have to meet again, I'm bringing Hans and Fritz with me, too."

Calvin began working on his commentary on the New Testament, and in 1541, established a theocracy in Geneva. His example revolutionized Christianity, and his followers spread to Scotland (the home of Adam Smith), England (the home of Thomas Malthus), and Holland (the home of Joop van Hoekstraaten),[6] carrying with them somber clothes, interminably long sermons, and of course the Protestant work ethic. Like Johnny Appleseed, wherever they went they planted the fruits of industriousness. Christians started making money, which meant they could pay back the moneylenders, who then had more money to lend to all those striving gentiles interested in expanding or starting businesses. Jesus might have been weeping, but Eliezer was smiling.

---

6. Which may mean nothing to you, but if you sold clogs in the seventeenth century, the man was a god.

CHAPTER TWELVE

LAND OF THE
REASONABLY PRICED

Hey, Shifty, not even you could unload this pile."

Lazar "Shifty" Sheftel took a sip of his coffee and turned toward his tormentor, Bancroft Cockburn,[1] who was standing at the board where properties were posted by the Guild of Realtors. In Lazar's fifteen years as the only Jew selling real estate in London, Cockburn had used his inherited position as a master guild master to prevent Lazar from becoming a member of the guild, and took every opportunity to remind him that as far as he was concerned, Jews had no business in the business. Still, the guild allowed him a table at Charrington's Coffee House, where trades were made, and when there was a property that was tough to unload, they dumped it on him. And that perhaps, more even than his being a Jew, was the source for Cockburn's animosity: He made sales that nobody else could make. When Lord Haaaaarcourt-Finchbottom wanted to sell the family funeral plot, he found a medical school to buy it. When the earl of Tet-de-Poulet needed to unload his Irish property, complete with an orphanage full of Hibernian urchins, he sold it to Jonathan Swift's younger brother, who went on to found the Swift meat-packing concern. He even managed to rent the floor above Maizy Doat's House of Trollops to a group of monks whose monastery had been confiscated by the crown, although in hindsight, that sale was actually pretty easy. Feeling that he had to prove himself, there was no challenge that Lazar couldn't rise to.

"What is it, Cockburn, trying to sell the family home?"

This brought appreciative laughter from the others in the coffeehouse.

---

1. The family claimed it was pronounced "Co'burn," but then, wouldn't you?

"No, Shifty," Cockburn responded through clenched teeth. "It's a prime piece of real estate, a million acres in our new colony in western Quebec that we just captured from the French." He was referring to the recently concluded French and Indian war, a long and bloody conflict, won primarily because the name confused the French into fighting their Indian allies. Cockburn continued. "From what I hear it's nothing but ice, unwashed, hostile savages, and Indians."

"I can sell it," said Lazar, matter-of-factly, taking another sip.

"You couldn't get twenty people to buy land there, even using all the 'ingenious' methods for which your race is so justly known."

"I could put twenty thousand people there, easily."

"Hah, Shifty, care to wager? I'd say we could make a gentleman's wager, but then, one needs to be a gentleman, eh wot?"

The whole coffeehouse was paying attention by this point, knowing the bad blood that existed between these two.

"Twenty thousand settlers? How does ten thousand guineas sound?"

The crowd gasped at the sum, all but one olive-skinned man who interjected, " 'Ey, I'ma sittin' right here."

"Sorry, Giuseppe. I meant ten thousand five hundred pounds."

The crowd let out another collective gasp. Wagering on sales was common, but not for that kind of money. It was a sum neither man could afford to lose. All eyes turned to Cockburn.

"Did you say ten thousand five hundred pounds? Is that pounds sterling, or pounds of flesh?"[2]

"Sterling, Cockburn. And I want the same terms that Stanhope gave Williams on the Ulster deal. One year per one thousand."

"So be it."

"And one more thing: If I win, I receive membership in the guild."

---

2. It should be noted that in Shakespeare's original version, a philo-Semitic revenge fantasy entitled *Shy Shylock's Badasssss Loan*, Shylock *got* his pound of flesh. While appreciating the sentiment, Shakespeare's editor, Elizabeth Hazenblatt, encouraged the young playwright to come up with an ending that was more palatable to British audiences.

Opposition was raised by the English Civille Liberties Union, which objected that allowing prisoners the opportunity to rebuild their lives in the fresh air of Canada would violate their rights to atone for their crimes through meaningless labor and tuberculosis in prison.

The crowd had been watching the two as if they were competitors in a tennis match. Now all eyes were back on Cockburn.

"Done. But if you lose, you must leave the business completely."

"Done."

Lazar went back to his large but not terribly lovely home on Jews' Street,[3] which he shared with his wife, Esther, and their six children, and began to plan. He spent a year exhausting every trick in his book. He built model bungalows in Quebec, and offered free weekends at Brixton for couples who would listen to a sales pitch. No takers. He entered into discussions with the government to open up a penal colony there, but opposition was raised by the English Civille Liberties Union, which objected that allowing prisoners the opportunity to rebuild their lives in the fresh air of Canada would violate their rights to atone for their crimes through meaningless labor and tuberculosis in prison. He did manage to send a few indentured servants to the colony, at his own expense, but as soon as their ship docked, they took off for the thirteen colonies south of the St. Lawrence. And that really was the problem. There were no shortage of Englishmen looking for opportunities in the New World, but England's other American colonies were too attractive an alternative for them to look to Canada. And so over a year passed with no movement whatsoever. It didn't help that Cockburn was busy spreading rumors about how awful conditions in Canada were. For example, that it was impossible to operate a business without paying protection money to the ruthless British-Columbian Sasquatch cartel.

---

3. It had been Jews' Alley before gentrification.

"So, Shifty," taunted Cockburn one day in Charrington's. "How are the sales going?"

"It's coming along," mumbled Lazar. "I've still got lots of time."

"You're going to need it. Maybe you should talk to Benjamin Franklin over there." He gestured to a gentleman sitting at a window table, in deep discussion with a group of men. "He's supposed to be the great genius of the American colonies. Perhaps he can help you."

Lazar looked and did a double take. Benjamin was the spitting image of a Jew he knew back in Poland. Lazar spent the next hour just watching Benjamin, and as he watched, an idea formed.

In addition to being a great inventor, wit, and ladies' man, Benjamin was a seasoned political wheeler-dealer, and since the end of the war, had served as a colonial agent in England. Essentially he was a lobbyist, representing the interests of Pennsylvania, Massachusetts, and several other colonies, as well as the CMA and the NAMBLA.[4] He heard a knock at the door of his room at the inn and opened it to find Lazar.

"Good evening, sir," said Benjamin.

"Good evening, Mr. Franklin. Or perhaps I should say 'vuz macht a Yid'?"

Benjamin was taken aback, but only for a moment. "I'm sorry, sir, but while I have a certain facility with the German dialects of my Pennsylvania neighbors, I have no more familiarity with your phrase than I do with you yourself, good sir."

"I'm Lazar Sheftel. And you I know as Benjamin Franklin. But tell me, what was it before?"

"Before?"

"Before it was changed."

Benjamin inspected his visitor closely, then checked the hallway of the inn in which he kept rooms, and seeing it empty, motioned for Lazar to come in and sit down.

---

4. The Colonial Musket Association, which advocated mandatory firearms ownership for free white men, and the North Andover, Massachusetts, Buffalo Lovers Association.

"Binyomin Frankel," Benjamin said with a sigh. "And it's actually a relief to finally tell someone."

Benjamin then briefly related the story of how his father, Gershon Frankel, had migrated to England from Poland to escape the chaos of that country's dissolution.

"It is an old joke, I know," he went on. "But in England, my large-nosed father yearned to breathe free."

What he found, however, was that while Oliver Cromwell, interested in creating an even more despised minority than his fellow Puritans, might have invited the Jews to England, the English proved to be bad hosts. His father never got to listen to the music he liked, never got to sit in the comfortable chairs, and most important, never got to practice his craft.

"And so my parents set out again, this time to the New World, where they hoped to reach that oasis of tolerance that was William Penn's Quaker colony. Alas, however, to my father, all goyim looked alike, and he settled down in Massachusetts. Too tired to run anymore, he endeavored to raise us secretly in the faith of our fathers. To be sure, we were not alone, and we, along with several other such families, used to attend secret Sunday school and secret sleep-away camp in the mountains. Despite my parents' best efforts, the whole experience soured me on organized religion, and when I came of age I left for Pennsylvania, where I made myself the man I am today. But although I practice the religion of my forefathers no more than any other, I still feel myself to be part of that race whose genius I claim and whose sufferings I share in my deepest of hearts."

Feeling a kindred spirit, Lazar opened up to Benjamin.

"Why, that's amazing," said Benjamin. "My father was also a Realtor...or at least he would have been, had it not been for this Bancroft's grandfather, Ogden."

Lazar then explained his plan: to create conflict in the thirteen colonies, so as to discourage immigration there, and ideally encourage immigration to Quebec.

"But I need an inside man, Benny, I need you."

Benjamin pondered this. "What you're asking me to do is serious. It could lead to hardship, violence, even death on a large scale. I don't know, even with my desire to revenge my father's persecution, if I can join you."

"I'll cut you in for 45 percent."

"Done. Just leave things to me."

Just then there was a knock on the door. Benjamin opened it, revealing the most beautiful identical twins Lazar had ever seen. He ushered them in, and then gestured for Lazar to leave.

"If you don't mind. I need to conduct an experiment to see if identical twins respond identically to certain stimuli."

"Do you think they will?"

"No." Benjamin winked. "But then, I also don't care."

Benjamin knew that matter of great import was about to descend on the colonies. Parliament had just passed the Stamp Act, which called for a tax on almost all printed materials, with a stamp affixed to show the tax had been paid. The only printed materials not taxed were so-called "bawdy novels," since the state didn't wish to be seen as profiting from licentiousness. Thus developed a black market in books masked with the covers of such materials, and some New England families still have Bibles bearing such titles as *Dame Chatsworth Goes Riding* and *The Stern Disciplining of Young Master Randolph*.

The colonists looked to Ben, their man on the scene, for direction on how to respond to what they saw as taxation without representation. He assured them that they had to be forceful and united, and to boycott English goods. Meanwhile, he made discreet payments to various hooligans of his acquaintance to form something called "The Sons of Liberty," which took it upon itself to enforce the boycott by tarring, feathering, ransacking the property of, and in general abusing those committed to enforcing the act or breaking the boycott. Parliament ultimately backed down, but Benjamin assured his friends in that body that the Americans were much less united than

It should be recalled that Franklin's genius and charm were both unquestioned on either side of the Atlantic. When his suggestions were challenged, he would respond with, "Oh, right, a bad idea . . . like bifocals, the Franklin stove, and the rocking chair?" If that didn't work, he would threaten to smite them with lightning.

they appeared, and that further action would break them. That led next year to the Townshend Acts; again, the Sons of Liberty put the squeeze on merchants to abide by the boycott. Moreover, Ben got a number of colonies to cease providing room and board for British troops as required by the Quartering Act, and then got the British to send more troops to Boston to enforce the various laws the Americans were flouting. That led to the famous incident in Boston where colonists, violating all decency and rules of war, began pelting British soldiers with ice balls. The British responded in a perfectly understandable manner. The headlines in the most important British papers shouted "Colonists Get Royal Spanking" and "Brave Britons Best Boston Bullies," but Benjamin's operatives, under his instructions to keep the heat on, made sure that the American press played up the horrors of "the Boston Massacre." For those who wonder how Benjamin could continue so successfully playing both sides against one another, it should be recalled that his genius and charm were both unquestioned on either side of the Atlantic. When his suggestions were challenged, he would respond with, "Oh, right, a bad idea...like bifocals, the Franklin stove, and the rocking chair?" If that didn't work, he would threaten to smite them with lightning.

For his part, Lazar was busy building homes in Quebec and printing up gorgeous full-color[5] brochures touting the many advantages of living in Quebec, such as number seven: "When the next war comes, you won't have to travel far to kill Frenchmen." In 1774, he made a good bit of change when Benjamin whispered in his ear

---

5. Which at the time meant black and white.

This copy of Lazar Sheftal's pamphlet is in the personal papers of Theodor Herzl, at Herzl House in Jerusalem. In 1894, Herzl made the following notation in the margin: "Surely, our natives are no more hostile than those of Quebec, and may be placated by the same methods: National Health, cultural autonomy, and hockey." Who knows how things might have turned out had Herzl succeeded in landing that NHL expansion team.

that he should invest heavily in coffee futures. Shortly thereafter, the Boston Tea Party took place, and all over the thirteen colonies Americans, many of whom were already boycotting British tea, now actively began drinking coffee as a way of voicing their anger. By that point, while Benjamin put in the bad word where he could, things had pretty much moved out of his control. He had just hoped for things to get bad enough to enourage a small migration. In 1775, the shot heard round the world was fired; in 1776, the United States declared independence, which he might not have intended, but after all was said and done, wasn't a bad conclusion. The war saw considerable violence directed at the Loyalists, those Americans who remained loyal to the British crown. As the Patriots asserted control over areas, the Loyalists faced the choice of death or flight. Thankfully for them, there were often ships at the ready (hired with Lazar's coffee money), available to transport them to spacious new homes in Canada. The surprising victory of the Patriots saw a massive exodus to the north, and Lazar easily filled his quota, albeit with only a year to spare. History records that Benjamin Franklin was one of three diplomats assigned the task of negotiating the peace with England. What it doesn't note is that on his way to the Paris peace talks, he made a brief stop in London, just popping into Charrington's in time to see Lazar officially inducted into the guild, an event that many at the time said propelled Cockburn into his grave the following week—although, to be fair, the man was seventy-eight and gout-ridden. Benjamin would be lauded (and more justifiably than anybody could imagine) as one of the fathers of the new republic. As for Lazar, he moved his family to more spacious digs on Jews' Lane,[6] and lived to dance at the weddings not just of his children, but his grandchildren, including one granddaughter who married an Italian Jew by the name of Isaac D'Israeli, and whose son also had a little something to do with imperial real estate.

---

6. As Methodists' Lane came to be known shortly after Lazar's family arrived there.

CHAPTER THIRTEEN

LIBERTÉ, *EGALITÉ*, CULOTTES!

Jew's a dope, Jew's a dope, thinks that he's a *philosophe*." The jeers of the altar boys echoed in Gonzago Pereira's ears long after he had passed by the church. While today his problems might be solved by a hearing test and a prescription, at the time Gonzago seethed with rage. While other French Jews might have borne the abuse with some equanimity, it was the central truth of the taunt that so enraged him. He did consider himself to be a product of the Age of Reason and, living in France in the late eighteenth century, refused to accept that in the center of the Enlightenment, he should be stigmatized for nothing more egregious than, as he saw it, an accident of birth. To be sure, conversion offered a solution, but while not particularly devout, Gonzago was too proud of his heritage, and too intellectually honest, to take that route. He felt sure that there had to be a better way to achieve the Brotherhood of Man that the new age promised, and felt equally sure that he would find it. He was right. While poverty, oppression, and the gross inequalities in the distribution of wealth in Bourbon France put the country on the brink of chaos, it was Gonzago Pereira who discreetly tipped it over.

While poverty, oppression, and the gross inequalities in the distribution of wealth in Bourbon France put the country on the brink of chaos, it was Gonzago Pereira who discreetly tipped it over.

Bordeaux's Jewish community, of which Gonzago was a prominent member, dated from the sixteenth century. Then, a number of Spanish Jews, who had adopted identities as Christians—whether this was in response to the expulsion or some sort of Halloween costume gone horribly wrong is not specified in the record—received permission to settle in that southern city. Although they continued to live openly as Christians for years, they were secretly practicing Judaism—for example, publicly raising pigs but privately giving them circumcisions and bar mitzvahs, and sending them to Ivy League schools. After the French expelled the Huguenots, both because they were Protestants and because even the French weren't sure how to pronounce "Huguenot," they realized that they had no religious minorities left to persecute, and allowed the Jews of Bordeaux to begin living openly as Jews.[1] While the French have achieved a certain reputation for tolerance, it should be noted that in the same way that Princess Di's "beauty" owed much to the contrast between her and the uggos in the royal family,[2] France's rep owes a lot to being located between the countries notorious for bringing you the Inquisition and the Holocaust. And so the Jews in eighteenth-century France were beset with numerous disabilities. Aside from the fact that they could only live in certain select cities (and of course their suburbs), Jews were forced to wear the previous year's fashions, and always one size too small. They were not allowed to have the really thin, twirly mustaches that the other Frenchmen had. And whereas it was sufficient for other Frenchmen to buss one another on the cheek when they met, the Jews of Bordeaux had to kiss one another open mouth, with tongue. Thus, while Gonzago might have been more obsessed with the matter than most, he was hardly alone among Jews in his desire to transform French society.

One day while in Paris conducting business after several years' absence, Gonzago couldn't help but notice how the population of beggars had grown. Indeed, in some *arrondissements*, the streets

---

1. In response to Sephardic demands that they also be able to look down on a population, France also annexed Alsace and Lorraine, thereby adding a larger Ashkenazi community. **2.** We're not saying she wasn't a decent person, but let's face it—when you're standing between Prince Charles and Prince Edward in the family photo, you have to be Quasimodo to not look at least reasonably attractive.

were literally paved with them. There had even been briefly a gazebo made entirely out of lepers that was used as a rain shelter by travelers waiting for the ferry across the Seine. At the same time that poverty was increasing, the shameless excesses of the wealthy were getting even more shameless and excessive. All the rage in Paris at the time was conspicuous nonconsumption, in which the wealthy sat in full view of the poor, their tables laden with all manner of delicacy, and pointedly *didn't* eat any of the food, which was then fed to their cats, which were then fed to their dogs, which were then turned into boots, which were very pointedly never worn, another example of conspicuous nonconsumption. In the same vein, some nobles forced their peasants to watch as they took the grain they had just collected as taxes, ground it into flour, and then snorted it.

But of course, France being France—except for those times when it was "Germany West"—what was really fashionable was fashion. Fashion in France had taken a drastically wrong turn in the mid-seventeenth century under the guidance of Louis Couture. Couture was chief fashion designer in the court of Louis XIV, who trusted him implicitly. This was fine in the early years of the Sun King's nearly seven-decade reign, but by the 1680s, Couture was deep in the midst of a syphilitic dementia that left his designs increasingly outlandish. A century later, the French ruling classes had been so influenced by this that they would essentially wear anything, as long as it was exclusive and expensive. During Gonzago's visit, he saw women traipsing about wearing capes made out of live chipmunks, men whose heels were so high that they used little stepladders to put them on, and a small clique of literal-minded fashionistas who let their smiles be umbrellas, with considerable ill-effect for the rest of their wardrobe. And while the wealthy paraded around, the poor—who were just as French and thus just as interested in fashion—watched and muttered angrily. It was clear to Gonzago that all the people needed was a push and they would go over the edge.

But Gonzago had a business to run and a life to live, and probably would have spent the rest of his days brooding and muttering as angrily as the peasants, but Dame Fortune, as has so often been the case for the chosen, fortuitously extended her hand to him. Gonzago's cousin Armando had been drawing up the specifications for some pants for his manufactory's seamstresses, when urgent business had sent him to Avignon. When he returned, he found that his foreman, seeing the designs and presuming they were completed had given them out, and fifty pairs of pants had been made, all too short. Armando was about to write it off as a major loss, when Gonzago saw the pants and got a brilliant idea. He bought the pants at cost and paid destitute but fashionable nobles a small honorarium to wear the pants around the capital. The culottes, as they were now known,[3] had all the elements of haute couture popular at the time—they were absurd, they were new, and they were wasteful, since it was well publicized that culottes weren't merely short pants, they were long pants that had been specially cut. Indeed, when after a few months competitors began putting out cheap knockoffs, Gonzago and Armando began packaging the severed legs with the culottes themselves to prove that they were the originals.

As culottes increased in popularity, Gonzago informed Armando of his ultimate plan, and the two of them went to the Jewish leadership of Bordeaux to get their assistance. Those Jewish leaders in turn spoke to the Jewish leadership in Alsace-Lorraine, and together they set aside their differences and arranged a "shortage" of wool, which led the cost of pants to skyrocket. Soon, the peasants found themselves increasingly pantsless, a condition that they found intolerable. To add insult to injury, there was actually a tax on pantslessness, so that in addition to their embarrassment, they were being driven into even further penury—which, incidentally,

---

3. When informed of Gonzago's plans, Armando supposedly responded, "You'd look like a perfect asshole in these short pants"; hence, *culottes*.

also made them liable for the penury tax. When it was brought to Marie-Antoinette's attention that the peasants had no pants, the lovely but ill-starred Austrian, being still unfamiliar with all the intricacies and idiosyncrasies of French fashion and presuming that culottes, being smaller, had to cost less, responded, "So let them wear culottes." When word of this reached the masses, they were enraged, thinking that the queen was mocking their misfortune. Desperate to stave off financial ruin and the impending social crisis, King Louis XVI summoned the estates-general to try to cure the nation's woes.

Soon, the peasants found themselves increasingly pantsless, a condition that they found intolerable. To add insult to injury, there was actually a tax on pantslessness, so that in addition to their embarrassment, they were being driven into even further penury—which, incidentally, also made them liable for the penury tax.

The king made numerous entreaties to the nobles to give up their culottes and accept taxation, even agreeing to replace the culottes with knee-length breeches from the hated British enemy's colony at Bermuda. The nobles, however, desperate to maintain their stature and distance from the people, refused to give up their culottes, which by this point had become a symbol of all the worst excesses of the *ancien régime*. But even had something been worked out, it might have been too late, as the rage of the Parisian crowds—egged on by provocateurs hired by the Jews—had reached fever pitch. When the deluge arrived, it was those crowds—the *sans culottes*—who would break the levee.

The reader is doubtlessly familiar with much of the rest of the story: the Tennis Court Oath, the storming of the Bastille,[4] the Declaration of the Rights of Man, the Reign of Terror, and so on. Gonzago had the satisfaction of converting his parish church into a

---

4. Brought on by Ginzbourg's Cinq et Dix Centime store's offer of 20 percent off to anyone who brought in a brick from the notorious prison.

After Eugene Delacroix painted an ad for Ginzbourg's Cinq et Dix Centimes entitled *Ginzbourg Leading the People . . . to Savings!* that was plastered all over the city and drew attention from the revolutionary authorities, they commissioned him to redo it in its more familiar form, *Liberty Leading the People*. Rather than start from scratch, he simply painted over Ginzbourg, a fact that remained unknown until 1987, when a deranged supporter of the restoration of the French monarchy tossed acid on the figure of Liberty, exposing the original underneath.

temple of reason, but after the Reign of Terror ended, found himself to be persona non grata. He and Armando fled to the United States, where they settled in Brooklyn and opened up an extremely successful pants manufactory, taking Armando's last name, Jordache.

CHAPTER FOURTEEN

FROM PRUSSIA, WITH LOVE

I'm sorry, Solly, but *mein herz* belongs to another." With those words, Solomon Luftheimer, sole heir to his family's successful Berlin distillery, was informed by his fiancée, Sarah Amplebrust, that their engagement was over, as she had found love in the arms of a Swabian spelunker of aristocratic mien. Heartbroken, Solomon repaired to a local *bierstube* to mourn his lost love in the company of his cousin and lifelong friend, Josef Luftheimer, owner and proprietor of a successful dry-goods emporium. Much to the surprise of Solomon, it turned out that Josef had been brought to romantic woe by the very same German, albeit in a very different way: He was in deep, but sadly unrequited, love with the handsome cave explorer. After overcoming his initial shock at his cousin's confession, Solomon decided that the two should put their heads together to find a way not only to win their loves, but to protect other Jewish men from similar suffering in the future. Thus was born an audacious plot: to turn the most desirable gentile men gay.

During the Middle Ages, Jewish men had very little to worry about in terms of sexual competition. Gentile men were seen as being unwashed, uneducated, drunken, wife-beating peasants whose sole redeeming feature was the ability to eat cheeseburgers, which, not having been invented yet, held very little actual appeal. All that changed with the nineteenth century, particularly in the German states. Hygiene improved, people went to school and got jobs above "entry-level serf," and improvements in medicine made beatings less serious. Moreover, German men were caught up in the Romantic Movement, which meant they spent a considerable amount of time hiking in lederhosen. While not the most attractive of outfits, they did show their calves off to good effect, which is about the most a nineteenth-century woman could hope to catch a glimpse of. But while the Gentile Man was radically transforming, most Jewish men were still strictly eighteenth century'sville, daddy-o, spending a considerable portion of their lives reading in a dimly lit room and subsisting on a diet consisting almost entirely of starch and, for the wealthy, fat. Indeed, when Abraham Warburg, from a distant branch of the prominent banking family (very distant—they ran a chain of check-cashing stores), suddenly dropped dead at the age of thirty-two, the autopsy showed that a chicken had actually formed itself out of the schmaltz in his veins. Physically, therefore, they weren't much to look at. Socially, most Jewish men had been given a traditional upbringing, and even the wealthy ones devoted themselves to business; this did not make for a race of scintillating conversationalists. Even so, the fact that Jewish men were still living in the past would have been fine—if Jewish women in the nineteenth century hadn't moved into the future.

Jewish women are hot. They were hot in the eighteenth century, and hot in the twentieth century, but in the early nineteenth century, they were smoking. While Jewish men were learning Torah or a trade, middle- and upper-class Jewish women were getting secular educations and learning to be charming ladies. Freed from traditional Jewish clothing, they were really visible for the first time, and their non-Jewish neighbors took notice of their appetizingly zaftig figures.[1] While in America blondes may have more fun, in Germany they were all too common. Jewish women, by contrast, were dark, exotic, beautiful, and smart, and the Brunhilde-bored

---

1. *Zaftig* literally means juicy, but when referring to a woman, means voluptuous (but in the way the term was originally used, not in the way morbidly obese women use it in personal ads—Delta Burke 1980 voluptuous, not Delta Burke 2000 voluptuous). Indeed, the word *juicy* itself is derived from *Jewessy*, with the change in spelling reflecting the influence of the Norman French equivalent, *juivesse*.

blond beasts of the time were lining up at their doors. For their part, many of these GOTMFPs[2] didn't really see their choice as a particularly difficult one to make. On the one hand, you had the husband/intended, who was pale, chubby, and socially awkward. On the other, you had the gentile paramour, who aside from the having the appeal of being forbidden fruit, was robust, could recite poetry, and had great calves. Given what they were up against, Jewish men didn't stand much of a chance, and the baddest mammelle-jammelles of the time were being removed from the tribe. Thus, the Luftheimers had no trouble finding allies to help them with their plot to turn straight things gay and vice versa.

In evaluating what was straight in the nineteenth century, it should be recalled that only a few decades earlier had men stopped wearing wigs and pantyhose. Ballet was straight. Poetry readings were straight. Crying was straight. Now, this may seem jarring to the modern sensibility, but let's look at it logically. Ballet at the time was seen as the height of athleticism, and involves one man surrounded by nubile, lithe, scantily clad ballerinas, periodically hoisting them aloft by their thighs. What's remarkable is not that it used to be considered straight, but that they ever managed to convince people it wasn't. As for poetry readings, they were conducted at salons filled with the most desirable society women, all ready to swoon at a well-turned metaphor. And crying? Well, let's just say that the poetry might get the girl to the bedroom, but it's the manly weeping that gets her in bed.

---

2. GOTMFP: German of the Mosaic Faith Princess. The acronym never really took off.

The plot was remarkably simple. Josef put the word out to his friends in the gay world, and Solomon did the same with his peers in the world of business, who were often called upon by their sophisticated wives to sponsor artists and performers. Slowly but surely, flamboyantly gay men were insinuated into the art world as dancers, singers, and poets. Although observers at the time didn't think it was possible to make dancing in tights anything other than supremely masculine, this first generation of gay artistes managed to do just that, by seamlessly introducing flouncing and mincing into the standard balletomane's repertoire of dancing and prancing. When it came to declaiming their poetry, they did so with the stereotypical lisp and limp wrist, and when they wept, it was not the manful weeping of poets gone by, but the shrill shrieking of a hysterical queen. Women, of course, still adored ballet and theater, but the nature of heterosexual men being what it is, it didn't take long for them to abandon these fields in droves.[3] But getting them to avoid the salons and opera houses was only half of the plan.

As noted above, the Romantic Movement had sent thousands of German men off into the countryside to discover the true nature of the German spirit. Groups like the Bruderbund and Turnverein were formed to gather Germans into organized groups, dedicated to manly pastimes. Josef Luftheimer generously opened the doors of his store, giving away hundreds of pairs of boots and other equipment to young men who joined the hiking and sports clubs he sponsored. As in any homosocial environment, pushing these groups into complete gayiousity[4] wasn't too difficult, especially with the generous donations of schnapps made by Solomon's distillery. Of course, they weren't completely successful. Efforts to transform football from a fairly asexual game in which you kick the ball from man to man, into what essentially was a clothed orgy, wouldn't bear fruit until years later, when American colleges began

---

3. Zoologically speaking, straight men travel in droves; gay men in gaggles.
4. Gayiousity, is, of course, a meager equivalent of the original German *freilichskeiten-shaftanschaunggeist*.

to adopt the German model, and American football became the rage of the Ivy League. This is all the more remarkable, considering how blatantly gay the positions were, such as "tight end," "wide receiver," and "between the thighs ball-grabber," although changing the last to "quarterback" may have helped. But even with the considerable success they did have, their plan only accounted for a fraction of German men. What they really needed to do was infiltrate an organization that included almost all young men: the army.

The problem wasn't getting gays into the army—at the time, the Prussian army was famous for two things: the efficiency of its soldiers and their tendency to have sex with one another. During the latter half of the nineteenth century, an average of eight soldiers a year were injured or killed when their partners forgot to remove their spike helmets before performing oral sex on them. Indeed, the greatest of all Prussian military heroes was Frederick the Great, who was known as Frederick the Gay until the Seven Years War, when he realized it didn't really inspire too much fear in his en-

What needed to be done was to transform the army's main role from the fairly gay task of marching around in fancy dress uniforms to something unquestionably hetero—like killing other men. And not with kindness, since that would be kind of iffy, too.

emies. What needed to be done was to transform the army's main role from the fairly gay task of marching around in fancy dress uniforms to something unquestionably hetero—like killing other men. And not with kindness, since that would be kind of iffy, too. A little bird whispered in the ear of Baron von Bleichroder, Jewish banker to Chancellor Otto von Bismarck, and the next thing you know, Prussia has beaten Denmark, Austria, and France, all in the space of six years. With that kind of record, German soldiers could bugger one another with no fear of negative repercussions. Indeed, the association of homosexuality with martial prowess later inspired the United States Marine Corps—which does have an awful

This was part of a series of Safe Sex posters put out by the German Army in the mid-1870s (the caption reads "Attention Solders! Take it off before you take it in."). Others in the series included "Bayonets are not for love," "Spurs hurt," and "Syphilis isn't just for artists and philosophers."

lot of fancy-dress balls—to adopt the motto "We're Looking for a Few Good Men," which is really better suited for a bathhouse than a branch of the military.

The gentile straight world responded to the Luftheimers' plan just as they'd hoped. As the old mainstays of the straight world became gay, gentiles turned to what they thought would buttress their heterosexuality. But not only did that increasingly remove them from contact with women, it also meant that when they actually did spend time with women, they would be unable to communicate with them, except to discuss sports. Jewish men, by contrast, diligently re-created themselves into the models of what women really wanted. It is no accident that the stereotype of Jewish men is almost identical to that of gay men—artistic, sensitive, witty, cosmopolitan. Of course, in terms of appearance, they may have left something to be desired, but insofar as the most attractive gentile men seemed to shooting, tackling, or buggering one another, that wasn't too much of a deal-breaker for Jewish women. Indeed, if anything the plan was too successful, and in their lifetime Jewish men became a hot commodity in the gentile marriage market.[5] As for their own love lives, Sarah had long since found that her troglodytic paramour wanted to spend all of his time with his new friends, exploring caves in which women were not welcome. Chastened if not chaste, she returned to Solomon and they had three children and a long life together. As for Josef, he soon tired of his spelunking and ended up with a nice kosher butcher, proof again of the superiority of kosher meat.

---

5. Although studies have shown that after brief exposure to Richard Simmons, even the most flagrant homophobes find hard-core gay porn to be relatively inoffensive in comparison, we have found no evidence that the conspiracy continues to this day. We freely concede, however, that we have also failed to uncover any logical explanation for either the length of Simmons's career or his ubiquity.

CHAPTER 15

READ THE FEIN PRINT

It was December 1842 and Ernst Fein, a typesetter at the Rotring Brothers Print Shop in Berlin, felt faint. Ernst was working his fifth consecutive double shift, and the unheated, dimly lit workshop wasn't exactly conducive to laying type. Ernst's fingers were numb, his vision was blurry, and the coffee he was drinking to stay awake was bitter, stale, and primarily composed of old ink—and even that wouldn't have been so bad if the Rotring Brothers offered something besides nondairy creamer.

"Back to work, Fein!" shouted Maximillian Rotring, one half of the Rotring brothers, fraternal twins with identically rancid dispositions. "We don't pay you five and a half marks an hour for you to sit around and grow dizzy." His boss was right. Ernst was originally hired to sit around and grow dizzy, but he was only paid four marks an hour for doing so.

Ernst went back to work. It hadn't always been that way. For centuries, the Fein family had served the German nation loyally as usurers. Indeed, one of Ernst's own forebears, as the reader might recall, had actually hatched the conspiracy to create capitalism in order to ensure that the Germans were able to continue paying back their exorbitant interest rates. But it was that very conspiracy that planted the seeds of Ernst's misfortune. Capitalism had been so successful in generating income for the goyim that they no longer needed the moneylenders. To be sure, the workers didn't have much, but when they needed money, they just got advances on their salaries, which had the added advantage (from the bosses' perspectives, at any rate) of making them virtual indentured servants. And so, with the family fortune gone, and with no experience in anything other than usury, Ernst had to make his way in the working world. As bad as working for the Rotrings was, he still saw it as an improvement over some of his earlier endeavors, such as ass master (which he'd presumed, incorrectly, involved livestock), human cog, and high school guidance counselor. Of course, working for the Rotrings wasn't just hard on Ernst, and even the non-Jewish workers weren't having an easy time. During a particularly frantic afternoon leading up to a deadline, Rudolph the bookbinder had inadvertently sewn one of his eyelids shut. Oskar the inker was combating a urinary tract infection that caused him to literally pee ink.[1] And Ludwig the paper cutter had just weeks earlier cut off his ring finger during a nightshift in which the workshop ran out of candles. What's worse, it turned out that fingers barely give off any light.

"If I were in charge, I would make the books out of solid gold. You could charge twice as much and make a fortune!" exclaimed Ludwig one day during their three-minute lunch break.

"No, that's stupid," said Rudolph. "What you need to do is break the books up into smaller books, only two or three pages, then people will have to buy dozens of them. That's the way to get rich."

"Neither of you know what you're talking about," stated Oskar matter-of-factly. "Books are old news. What I would do is print the words on slices of bread. Sliced bread is the best thing since cholera-free water. Everybody buys the bread-book, eats it, and then has to buy another one for their library."

Idiots! thought Ernst. *If these guys were in charge, this print shop would be bankrupt in a week.*

Wait a second, that's it! thought Ernst. *The problem isn't that the goyim are running factories; it's that the* smart *goyim are running factories. Find a way so that they relinquish control of their*

---

1. This gave the Rotring Brothers the idea to replace the quill, which had to be dipped into ink, with a new writing device, which contained the ink within. When the patent office rejected the application for the *penis,* they shortened the name, calling it the *pen.*

businesses to their workers and these businesses will go broke in no time. Soon they will need the moneylender again. I will then re-open the family business and never have to squint over another damn bit of type again. But how?

He looked down at the type he was setting for a title page. It was called *The Mensch and History* and it was the first published work by an unknown twenty-four-year-old named Karl Marx. Yes, Karl Marx had at a young age developed a serious addiction to Judaism, which at the time was actually used in drug-treatment programs as a way of weaning people off opium. This would inspire his later aphorism "religion is the opiate of the masses," though a more correct translation of the original German is "religion is the methadone of the masses." The catalyst for Marx's interest in religion was a rift with his father, Heschy.

Yes, Karl Marx had at a young age developed a serious addiction to Judaism, which at the time was actually used in drug-treatment programs as a way of weaning people off opium. This would inspire his later aphorism "religion is the opiate of the masses," though a more correct translation of the original German is "religion is the methadone of the masses."

Heschy Marx was a moderately successful civil rights lawyer in Trier who planned to leave his practice to his son. The civil rights business was a good one ever since Napoleon, outraged by the savage treatment of short people in Germany at the time, instituted the Napoleonic Code in the area. Other oppressed groups, such as lepers, mimes, and men with bad comb-overs, would witness the success of short people in attaining basic civil rights and soon clamor for their own, making civil rights law a most lucrative field. So, after graduating from gymnasium, where Karl demonstrated a natural flair for kickball, he followed suit and enrolled at Bonn University to study Law. Marx had always been a gifted student, so it is no surprise that he became a straight-A student.[2] All was going well for Karl until a fateful afternoon in February 1841 when he opened the letter from his father in which the latter announced his conversion to Protestantism.

Even though Marx had never been religious his father's conversion and subsequent name change triggered a religious awakening within the young man. At first, Marx practiced Judaism just to get under his father's skin, but after some time, really took a liking to it—the legal arguments that had gone on for centuries, the sense of a historical community combating persecution and courageously marching forward—not to mention the herring in cream sauce, the absence of social prohibitions on interrupting, and jokes about Reform rabbis—all of it tugged at his heart. Medical historians today believe he might have just had an enlarged aorta, but at the time, he gave up the study of law, moved to Berlin, and immersed himself in the full spectrum of religious scholarship including Talmud, ethics, Hasidic thought, and origami.[3]

Ernst normally didn't give a second thought to the texts he was assembling, especially the religious stuff. But Marx's messianic tome captured his attention for some reason. Behind the words of this religious text, pulsed the heart of a revolutionary:

> The Jew must simultaneously say yes to the world to come and no to life as it is—yes, to a future in which the G-dly truth concealed within every created being is revealed. No, to the alienation and misery that is contemporary secular life. This life is defined by materialism. In the world to come, we will be spiritual beings. So when you raise your Kiddush cup this Shabbes, do not say l'chaim (to life!), for this life is but a paltry thing. Raise your

---

2. He actually got a B-plus while fulfilling his Spanish requirement, but the professor was a total a-hole.
3. Rabbis at the time generally didn't earn regular salaries, and often supplemented their meager incomes by making decorative centerpieces for weddings, bar mitzvahs, and pogroms.

This photo of Karl Marx was taken at the wedding of his distant Orthodox cousin, Simcha Bunim Eger, in 1868. The photo would resurface on Trotsky's desk fifty-six years later, and share the same frame as the picture of the Red Army's Commissar at his bar mitzvah being kissed on each cheek by a thirteen-year-old girl.

cup to the world to come: Rabbis of the world unite. You have nothing to lose but your *chaims!*

Now, Ernst was not a religious man, but he could not help but feel pangs of inspiration bubble up from within. This man Marx, with his messianic yearnings, understood him and his alienation, his endless toil and unhappiness. This man Marx yearning for redemption wasn't so different from him, yearning to clock out on a Friday afternoon.[4]

Ernst turned to the back page of the book to a photo of the author, bearded, in a black suit, standing in front of a small house: a house that Ernst used to walk past on his way home from work.

I wonder if that's where Marx lives? thought Ernst.

That's when the idea came into Ernst's head: If this guy can warm the embers of faith within my cold heart, then he'll have no problem inspiring workers to revolt. With his flair with words and my devious machinations, we're certain to rouse the workers into demanding their fair share of the pie.

Feeling that Marx would be suspicious of an assimilated Jew, Ernst disguised himself as best he could: He wore a black suit that hadn't been to the cleaners in five months and showed up in a wood-paneled station wagon with eleven children all named Menachem Mendel. Then he waited across the street from the house depicted in the photo. Not even half an hour later, Marx exited the house, took a left turn on Freiedrichstrasse, and headed toward the synagogue in Mitte, where he was to give a sermon. Just as Marx was about to enter the house of prayer, Ernst tapped him on the shoulder.

"Do I know you, sir?" asked Marx.

"Rabbi Marx," replied Ernst. "The goyim have a saying: 'You are preaching to the choir.' Certainly you can use your persuasive

---

4. Saturday mornings, the Rotring Brothers allowed their workers to come in an hour late at 5 A.M.

powers on traditional Jews, but what of the growing number of our people who no longer identify as such?"

"Tell me more, my friend," replied Marx.

Ernst continued: "If redemption is as imminent as you say it is, don't you want all of the Jews to experience it?"

"Of course," replied Marx.

"Well, then you must be willing to speak their language. Jews are becoming secular so quickly that the only way to reach them is through a secular language. The people in this synagogue are the choir. They aren't the ones you should be preaching to."

Ernst knew he had a catch. He went in for the kill:

"Did not the Alter Rebbe[5] teach that in every generation there is one righteous person who is a potential messiah? What if you are that messiah? What if you are the one to bring about the redemption?"

"Me?"

"Is it not true that you live at 740 Kramgasse?"

"It is," replied Marx.

"And is it not true that every Hebrew letter has a corresponding number?"

"Of course."

"Then certainly you know that 740 is also the numerical value of the words 'The house of the messiah.'"

Marx stood in silence. He was, of course, familiar with *gematria*. The style of letter calculation was one of the ways that the rabbis of the Talmud used to show the hidden spiritual

Marx stood in silence. He was, of course, familiar with *gematria*. The style of letter calculation was one of the ways that the rabbis of the Talmud used to show the hidden spiritual meaning in the text as well as let one another know when they had a girl in the dorm room.

---

5. The prominent eighteenth-century rabbi and founder of the Chabad Chasidic movement. Not to be confused with "The Alter Kocker," the prominent eighteenth-century nudnik and finder of flaws in those around him.

meaning in the text as well as let one another know when they had a girl in the dorm room. Lucky for Fein, Marx didn't do the math, since the numerical value for the house of the messiah was actually 770; 740 is the number for "the house of the guy who shows up at the Kiddush to fill his pockets with black and white cookies."

Learning to speak a "secular religion" wasn't as difficult as it sounds for there already was a secular religion in Germany. Centered at the University of Berlin, the religion was called Hegelianism, a school of thought largely derived from G.W.F. Hegel's[6] *Phenomenology of the Spirit*. Opaque as even the most obscure forms of mysticism, it was not surprisingly regarded with religious awe and reverence. Marx enrolled at the University of Berlin extension school and began taking correspondence courses from an adjunct named Ludwig Feuerbach. At first, Marx was uncomfortable with Feuerbach's insistence that religion could only bring more alienation to human life and told Ernst that the University of Berlin was not for him. But Ernst convinced him that if he wanted to bring people closer to God he needed to learn the language of the atheist. Marx went back to school and focused on the parts of it he liked—the Hegelian notion that history unfolded dialectically, which he misinterpreted to mean "dietetically," that in the future there would be no more alienation or struggle, since everyone would be slim, happy, and well adjusted.

Convincing Marx to learn the secular religion of Hegelianism was one thing, convincing him to encourage rebellion among the working class was another. It was, in fact, just as difficult as it was for Eliezer Fein to convince Calvin to encourage capitalism three hundred years earlier. So when his attempts to convince Marx to attack private property based on Judaism's rich commitment to social justice[7] fell upon deaf ears, Ernst promised him 25 percent on

---

6. If your name was Georg Wilhelm Friedrich, you'd go by G.W.F., too.

7. Which some rabbinic authorities interpret as "a social commitment to rich justice."

all revenue that his writings would generate. Ernst also made sure to get a big cut of the take from protest slogans and placards. His summer home in Marienbad was purchased with the royalties from "Hey hey, ho ho [insert politician/product/corporation here] has got to go!" alone.

Since Marx was cut off from his father's wealth, the deal was too good for him to refuse and he began his career as an agitator against capitalism. In 1843 alone Marx wrote seventeen pamphlets, eight essays, and a screwball comedy in which he himself would costar with a flatulent Saint Bernard. Ernst made sure that Marx's writings got into the hands of the workers, even after Marx moved to Paris, away from anyone who knew about his religious past. It would take a few years, but the workers would eventually come under Marx's spell. In his writings, they heard the language of modern life but the spirit of a herald, and were moved with religious-like zeal.

Ernst anonymously served as Marx's editor until the end of his life. It was Ernst's idea, for instance, to change "rabbis of the world unite" to "workers of the world unite." Even though the revolution didn't happen during Ernst's lifetime, he did manage to sell three million copies of *The Communist Manifesto*, thereby restoring the family fortune and convincing him that the future was in publishing, not moneylending. As for Marx, he kept his Hasidic beard and secretly refrained from all forms of labor on the Sabbath. In order to avoid suspicion, he eventually refrained from all labor during the rest of the week as well, a practice subsequently adopted by most Marxist intellectuals. For appearance' sake, he joined the Communist Party in Paris, but not before writing one final religious text, entitled *On the Jewish Question*. A greatly misunderstood text, it was actually created as an absurdist spoken-word parody, delivered by a man wearing a priest's cassock and dunce cap, and dripping with obviously satirical lines like, "What is the worldly basis of Judaism? Practical necessity, selfishness. What is the worldly culture of the Jews? Commerce. What is his worldly God? Money. All right!" The problem was that without Marx's delivery, and with no italics available to show which words to stress,[8] the essay was taken seriously instead of as the joke it was intended to be.

---

8. *Italics* is short for *Italian licensed* and was a typeface developed in 1867 as an effort by the recently unified Italian state to capture on paper the stresses and vocalization that Italian nationalists felt to be essential to the Italian language.

CHAPTER SIXTEEN

GRAND DRAGGIN'

At the beginning of 1865, Moritz Gelbfisch was a happy man. For some, the Civil War (or as it is still quaintly known to many Southerners, "The War in Which Those Damn Yankees Robbed Us of Our Constitutional Right to Wear Hoop Skirts, Drink Mint Juleps, and Own Other Humans") was a tragedy; but for Moritz, the owner of a "Jew Store"[1] in Pulaski, Tennessee, it was a gold mine. As the war progressed, Southern efforts to replace Northern industrial goods with 100 percent cotton substitutes proved at times both fruitless and fatal. While lauded for its comfort and washability, the denim suspension bridge over the Chattahoochee River proved wholly inadequate, leading to the deaths of over fifty people when their train crashed crashingly into the river. The event proved particularly tragic, since the train in question was carrying a contingent of circus entertainers en route to entertaining troops at the front. Among the survivors were numerous clowns, whose ironic sorrow added an extra poignancy to the tragedy while at the same time inspiring a genre of painting that continues to haunt us to this day. Consequently, goods smuggled

---

1. While this may be jarring to sensitive modern ears, it was not considered a pejorative, and should not be placed in the same category as the considerably more offensive "Jew Racks" and "Jew Thumbscrews," which were as ubiquitous in fifteenth-century Spain as Jew stores were in nineteenth-century Dixie.

through a network of Southern Jewish merchants and their Northern coreligionists and partners proved vital.

With his connections, Moritz branched out and his line of ready-made uniforms for officers became as famous for its motto—"Don't just secede...Succeed!"—as for the quality. As the war wound down, Moritz found himself in an enviable position, but like a character from a Greek tragedy, his hubris led him to take a step that, though not as stomach-churning as sex with his mother, brought him nearly as low. Like many, he presumed that the Confederacy as a whole would never surrender and that instead, resistance would continue for years in the form of individual guerrilla groups. Betting that small-unit surrenders would take place all over the South, he ordered a huge quantity of white cloth to be sold as white flags for surrenders. His credit was overextended and his warehouse was full, but he happily awaited the bitter, drawn-out end.

News of Appomattox hit Moritz like a ton of bricks, as all that he had achieved in his two and a half decades in the States of America, United and Confederate, seemed on the verge of collapse. Moritz was desperate to unload his white cloth, but there were only so many bedsheets and bandages that people needed. He had to find another use for them, and then one day it hit him. In the wake of the surrender, the newly freed slaves had begun to act "uppity"—learning to read, objecting to being whipped, refusing to use coasters, and the like—and Southern whites were none too happy with it. As they did elsewhere in the South, angry whites engaged in acts of terror against the freedmen in Pulaski. And, as elsewhere, federal troops—at least those led by officers of an abolitionist bent—took action against them. After one such incident, the local commander, from a fine old Quaker family that abhorred all forms of race hatred not directed against the Irish, summoned the good citizens of Pulaski and informed them that while "the men responsible for this action may see themselves as heroes of the white race, I am here to tell you that they are nothing but hoods, white hoods, and they shall be treated as such by the military authorities." For some weeks, the word *white* had captured Moritz's imagination, in such a way that writers more skillful than ourselves would make some clever connection to his state of mind and that of Captain Ahab's, since both involved obsessions and the same color. So when he heard the phrase "white hood," it stuck in his mind, and as he thought about it, an image came to him of a different sort of white hood, fashioned from the cloth in his warehouse. He went home and began to sketch patterns (he had apprenticed to a tailor in Strasbourg in his youth), coming up with a hood-and-cloak combination. An initial effort to market his design, however—which was, after all, essentially a muumuu and matching hat—left much to be desired. "No offense, Mr. Moritz," said Jeb Crawford. "But ef'n I was to wear a dress to a lynchin', they'd string *me* up."

Fortunately for Moritz, besides being the place where the KKK was about to be founded, Pulaski was also home to a fairly thriving gay community. Due to its dance music, cheap liquor, and notoriously ugly women, it was the sort of place where a discreet Southern gentleman of a certain persuasion could enjoy quite the active social life. Although most of Pulaski's citizens remained blissfully unaware of their town's reputation as the Sodom of the Appalachians, one could only provide so many specially made extralarge crinolines, corsets, and high heels to men whose "matron sisters" had never been seen, before you realized that something was going on. Moritz's youthful experience in *le monde* of French couture gave him a certain stature in the community. Thus, when Moritz approached Colonel Eustace T. Pettibone with his new design,

> Although most of Pulaski's citizens remained blissfully unaware of their town's reputation as the Sodom of the Appalachians, one could only provide so many specially made extralarge crinolines, corsets, and high heels to men whose "matron sisters" had never been seen, before you realized that something was going on.

he felt assured of a receptive audience, and he was not disappointed.

The elderly Pettibone, a hero of the Mexican-American War whose looks had, shall we say, gone with the wind, had been the local militia commander both before and during the recent conflict, and had seen his star dim considerably since the town had filled with better-looking younger men with more distinguished records. His arch rival was Captain Calhoun Rivington, a dashing cavalry officer who had taken time during the Pennsylvania campaign to loot the boudoirs of the stoutest and best-dressed women of the Keystone State. With Pettibone about to hold his annual drag ball to celebrate the beginning of the summer mint julep season,[2] he was looking for some way to upstage the upstart, and Moritz convinced him that this was just the thing. The flowing gown would help to mask his girth, the hood with removable veil would cover the cruelties that age and dissipation had heaped upon his face, and the genius of the white sheet was its simplicity—you could accessorize with anything. Moreover, having been cut off from Europe for some years, Pettibone had to take Moritz's word for it that this represented the cutting edge of Parisian fashion. Finally, Moritz was actually willing to give the colonel the dress gratis, and all he wanted in exchange was one small favor.

On the big night, the colonel descended his staircase, bedecked in as many jewels as he could beg, borrow, or steal. According to legend, Captain Rivington, who had up to that time been the belle of the ball, commented cattily that "The colonel's wearing so many stones it's a wonder he can drag himself down the stairs." To which an onlooker replied, "He may be draggin', Captain, but he's *grand* draggin'." By the time he reached the bottom of the stairs, the colonel was besieged with demands that he reveal where he got the gown. Although his natural inclination was to keep it a

---

2. There were also fall and spring mint julep seasons, but it was considered gauche to celebrate them in full drag.

delicious secret, he was a Southern officer and gentlemen, and his word was his bond. Thus, not only did he tell them, he directed them to the next room, where Moritz was waiting, his white cloth on hand to fit all those in attendance. With the exception of the humiliated Captain Rivington, who fled Pulaski that night, the entire party bedecked themselves in the white hoods and gowns.[3] As the evening went on, and mint julep after mint julep was consumed, the colonel decided it was time to move the ball to a local black church, which the gay veterans promptly burned down as the defenders of Christian morality that they were.

After it became clear that efforts to ascertain the attackers' identities were foiled by their hoods and gowns, more and more people were eager to dress the same way for their own night rides. The heretofore informal group adopted the name Ku Klux Klan[4] and although these riders formed around the nucleus of the colonel's gay clique, by summer's end, the torch had (literally) been passed to a new generation (since none of that crowd would wear white past August, and by next summer, white hoods and gowns were *très passé*). Although rumors dogged the group for years (local wags dubbed it the "Gay-KK"), it recruited a new leader, the great Confederate general Nathan Bedford Forrest, and distanced itself from its past. By the twentieth century, gay white supremacists would be drawn almost exclusively to the leather boots and Sam Browne belts of the Nazis and their offshoots and imitators. As for Moritz, he soon emptied his warehouse and, his fortune made, joined his cousins in Cincinnati, where he and his descendants became prominent philanthropists, giving heavily to the NAACP.

---

3. The captain went to seek his fortune in the Wild West, where he would become a footnote in history as the man whose loud snoring—some say he was actually sobbing into his pillow—prompted "shootist" John Wesley Harding to add him as another notch on his gun.

4. *Ku Klux* is a corruption of *Kuklos,* the Greek word for circle, and referred to the "Greek Style" circle jerks the group favored at the conclusion of a boisterous night's lynching and cross-burning.

This lithograph comes from the second issue of *The Louche Leroux: A Magazine for Discriminating Gentlemen*. Put out between 1866 and 1873 by Gaspar Leroux, an artist and journalist from New Orleans, the magazine was aimed at Southern gays unhappy with Reconstruction. It went broke partially in response to the Federal government's Force Acts, and partially due to the fact that it was a gay magazine in the 1870s.

CHAPTER SEVENTEEN

MATCHBREAKER, MATCHBREAKER

Guess what, Mutti, we're all getting married!" Thus did Julius Grunglass introduce to his mother, Frieda, the fact of the upcoming nuptials of not just him, but his brothers, Otto and Ismar. These normally glad tidings brought little joy to Frieda's heart, however, since *die Brudern Grunglass*, proud proprietors of the bookkeeping firm of the same name, thereupon informed her that their betrothed, delightful girls though they may have been, were not members of the tribe. Had Frieda not, in fact, been in a state of perpetual mourning since the death of her beloved husband, Jakob, some eleven years earlier, she doubtlessly would have sat shiva then and there. For those of you who do not know, shiva is the Jewish mourning ritual, which lasts seven days following the burial of a close relative. Also done when a child marries out of the faith, a practice that began when Hershel Gribniss married Lakshmi Pandarawal, a practicing Hindu, whose worship of the androgynous Indian deity of destruction and rebirth gave the custom its name.

So instead of crying, Frieda turned Jakob's portrait to the wall, set her stern countenance on her sons, and, much to their shock, pronounced her acceptance of the engagements. "After all," she declared, "we live in modern times, and as Germans of the Mosaic faith, why should we remain separate from our fellow countrymen, whose only difference from us is that of confession?" Why indeed, particularly since by 1878 Jews had become fully accepted, if not actually admired, by their non-Jewish neighbors. The popularity of the Jews expressed itself in myriad ways. Imitation is the highest form of flattery, and German comedians frequently favored humor featuring characters with Jewish dialects.[1] German cartoonists couldn't seem to draw a single panel that didn't feature some prominent Jewish figure in the background. And, in fact, there were many neighborhoods in Germany where a Jew couldn't walk without being pursued by a mob, sort of like a nineteenth-century version of Beatlemania. In short, Jews were the new black. Indeed, the original phrase used to refer to the hottest new trend was "the new Jew." Anti-Semitism came late to America, and the phrase was still in use by the 1910s, when blacks became all the rage, what with jazz, Jack Johnson, and the starring roles in the country's biggest cinematic blockbuster *Birth of a Nation*. By the 1920s, blacks were "the new Jew," as popular in the U.S. as Jews had been in Europe in the 1870s, and they soon became the standard by which hot new trends would be evaluated.

So if the brothers were surprised by Frieda's response, it was not because they didn't see their decision as a perfectly reasonable one, but only because they saw her as being hopelessly retrograde. She did have one request: Given the need to prepare various relatives—not as modern as she, of course—for the shock of their decision, could they refrain from marrying for a year, and from announcing the engagement for nine months? In light of the titanic conflict they had been prepared for, this was a tremendous relief, and with a grateful "Ja, Mutti," they kissed their mother and went off to tell their beloveds the qualified good news. Frieda waited a respectable few minutes, then turned Jakob's picture around and assured him that these marriages would never come to pass. In death as in life, Jakob kept his counsel to himself.

---

1. Readers may be puzzled by the obviously oxymoronic "German comedians." The term, in this context, is a loose translation of what at the time were referred to as "Drunken Louts haranguing Jews in beer gardens." If this seems a stretch, the reader should be informed that this was, in fact, the origin of both the comedy club, when Jews responded with their own humorous ripostes, and darts, when the aforementioned drunken louts responded to the Jews' responses, by throwing pointy things at them. Eventually, the Jews chose to make humorous observations at other venues, and were replaced as targets by cork boards. British sailors in Hamburg then took the practice back with them.

The very next day, Frieda gathered all her friends for strudel and coffee, and to discuss what could be done. Frieda's story was one with which they were all too familiar. "But," so the chorus went, "what could be done, since as long as Jews were so highly esteemed, they would be highly sought after." And that, Frieda recognized, was precisely the solution. If Jewish popularity was the source of their woe, then Jewish unpopularity would be their salvation. A woman of less fortitude might have blanched at the thought of trying to undo decades' worth of social advancement in the space of nine months, as might a woman of stronger ethics, but Frieda was made of sterner stuff. She looked around her and recognized that she had assembled a treasure trove. There were the wives of journalists, and publishers, and bankers, and doctors, and lawyers—some of the finest middle- and upper-middle class families in Frankfurt were represented. If they couldn't make the Jews unpopular, nobody could.

Panel from 1872s *Fluffi und Hoppi Spendieren die Erdbeerbowle* (Fluffi and Hoppi Make the Strawberry Punch) from the extremely popular Fluffi and Hoppi series.

Of course, the first thing they needed was a public face for their efforts. Yetta Hirschkopf had just the man—Wilhelm Marr.

Marr had been a hotshot reporter at the *Frankfurter Mitkraut Tagliche Gazette*, the paper at which Yetta's husband was city editor. Marr's career had taken a nosedive when his drinking led to a drastic decline in the quality of his work. Unwilling to take responsibility for his actions, he instead chose to blame the Jews. Some observers have suggested that with three Jewish ex-wives, Marr's feelings toward Jews had to have been convoluted and ambivalent. We would suggest that these observers haven't had to deal with either ex-wives or their attorneys. At any rate, Marr seemed to have little difficulty in scapegoating the Jews, but given the previously noted popularity the Jews enjoyed in Germany, he had considerably greater trouble in finding an outlet for his screeds, and had been reduced to writing puff pieces for the *Frankfurter Pfennig Pfincher*, at which the worst he could do was make oblique references suggesting that prices were lower at the stores of gentile shopkeepers. Gertrud Schlosser's husband was a theatrical impresario, so it wasn't difficult to find an actor to pose as a "representative of concerned parties who wish to remain anonymous" and approach Marr to ask his help in exposing the truth of Jewish perfidy. Marr was more than willing to show Germany just how cunning and manipulative the Jew could be (though, as should be clear, even he had no idea); what he needed was a platform and stories to present on it that could provide more substance than his paranoid speculation. Frieda and her friends would provide both.

As to the former, it wasn't difficult for all of them to pool some money to rent a storefront and printing press. The stories were also not too hard to come by. There was no shortage of Jews involved in scandalous, if not outright criminal, behavior. Moreover, they could kill several birds with one stone by targeting only those Jews who had married out of the fold (in some cases, their own ex-husbands who had traded them in for younger, shicksaier models). This played well into their grand scheme, since they wanted to convince gentiles that it was particularly those Jews who were the most acculturated that they should watch out for, and keep their marriage-age children away from. They culled their husbands' desks, files, and after-dinner conversations for the juiciest morsels to feed to Marr. There were directors corrupting ingénues (followed by trips to the doctor for abortions and treatments for syphilis), there were financiers misappropriating funds, there were Jewish shoemakers who intentionally mislabeled shoe sizes—you name it, Jews were doing it. These revelations came as a shock to the German Jews and German Germans alike. The former had come to feel at home in Germany, and to believe that any residual anti-Jewish sentiment was due to the continued existence of traditional Jews. But if the old Jew hatred, or *Judenfeindschaft*, was based on hatred of the Jew as outsider, this new bias was fundamentally different. Not only did it target Jews who had become insiders, but it alleged that it was precisely that assimilation that made them particularly dangerous. As Marr himself wrote:

It is not the Jewish kosher butcher I fear, except, you know, in the sense that he has a cleaver and a certain amount of skill with it, but the Jewish interior decorator. For the butcher is what he is, and is unmistakable as such, with his bloody apron, pungent smells, and large sign saying "Jewish Kosher Butcher," and thus is not a threat to the *volk*. But the Jewish decorator, he is a danger. For with the sheen of his skillfully pomaded hair, his colorful but not flamboyant cravat, and the subdued way he has of gesticulating—not *too* wildly—when he speaks, is there even one German in ten who would not say to him, "Come, come in to my house, my metaphor for the German nation, and move my divan as you see fit"? It is this that is the great threat, against which we must be vigilant.

In the face of this new threat, Marr had crafted a new hatred, with a new name: anti-Semitism, the hatred of Jews based not on what they do, but on what they are. To the anti-Semite, the Jew is immutable, and he can call himself anything he wants to—including "Christian"—and it won't affect his inherent nature. It has been suggested that this was payback for the breakup with his third wife, who told him, "Willi, I'm not leaving you because of something you *do*, I'm just leaving because you're you."[2]

> **Whereas previously they had seen the Jew as a lovable, brilliant nebbish, who made one more sophisticated merely by association—like Woody Allen in 1972—now they saw him as a malignant, morally stunted troll who corrupted all those he touched—like Woody Allen in 1992.**

German Germans began to see their neighbors in an entirely new light. Whereas previously they had seen the Jew as a lovable, brilliant nebbish, who made one more sophisticated merely by association—like Woody Allen in 1972—now they saw him as a malignant, morally stunted troll who corrupted all those he touched—like Woody Allen in 1992. As the public mood turned against the Jews, Marr no longer needed the support of the ladies and in 1879 founded his League of Anti-Semites, which, as the name suggests, he envisioned as a group of Jew-fighting superheroes. This might have been another example of Marr's tendency to drunken delusion; in point of fact, no one in the league had superpowers, although one member in Düsseldorf was reputed to be uncanny at charades. If the reality proved less than super, and if his motives were loathsome, in this age where real estate developers and industrialists adopt deceptive fronts like the "National Wetlands Council" and the "Clean Air Working Group," you can at least respect his honesty. His group was everything it

---

2. And, since it is specifically directed at Jews, contrary to the claims of some apologists for Arab anti-Semitism, being Arab is no more a defense against being an anti-Semite than being fettucini is a defense against being an antipasto.

claimed to be and soon inspired imitators all over Europe. Eventually the proliferation of European anti-Semitic groups became so confusing that for the sake of simplicity they decided to just go by the term *Europeans*. A new age had begun.

Eventually the proliferation of European anti-Semitic groups became so confusing that for the sake of simplicity they decided to just go by the term *Europeans*. A new age had begun.

As for our protagonists, over the course of the two weeks preceding the date their wedding announcements were planned, the engagements were all broken under pressure by their fiancées' families. By a remarkable coincidence, several of Frieda's friends had daughters whose engagements had also recently been broken. Introductions were made, dates were chaperoned, chuppahs were stood under, and the brothers Grunglass and their families all lived happily ever after.

CHAPTER EIGHTEEN

CHINESE TAKEOUT

Hung Lo positively quivered with anticipation; this was the sort of thing that could make or break a restaurant. In the name of the five-year-old emperor Pu Yi, the imperial regent, Prince Chun, had requested that he provide the food for a banquet at the Imperial Court in the Forbidden City. Apparently, one of the emperor's eunuchs had stopped by the deli for some of Hung's Romanian pastrami and raved about it to the Son of Heaven. While the gastronomic addiction of Jews to Chinese food is the stuff of countless tiresome jokes, considerably less well known is the affinity the Chinese have for deli. New York's Chinatown, of course, is located on the Lower East Side, and Chinese immigrants developed a taste for the exotic fare, which they brought back with them to the Middle Kingdom and elsewhere in the Chinese diaspora. Hung had been developing a reputation for having Beijing's best bicjles (formerly known as Peking's best pickles), and word was that his farfel was to die for, especially for the Buddhists, since they could then get reincarnated and have seconds. But word of mouth from all the Mandarins in China couldn't do as much for Hung Lo as one favorable review from the emperor himself.

It had been a strange trip for Hung. As a young man, he had traveled to New York to work as a houseboy for a wealthy merchant, only to find that the merchant had purchased one of those newfangled mechanical Chinamen that were all the rage at the time. Disconsolate, he stumbled through the streets of the Lower East Side until he found a storefront with a Help Wanted sign in front. By a bizarre coincidence, the letters that make up the Yiddish words for Help Wanted look remarkably like the Chinese characters for "Good job within for those willing to work hard; see Ms.

Galtieri in Human Resources." Hung got the job and began as a busboy in Bercovici's Kosher Romanian Delicatessen, working in exchange for a cot, meals, and English lessons. When he found out that old man Bercovici had actually been teaching him Yiddish, he was understandably upset. His ire was mitigated, however, by the fact that he had found love, with Ida Bercovici, younger daughter of the proprietor. Mr. Bercovici was not thrilled with his daughter's choice, but he doted on his daughter. Being a man of some learning, he decided that like the spouse of the biblical Ida,[1] he would make her suitor work for him for seven years before giving him her hand. Also, during that time, Hung would have to prepare himself to accept her faith, just as the biblical Hung had.[2] Becoming a Jew was fairly easy for Hung, since he already wore a skullcap, played the violin, and never quite got the whole virgin birth thing. The bris would have been difficult, but Hung was actually able to avoid it. According to Jewish law, if a baby is jaundiced, you delay the bris until the telltale yellow complexion goes away. Hung had learned his lessons well and

> **Becoming a Jew was fairly easy for Hung, since he already wore a skullcap, played the violin, and never quite got the whole virgin birth thing.**

was able to convince the mohel—who doubled as the slicer at the deli—that in his case, there was just no way to tell, so the bris couldn't be performed. As a member of the family, he was brought into the business. When Mr. Bercovici died in 1910, however, the deli went to his son. Hung and Ida talked about it and decided to pack up the recipe book, grab their twins Zelig and Wong, and take a slow boat to China, which at the time was actually the fastest way to get there.

By the time the emperor had placed his order the deli had been open for nearly half a year. Business wasn't bad, but one thing that

---

1. Actually, he was a man of very little learning.
2. All right, he was an idiot.

134

Hung hadn't counted on was the deep conservatism of the Chinese people. As a cosmopolitan New York Jew, he was willing to try new things, but for years, the Chinese of Beijing had gone to Chiang Kai Shecky's for their deli. Shecky had merely been the cook on a ship that made a lot of stops in Eastern Europe, so his grasp of the cuisine was always a little sketchy, but then it was the same for many Chinese as well, so if anybody noticed something was amiss with the hot-and-sour matzo ball soup, they weren't mentioning it. More problematic from Hung's perspective, Shecky's place was only kosher *style*, while his strictly observed all the dietary laws. Still, despite the clear superiority of Hung's product both gastronomically and theologically, the customers just weren't coming in the numbers he'd hoped for. Thus, the order from the palace seemed to him to be a real godsend. Sparing no expense, he prepared his most magnificent spread—known as the Feast of the Divine Personage,[3] and personally delivered it to the palace gates. Confident that the imperial palate would be satisfied, he sat back to wait, for both the review and the payment of the substantial bill. And waited. And waited. He waited so long that had this episode been depicted on a TV show, he would be shown sitting there while a calendar's pages flipped several times. At last, with bills due and business unimproved, he gave in to Ida's imprecations and went to see the August Personage Responsible for the Emperor's Satiation. The eunuch informed him that the emperor was most satisfied by the banquet, and that a proclamation to that effect, as well as generous compensation, would be issued by the August Personage Responsible for the Emperor's Gustatory Proclamations and Compensations at the earliest possible date, *eight years hence.*

Hung was stunned, but anybody who'd had any experience with the Chinese civil service wouldn't have been surprised. Although it

---

3. Actually the same as the Banquet of the Celestial Master, but you got both coleslaw *and* potato salad.

had been the envy of the ancient world—though, when your nearest neighbors are the Mongols and the Huns, your civil service doesn't exactly have to shine to be considered exemplary—by the late nineteenth century, the civil service had entered into a sad state of decay. There was nothing that Hung could do but go home and wait, and hope that he still had a business in eight years.[4] And what, after all, was eight years in comparison to the four-thousand-year history of imperial China? But if Hung was resigned to his fate, Ida was not. Although her family was religious, many of the deli's workers were Socialists, and she had grown up steeped in radical ideology, which may sound unpleasant, but when one considers that most things that steep do so in boiling water, Ida really got off pretty easy. If they couldn't get their money from Pu Yi, they'd get it from his replacement. Hoping to explain how different things were in China, he gave Ida a crash course in Chinese history and government. What struck her most was the notion of the Mandate of Heaven. Essentially, a ruling dynasty ultimately derived its authority from the belief that the gods had granted them the right to rule, bestowing on them their divine mandate. When, for whatever reason, that mandate was withdrawn, disasters like earthquakes, famine, or floods would follow, making it clear that the dynasty was no longer favored, and a new dynasty would rise up to supplant it.

"Well," said Ida, "that's it. All we have to do is make this emperor look like he's lost the Mandate of Heaven and he's finished." Although theirs was a Yiddish-speaking home, they spoke English when they didn't want the boys to understand what they were talking about.

Hung laughed sweetly at what he saw as her naïveté.

"Idale, so simple, it's not. Da Empera's a big *macher*." It should be recalled that while Ida had attended public school in New York, English was Hung's third language, and he learned it from people for whom it was a second language.

---

4. He could have filed a complaint, but there was a ten-year waiting list to do so.

"Emperor, schmemperor, you said yourself there have been almost a dozen dynasties, so why is this one so special? This Pu Yi is a five-year-old pisher! All we have to do is make him look like one. Why should that be so hard?"

He began to laugh again and then stopped as it dawned on him: Why should it be so hard?

"Nu, youse are, maybe, on to sumtin'. If we make, maybe, a big enough *tummel*..."

"Look, Hung, politics is all the same wherever you go," Ida continued. "All you need to win is to control the political machine."

Like most machines, however, those were in short supply in China. Luckily, Hung knew of one that they might be able to use.

Dr. Sun Yat-sen had gotten his primary education in Honolulu and his medical degree from the Hong Kong College of Medicine for Chinese, which did not yet have the reputation as a party school that it would later develop. His political intrigues had led him to be exiled, and he had lived for several years in New York's Chinatown. From his table at a popular Mott Street business establishment, he offered prescriptions for medical treatment and political reform at home, a mix that led to one tragedy when a tubercular patient got confused by the advice and divided himself into equal plots of land for the peasants instead of going to Colorado for the climate. Hung had often brought deli to Dr. Sun, and the two had become friends. Although Dr. Sun was still back in the USA, perhaps his supporters in China would help them. Hung sent a cablegram to Dr. Sun, who was outraged by Hung's plight and offered him whatever support he could.

Ida and Hung hit the scrolls to figure out how to bring down a dy-

> **From his table at a popular Mott Street business establishment, he offered prescriptions for medical treatment and political reform at home, a mix that led to one tragedy when a tubercular patient got confused by the advice and divided himself into equal plots of land for the peasants instead of going to Colorado for the climate.**

nasty. Assisting them was a young busboy whom Ida nicknamed "Ketzelle," or "Kitten." A well-educated teen from a peasant family, Ketzelle reminded both Ida and Hung of themselves. This was because he was an industrious Chinese busboy interested in Socialism, not because of some freaky Chinese transgender M. Butterfly thing. Ketzelle displayed remarkable organizational and leadership ability, and in addition to providing invaluable insight into the mindset of the Chinese, the young man handled the most sensitive and complicated tasks. It didn't hurt that he had become reasonably fluent in Yiddish, so that like the Navajo windtalkers in the Pacific, they could send him messages in a virtually indecipherable code.

Little by little, the pieces came together. The dynasty was already widely held in disdain because of its inability to resist Western domination; all the people needed was a sudden jolt to push them over the edge from discontent to rebellion. One of the pillars of a dynasty was supposed to be its ability to predict the future and foresee whatever trouble may arise. The imperial seers read the oracle bones, then sent their predictions out among the people, wrapped in fortune cookies. While these predictions were originally fairly specific, the quality of fortune-telling had gone down considerably, so that by this period, fortunes had taken on the vague, generic form we know today. Using meticulous planning, Dr. Sun's network of followers staged a series of fortune-cookie hijackings, replacing the generic predictions with very, very specific ones delivered to them by Ketzelle. Few people in China could argue with a prediction like "A dark-haired man will enter your life" or "You will have trouble reaching groceries on the top shelf." But when people started reading absurd prediction like "You will find that your hat is now three sizes too small" or "One day, an enormous American automobile factory will be erected in your rice paddy," people began to mutter that the emperor had lost it. To make them even more perplexing, they were actually written in English. For the next step, the conspirators decided to kick it old school—*really* old school— and conduct a series of Chinese fire drills.

Now this may seem just a strange and inexplicable slur, but the first Chinese fire drill actually played an important part in Chinese history. In the eighth century B.C., King You of the Zhou dynasty, in order to please his new concubine, set off the warning beacons, signaling to his vassals that he was under attack. They all came running, only to find the emperor and his woman laughing at their error. Predictably, the emperor later did come under attack, but this time nobody came to assist him, presuming it was another false alarm. Centuries of chaos followed, and from then on the Chinese have been very hesitant to sound fire alarms, so when they do, people know its really, really serious and freak out, running around in a comically confused manner. On the other hand, they also developed paper, silk, gunpowder, and the egg roll, so let's not be too dismissive.

The revolutionaries set off alarms—fire alarms, flood alarms, Round-Eyed Devil alarms, you name it—all around the capital and the surrounding prefectures, paralyzing the country. At first the government did respond but eventually decided not to bother. The stage was set for the next phase. In Wuchang prefecture, some of Sun Yat-sen's revolutionaries who were soldiers in the army began a mutiny. Presuming that the alarms were merely more hysteria, the government did nothing for several weeks and the rebellion spread, eventually reaching the capital. Even so, a strong show of force may have still saved the day. Hoping to do just that, Prince Chun sent his vizier to address the crowd that had gathered near the Forbidden City. This was the moment Hung and Ida had been waiting for. The deli in New York had been a favorite spot for Yiddish comedians, and they had sent back to their old acquaintances for some material.

"I assure you," the eunuch called out, in his falsetto, "Pu Yi still has the mandate."

"Well then," shouted Hung, "I hope the emperor at least brings him some flowers."

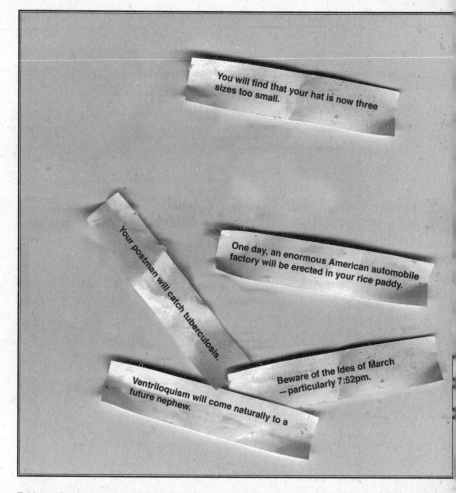

You will find that your hat is now three sizes too small.

One day, an enormous American automobile factory will be erected in your rice paddy.

Your postman will catch tuberculosis.

Beware of the Ides of March —particularly 7:52pm.

Ventriloquism will come naturally to a future nephew.

Evidence for the impact that these fortunes had on China's fortune can be found in the fact that when Mao Zedong died, he was clutching them in his hand. The fact that he was clutching his belly with his other hand suggests that consuming the sixty-year-old cookies might have been a contributing factor in his demise.

"Mandate?" shouted Ketzelle. "Don't you think a five-year-old is too young to date?"

And so it went. Soon, the country was awash with jokes about poor Pu Yi. The Manchus had withstood hundreds of years of foreign humiliations and native rebellions—but in three thousand years, no dynasty had faced the complete loss of face suffered by them in the weeks to come. The people might consent to be ruled by an emperor they loathed but not by one they mocked. The emperor stepped down, and a new "Sun" rose over China. One of the first acts of the new government was to cut a check for Hung. After Hung and Ida died in the 1920s, Zelig and Wong took over the deli, which remained the main purveyor of cold cuts to the Kuomintang until the Communist takeover in 1949. Given their connections to the Nationalists, the twins had good reason to fear for their future. It was with some surprise, then, that they were informed that they would not only be compensated for their property, but they and their families would be allowed to emigrate with their wealth to Israel, where they became the largest importer of Oriental products in the fledgling Jewish state. Even more surprising was the party that saw them off at the airport. It was Mao Zedong, whom all those years ago Ida had nicknamed "Ketzelle" because his name reminded her of a cat's meow, and who, luckily for Zelig and Wong, retained a soft spot for the place where he had his first taste of both revolution and pastrami.

CHAPTER NINETEEN

THE WAX TO END ALL WAXES

gnatz, not again!" Ignatz Schmeckgut's long-suffering fiancée, Hilda Lowensohn, shouted tearfully. "You can't keep wasting your time and money on these get-rich-quick schemes."

"No, Hilda, this one is different," Ignatz reassured her. He patted the large box he'd just placed on the table. "This box records your voice and plays back what you said. I tried it myself. Think about the potential uses! Here, watch."

He pulled a lever on the box and spoke into a small horn-shaped opening that led into the box. "My name is Ignatz Schmeckgut."

There was no response. He tried a few more times, again with no luck. While trying to soothe Hilda, whose tears by this point threatened to flood his small apartment, he took out a screwdriver and opened the box, revealing a dead parrot. As he pondered the dozen or so similar boxes he had enclosed in the back of a delivery wagon downstairs, the floodwaters continued to rise.

Ignatz Schmeckgut was, for lack of a better term, a *luftmensch*, a "man of air"—essentially that one relative nobody likes to talk about, who never seems to have a livelihood (unless borrowing money is a livelihood) but who always has a big plan that's going to pay off any day now. Although this is a concept more usually applied to the Jews of Eastern Europe, there was a Western European variety as well, and Berlin, as a thriving Jewish center, had more than its fair share. Desperate to avoid the humdrum future as a shipping clerk or salesman that life seemed to have in store for him, Ignatz went through a string of dubious inventions and get-rich-quick schemes by the time he was thirty. Among the "can't miss" ideas Ignatz involved himself with either as inventor or entrepreneur were "Corset-in-a-Bottle," The Singing Telegraph (messengers sang out a series of dots and dashes), and super-realistic toupees made from gorilla scalps. After the parrot episode, Hilda tearfully implored him to take the job her uncle Josef had graciously offered at his thriving import/export business, or she would leave him. Thus, 1882 found Ignatz sitting in the shipping offices of Lowensohn Imports, Ltd., located near the headquarters of the General Staff, next to an apothecary. All day long, when not filing papers, Ignatz would watch the officers going in and out of the pharmacy, replenishing their supply of wax for their pointy handlebar mustaches. What academic historians don't realize, for all their fancy diplomas, Naugahyde chairs, and elbow patches, is that it would be that wax that ultimately set Europe on the road to the Great War.

To understand why these mustaches were so important, it is necessary to know a little about a little-known theory that had gained popularity in German military circles in the latter half of the nineteenth century. The fairly new and not terribly scientific science of anthropology had spawned several bastard children, even newer and less terribly scientific sciences that claimed that one could "read" the physical attributes of a person to gauge his character. The most well known of these today is doubtlessly phrenology, the reading of skulls, but very well respected at the time was also Lombroson-ism, popularized by the criminologist Cesar Lombroso, who believed that all criminal types shared certain common facial features.[1] Considerably more obscure was the science of martial folliclism, the notion that facial hair was a reflection of military prowess. German theorists of martial folliclism looked at the effete thin mustaches of the Frenchmen and the long bushy mustaches and muttonchops favored by the Austrians and saw in them signs of decadence and inadequacy. By contrast, the smart, stiff, sharp handlebars of the German officer corps were seen as a symbol of their own vibrant virility. Consequently, maintaining your mustache at peak pointiness was seen as a prerequisite for advancement. Given the state of mustache wax technology at the time, this required frequent reapplications during the day, which was costly, messy, and time-consuming. In fact, the Germans almost lost the decisive battle of Sedan during the Franco-Prussian war when an adjutant bearing crucial orders to the crown prince of Bavaria spent several precious minutes waxing his mustache, almost allowing the French forces to extricate themselves from the trap.

And so it happened that Ignatz was staring out the window at the parade of officers, while absentmindedly playing with some liquefied rubber, samples from an experimental plantation in the German colony of Cameroon. He accidentally got some in his beard and, as he tried to comb it out, noticed how stiff and pointy it made his Vandyke. Although it was too thick and gummy by itself, he realized that if he could find a way to dilute it while still maintaining its stiffening abilities, he was sitting on a gold mine. Over the next few months he managed to develop a formula that fulfilled all his requirements (all the while keeping his experiments secret from Hilda, who was tearfully—from joy, this time—planning their wed-

---

1. This had serious consequences. Whereas for centuries, girth had been associated with good health, Lombroso diagnosed large jowls as being indicative of the sort of lowlife who would file fraudulent medical malpractice suits. As a result, many doctors refused to treat overweight patients, which led them to develop serious medical conditions, which were then attributed to their weight. While most doctors today realize that isn't true, they are too terrified of the diet industry's leg breakers to speak out.

ding). Formula in hand and patent in pocket, he went out to find a backer. Unfortunately, years of peddling snake oils and technological wonders had given him a reputation as a bipedal money-pit among his friends, family, and Berlin's financial institutions. One day he was at synagogue bemoaning, to no one in particular, his dismal fortune. Most congregants had long ago learned to ignore him, particularly when he was in his cups after a few glasses of schnapps. One congregant, however, who was concerned with his own financial well-being was willing not only to commiserate, but to help.

During the 1860s, Felix Kleinstuck had achieved a fair amount of success as a midlevel arms merchant to Prussia's expanding and expansionist military. The 1870s, however, had seen a considerable decline in his fortunes. With the successful conclusion of

This photo, discovered amid the rubble of a house destroyed in Colmar, shows an intensely patriotic German family in the late nineteenth century that has clearly taken to the extreme Kaiser Wilhelm II's "Starke durch Schnurrbarte" (Peace Through Mustaches) program.

the Franco-Prussian war and the proclamation of the German Empire, Germany was the most powerful country in Europe, and bolstered by the recent alliance with Austro-Hungary and Russia, there seemed little chance of Germany ever going to war, which was bad news, if not for the Jews, then at least for those like Felix who were military contractors. When Felix heard of Ignatz's idea, it was like a gaslight went off above his head. Whether genius, drunkenness, or insanity,[2] he saw with perfect clarity what he could do with Ignatz's invention. He became Ignatz's silent partner, and thus financially fortified, Ignatz opened up a small factory, which led Hilda to tearfully break off the engagement. Before releasing "Schmeckbesser's Twelve-Hour Handlebar Holding Gel"[3] on the open market, Felix conducted some marketing research upon a small but very influential test group. Under the pretext of demonstrating some new high-explosive shells from Sweden, he invited a group of high-ranking officers, including Crown Prince Wilhelm, the grandson of the kaiser, to his proving grounds outside of Berlin. It was a sweltering summer's day, and as was expected, the mustaches began to wilt. Felix had managed to insinuate himself into the prince's retinue and offered him his own mustache wax. Although Wilhelm was affronted by the commoner's presumptuousness, it would have been bad form to refuse, and besides, it was a new tin. As the day went on, Wilhelm was amazed and delighted to find that he didn't need to reapply the wax, a matter of particular concern for him, since, his left arm withered, it was only with difficulty that he was able to wax his left handlebar. Soon the staff officers and nobles who surrounded the prince were also

---

2. Or Alcohol-Induced Genius Syndrome (AIGS), a very rare disorder that unfortunately has virtually identical symptoms as Delusional Alcohol-Induced Genius Syndrome (DAIGS), a condition that is found in the vast majority of people who drink to excess. Tragically, there's no way to tell the two apart until the plans developed while under the syndrome's grasp are actually put into effect. At that point, it is fairly simple, as AIGS-induced plans almost never lead to the emergency room.

3. Aside from the desire to head off the likelihood of a competitor claiming the name "Schmeckbesser's..." Ignatz felt that the name change was appropriate considering his change in status.

begging to try the wax, which Felix graciously provided. They left the proving grounds with three weeks' supply of wax and the certainty that they would never use anything else. When the product went on the market a month later, there were already so many pre-orders that it became instantly profitable.

In 1888, the crown prince was coronated as Kaiser Wilhelm II. Unlike his predecessors, he felt no particular need for alliances, preferring instead to rely upon the supremacy of Teutonic mustachery. Aside from his resentment over being overshadowed by the architect of German reunification, Wilhelm had nothing but contempt for Otto von Bismarck's bushy, unwaxed mustache. He soon dismissed Bismarck, abandoning the diplomatic framework the "Iron Chancellor" had spent years building up. Over the course of the next few years, Felix discreetly bought up and shut down numerous rubber plantations in Germany's African colonies. Eventually, "shortages" of liquefied rubber began to threaten the supplies of mustache wax, and with it, as the theory went, German military supremacy. The kaiser soon embarked on a policy of colonial expansion designed to secure access to rubber plantations, most of which were already located in French and British colonies. Furthermore, to guarantee these supplies, he began dramatically expanding the German navy, which placed him on a direct collision course with the British Empire. Felix found his military supplies again in high demand, and given his close ties with the kaiser, became one of the most prominent military contractors in Germany. As for Ignatz, after the factory took off, Hilda tearfully begged him to take her back, which he gladly did. They had a long and happy marriage, and when handlebars fell out of favor following the Great War, the Schmeckbesser Gummi Fabrik successfully converted to condom manufacturing. During the 1930s, his grandchildren migrated to Palestine, where they became the largest manufacturers of condoms in the Middle East. And if that isn't exactly a happy ending considering that it all resulted in the Great War, well, that's the best you're going to get.

CHAPTER TWENTY

CRASH COURSE IN PSYCHOLOGY

Doctor Leo Gerstner, graduate of the University of Vienna and formerly one of that city's most prominent psychoanalysts, listened carefully to the man's story. He was feeling stressed out, as his wife and children expected so much from him and his boss was always on his back. Leo nodded thoughtfully, evaluated the man's condition—"Clearly a repressed homosexual who is stricken with guilt over his secret love for his boss"—and prescribed the cure.

"You need a Manhattan, easy on the vermouth."

He mixed the drink and offered it to the harried stockbroker. The man took a sip and the stress melted away.

"Leo," said the man, "I just don't know how you do it."

Leo just wiped the glasses and thought about how he did it. He did it by having been first in every class he ever took. He immersed himself in the field of psychoanalysis, to the point where no less of an expert than Carl Jung himself declared Leo "without question, Freud's most brilliant disciple," though it should be noted that at the time, Leo was thrusting Jung's head repeatedly into a toilet, commanding him to "say it, bitch."

> **Carl Jung himself declared Leo "without question, Freud's most brilliant disciple," though it should be noted that at the time, Leo was thrusting Jung's head repeatedly into a toilet, commanding him to "say it, bitch."**

Leo's stratospheric career might have known no limits had the Vienna psychoanalytical board not objected to some of his more controversial methods, such as hypnotizing and sleeping with his female patients. He argued that this was done so that they would get their sexual desire out of their system, and thus the doctor/patient relationship wouldn't be strained by a misplaced Electra complex. He had no explanation, however, as to why he only did it with the really hot ones. Given his prominence in the field, the review board felt that revealing the truth for his disqualification would reflect poorly on the whole profession, so they just attached a note to his record stating that there was no room in Vienna for his "funky, street style" of psychoanalysis.

Banned from practicing in Austria, Leo contemplated moving to Germany. Without question, there was no shortage of patients there with serious mental illness, including depression, which was his specialty. But in 1923, the German economy was a complete shambles, and so instead he came to the United States, presuming that a psychoanalyst of his stature would have no trouble finding clientele. The problem here wasn't the money, it was the fact that things were going so well that nobody needed a shrink. With European industry having been devastated by the war and by the emigration of the most hardworking Europeans to the United States, U.S. industry was producing like there was no tomorrow.[1] The moneyed classes in America were not just happy, they were extravagantly optimistic, believing that the good times would never come to an end. Thus, there was nothing for Leo to do as a psychoanalyst, so he was left with little choice but to fall back on his one other skill: bartending. During his days in the university, he had tended bar at the campus rathskeller, and that experience would come in handy in America, where he worked at the Hole on the Wall, a speakeasy on Wall Street. The bar attracted a large clientele from the Street, not only due to its proximity, but because of Leo's unerring ability to ascertain what drink best suited their psychological needs at the time. Consequently, all the big brokers and money-men passed through the doors of the Hole, and seated themselves at Leo's bar.

---

1. Also no child labor, workplace safety, or overtime laws.

One day in the fall of 1929 a man whom Leo had never seen came in and began to treat the whole bar.

"Who's that?" Leo asked a customer, curious about a man whom he had never seen, but who seemed to know and be known by everyone.

"Oh, him? That's Oscar Cohen II."

Oscar Cohen's father, Oskar Kahn, had been one of the great German-Jewish financiers who were as ubiquitous in 1890s New York City as skinny, siliconed Eastern European "models" would be a century later. Like many German Americans, the Kahns took measures during the war to mask their ethnicity. Aside from changing their name, they stopped eating sausage, stopped wearing sandals with socks, and arranged for the weekly public beating of a chubby, lederhosen-clad blond boy. Oskar had made a fortune on Wall Street, primarily trading in immigrant futures,[2] and he expected his son to follow in his footsteps. Unfortunately, the apple had fallen some distance from the tree. Although his father, shortly before his death in 1921, had warned his son to get out of immigration futures, Oscar refused to listen, and the National Origins Act of 1924 took a big chunk out of the family fortune. Since then, Oscar had been going through the inheritance at a fairly rapid rate, trying to make his mark and his money back through various dodgy deals. It was a mark of his stellar incompetence that he managed to lose money even in the most taurine of bull markets. It had reached the point, in fact, where he

---

2. The market on Jews and Italians was going through the roof, and he managed to get out of the Japanese market just before it collapsed.

had become a bellwether for the market, and people watched him for signs of how a particular stock was going to do. He sold, they bought, he bought, they sold. And by and large, the system worked. Leo had never seen Oscar because he had never had any reason to celebrate, and his years of loss had left him scraping the last million his father had bequeathed him. But on that day, his stock was rising and he was feeling generous. The cocktails were flowing freely and it looked like Oscar's luck had finally turned.

"Hey, Oscar," called out one reveler. "Aren't you going to tell us what the stock is?"

"I think I can share the wealth. It's United Amalgamated Confederated. Now go on, sell your shares if you want to—it's your loss."

Half the bar ran out. A man came out of the bathroom, looking at the empty seats.

"You might want to join them, Oscar. According to the tickertape in the bathroom, UAC is dropping like an anchor."[3] Oscar ran into the bathroom, then came out a moment later, ashen faced. The man who'd given him the dire news ushered him to the bar, sat him down, and signaled to Leo.

"Two more right here, Leo."

Through the remainder of the afternoon and evening, Oscar sat at the bar nursing drinks and pouring his heart out to Leo. As the night wore on, the latter began to develop a plan...

The next morning, Oscar woke up on his couch, his head pounding. He smelled pipe smoke and struggled to rise. A hand gently but firmly held him down and offered him a glass.

"Here," said a man with a German accent. "Drink this, it will help with the hangover."

"Hey," Oscar replied, recognizing his interlocutor. "You're the bartender."

"Oh, no, *mein freund*, I am much, much more than that...."

---

3. UAC actually managed to weather its collapse and the crash, and went through several reconstitutions before achieving its current form, Mary-Kate and Ashley Olsen, Inc.

The plan was devilishly simple. Oscar had achieved such a terrible reputation that Wall Street would do exactly the opposite of what he did. It was time he made that work for him. What he needed was a confederate. Oscar would very visibly buy blue chip stocks. The prices of those stocks would then plummet. Leo would then purchase shares of those stocks at discount rates, at which point Oscar would unload those stocks, immediately driving the price up again. At the same time, Leo would have purchased the same worthless stocks that Oscar already had in his portfolio; then, when Oscar sold them, the price would rise and Leo would unload those for a tidy profit.

"It sounds like it could work," conceded Oscar, still on the couch. "But even as bad as my reputation is, how are we going to get people to unload stocks like U.S. Steel and Standard Oil at discount rates?"

"Ah, that's where I come in. By the time you step into the picture, I guarantee that the Street will be primed and ready to sell."

For the next few weeks, Leo turned the speakeasy into a laboratory for subliminal suggestion. Using a trick Freud had used when his landlord had come to collect the rent, he set up a metronome behind the bar to help facilitate a hypnotic state in select customers. Once he had them in a suggestible mood, he would begin the suggestion. Some of this was visual, some of it verbal. For example, by stressing certain words and syllables in the phrase "Did Hugh steal the chairs that were down in the basement?" he ensured that listeners heard "U.S. Steel shares down in the basement," and would be so subconsciously troubled that they wouldn't wonder what the hell he meant. Visually, he would set up objects behind the bar to accomplish the same thing. For example, he would begin a shift with a Ford Motor Company calendar posted high on the wall, and then slowly, slowly move it down the wall, so that by the time people finished their drinks, they couldn't help but feel that Ford was moving down. Leo did this for several weeks, and by the end of that period, the biggest names on the Street couldn't explain it, but they felt that something was horribly, horribly wrong. Then came Monday morning, October 28, 1929, and Oscar began to play his part.

Primed by Leo, the movers and shakers saw Oscar buying the blue chips and they began to panic. A massive sell-off ensued, and Leo picked up a lot of bargains. At the same time, Oscar's sale of his garbage stocks convinced many that they were the ones to buy, and Leo was the man to buy them from. The pair made a nice bit of change, and the next morning it was time for both Leo and Oscar to sell their blue chips. That's when things stopped going according to plan. Convinced by Leo's subliminals that those stocks were going down, people refused to buy them back. Moreover, when people saw that the big men in J.P. Morgan, Merrill Lynch, and the other major firms were unloading their best stocks, it led to a massive sell-off all across the board. By the end of the day, the stock market had crashed. To make matters worse, many learned over their late-night cocktails at the Hole on the Wall that dozens upon dozens of investors jumped out the windows of skyscrapers upon learning of their financial misfortunes.[4]

It was not entirely true to say that things weren't going according to plan. More to the point, things didn't go according to the plan that Leo had told Oscar. But from Leo's perspective, things couldn't have been going better. Thousands and thousands of Americans found themselves in the midst of a great depression, and not only did they need help, but the fledgling American psychoanalytical profession needed guidance. All eyes, and numerous wallets, turned to Leo. As for Oscar, he was not forgotten. For the first time, he had actually made money and was ready to plunge his earnings back into the market. Leo, however, gave him some free sessions, and in a few weeks made him realize that he was trying to be Oskar Kahn, instead of Oscar Cohen II, and that all the success in the

---

4. They learned this, of course, from Leo. Less convincing was the rumor he spread that they could restore their wealth by helping him get back his fortune from Nigeria.

f The United Stat

TOP SECR

Name: Cookies

Code Name: SICA-18

Military Grade Equival
Lieutenant-Colonel

As per an 1824 Supreme Court ruling (*Aaron Burr v. Aaron Burro*), government documents regarding actions by animals may be classified, but not information about the animal itself. Consequently, our Freedom of Information Act request regarding "Cookies" the chimp produced this partial record. "SICA" stands for Super Intelligent Chimp Assassin, and we can only presume that "18" means that he was the eighteenth such chimp in the program.

markets couldn't buy him happiness. He also reminded him that he had a few thousand shares of U.S. Steel, Standard Oil, and Ford that would be worth a hell of a lot when the stock market recovered. Thus enlightened, Oscar gave up the dreams that he now realized were not his, but his father's. It took him a few years to find himself, but he eventually went on to achieve great success and fulfillment as a breeder of superintelligent chimps for the military.[5]

---

5. The program remains classified, but let it simply be noted that for many years, the American intelligence community used to deny involvement in assassinations, coups, sabotage, and the like with the curiously worded statement: "To the best of our knowledge, no human agents of this government took part in..."

CHAPTER TWENTY-ONE

JEWISH MEMBERS

I'm sorry, sir, but members of the Hebrew race are not permitted into the club." It was 1928 and Max Wolf, only in his twenties and already founder and absolute tyrant of Wolf Pictures International, was trying to enter the tony Suncrest Club in order to make a date he had finally wrangled out of Shepard Flintjaw, daughter of one of L.A.'s finest and first Anglo families. He had been imagining a magical evening, but the majordomo's words were punctuated by the door's being slammed in his face. What really hurt, however, were the cruel smiles on the faces of the club's elegant denizens and, most painfully of all, of Shepard's herself. Burning with shame and a desire for revenge, Max arranged a meeting with all of Hollywood's major players. Even those who normally would have never given a minor operator like Max the time of day agreed to attend—they'd all had similar experiences themselves. At the meeting, it was decided that no matter how long it took, they would use their considerable resources to make sure that the day would come when Jewish men were not only accepted, but adored.

The first thing to do was to eliminate the current crop of stars. Hollywood's power brokers had been aware of a process to add sound to film, but up to that point saw no reason to do it, as it would jeopardize their stables of talent who sounded considerably worse than they looked. With their new mandate in mind, however, they decided not merely to make a "talkie," but to do so with a bankable Jewish star, whose life story—the basis of the film's plot— was a paean to the ideal of toleration. And thus was born *The Jazz Singer*, a franchise that over the course of the twentieth century would provide lead roles for three Jews and one Lebanese Christian.[1] More important, though, it completely overturned Hollywood's old order, as star after star proved either unintelligible or simply laughable. In their place, a generation of rugged, tough Jewish leading men like Paul Muni and John Garfield lit up the screen. In order to make the Jewish leads look even better in comparison, the moguls elevated men like James Cagney, Humphrey Bogart, and George Raft, who, let's face it, weren't exactly beauty pageant winners, to the top of the non-Jewish field.

The rise of totalitarianism in Europe presented Hollywood with a unique opportunity. If America would grow to accept Jews by seeing Jewish actors depicting heroes on the big screen, how much quicker would they do so after seeing Jews themselves depicted as war heroes? The Hollywood bigwigs had FDR right where they wanted him—by the balls, literally, since only they could provide the fairly esoteric pornography that was the patrician Knickerbocker's greatest shame: his desire for stout, prognathic Irishwomen in scullery maids' uniforms. They nudged him, he nudged the country, and once the bullets were flying, the Dream Factory began churning out grist for the assimilationist mill. Some early efforts, like *J. A. P. S. vs. the Japs*[2] and *The Rabbi Wore a Helmet*, were, to put it mildly, blunt. After a few such failures, however, the moguls realized that while the American people might not flock to see films starring explicitly Jewish heroes, they would see films that included Jewish heroes among others, and thus was born the ensemble army film. In thousands of wartime movies, multiethnic squads portraying the full glorious rainbow of nonblack America went into battle, and in each of them the scrappy Jewish kid from Brooklyn or the Lower East Side would die heroically. In 1942 alone, Wolf's studio had killed off: 432 Jewish servicemen falling on grenades, 345 leading suicidal bayonet charges, 83 heroically crashing their plane/ship/tank/jeep into an enemy position, 34 being tortured to death by brutal interrogators,

---

1. Alas, the Lebanese Christian was Danny Thomas. Outside of our most special dreams, the world has yet to see *The Jazz Singer* starring Jamie Farr.
2. J.A.P.S.—Jewish American Paratroop Squad.

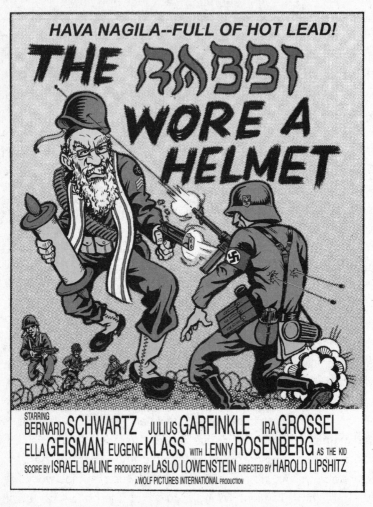

The Rabbi Wore a Helmet was Wolf Pictures International's first and, arguably, worst foray into wartime propaganda, featuring lines like "You just entered the slaughter-house . . . and I'm the shochet." The poor quality is all the more remarkable since many prominent Hollywood Jews actually lent their services, albeit under their original names. It was their influence that kept the film out of the public eye, and it took an exhaustive search of the Motion Picture Association of America's Library of Cinematic Promotion to turn up even this poster.

32 catching a sniper's bullet (in 29 cases, a bullet intended for someone they would push out of harm's way), 19 being bayoneted, and 1 clubbed to death by a cyclops in the rarely shown conceptual nightmare *The Marines Meet Hercules*. It has been estimated that had the depiction of Jewish war dead in wartime films been accurate, the Brooklyn Jewish community would have actually become depopulated by mid-1944.

In 1942 alone, Wolf's studio had killed off: 432 Jewish servicemen falling on grenades, 345 leading suicidal bayonet charges, 83 heroically crashing their plane/ship/ tank/jeep into an enemy position, 34 being tortured to death by brutal interrogators, 32 catching a sniper's bullet (in 29 cases, a bullet intended for someone they would push out of harm's way), 19 being bayoneted, and 1 clubbed to death by a cyclops in the rarely shown conceptual nightmare *The Marines Meet Hercules*.

Hollywood would exploit the wholesale slaughter of the Jews in Europe to produce such anti-anti-Semitic fare as *Gentleman's Agreement* and Wolf's lesser-known *Paging Dr. Hate*, about a snobby doctor and country club officer who turns out to be a deranged Nazi-sympathizing vivisectionist. The late forties and the fifties saw the continued presence of tough, attractive Jewish leads like Tony Curtis, Kirk Douglas, and Jeff Chandler. Meanwhile, non-Jewish stars were made to seem almost completely incoherent—like Marlon Brando, James Dean, and Robert Mitchum—or "questionable"—like Rock Hudson and Tab Hunter. Of course, part of the goal was not only to make Americans see Jewish men as likable, but sexually attractive, as well. Thus, during this era, carefully orchestrated life imitated art. When the moguls arranged for screen sex goddesses like Marilyn Monroe, Elizabeth Taylor, and Carroll Baker not only to marry Jews, but to convert, the message to the world was clear: If Arthur Miller is sexy, what Jewish man isn't?

As the 1960s progressed, America was ready for actors who

they could identify with. So Hollywood produced stars like Alan Arkin, George Segal, and Richard Benjamin. The Vietnam War had cast a pall on traditional gentile masculinity, allowing Hollywood to push stars who better represented the less manly Jewish version. While Wolf nixed production of *Psychadelicatessen*,[3] it is worth noting that the most successful war movie of the era was not John Wayne's *The Green Berets*, but *M*A*S*H*, starring Elliott Gould.

Critics of Hollywood have noted the increased explicitness of cinematic sex since the sixties, charging that this helped loosen the morals of America. It was no accident that this was taking place at the same time that celluloid Semites became more accepted. But critics and conspiracy theorists are wrong in suggesting that Hollywood was trying to corrupt Americans in order to get them to sleep around; they were only trying to get them to sleep around with *Jews*. After all, what was the point in having a sexual revolution if the only beneficiaries would be gentile men? Nothing expresses the transformed sexual ideals of America better than the fact that this was an era in which executives casting *The Love Boat* would say: "We need to find a real ladies' man to play Doc. You know who's *really* suave and handsome? Bernie Kopell, that's who!"

Similar criticisms have been made regarding cinematic violence in the same period. But Jews in Hollywood weren't trying to increase violence in America; they were trying to transform violence, that last bastion of gentile masculinity, from something that was heroic to something that was terrifying. When you saw John Wayne pull out a gun, you knew he was going to use it to save the girl; when you saw Charles Bronson with one, you were afraid he was going to use it to pistol-whip her. In the seventies, Jewish Hollywood would promote gentile actors like Robert De Niro and Al Pacino, who were physically indistinguishable from the Jewish

---

3. The plot involved a kosher deli in San Francisco being run by the Huttmachers, two hippie brothers who serve up hallucinogenic cold cuts to the city's nonvegetarian flower children, and in the denouement, a banquet at a local military base.

stars of the period. So if you had to date the guy from *Kramer vs. Kramer*, or the guy from *Taxi Driver*, whom would you choose? Again, the message was clear: Jewish men look as good as their non-Jewish counterparts, and are much less likely to be homicidal sociopaths.

In the 1980s, the moguls moved into their endgame: As the Jewish actors who most closely resembled the Hollywood moguls themselves, the repulsive Jewish types, like Corey Feldman, Ian Ziering, and Herschel "Yoda" Yodawsky, became sex symbols. And it's an open secret in Tinseltown that before he became Orthodox and moved back to Israel, E.T. slept with almost every major female star in Hollywood. We have today reached the stage in which Jewish men are seen as catches, no matter how trollish they may be. Challengers of this assertion are free to check out the *Playboy* Playmate who married the truly Rondo Hatton–like Ziering. It took seventy years, but Hollywood's founding moguls succeeded with their conspiracy. Of course, Max Wolf never did get that magical evening with Shepard. But many years later, as president emeritus of the Suncrest Club, he did spend one particularly satisfying afternoon in his office there with her ingenue granddaughter.

So if you had to date the guy from *Kramer vs. Kramer*, or the guy from *Taxi Driver*, whom would you choose? Again, the message was clear: Jewish men look as good as their non-Jewish counterparts, and are much less likely to be homicidal sociopaths.

CHAPTER TWENTY-TWO

THERE'S **NO** BUSINESS LIKE *SHOAH* BUSINESS

In late 1940, when Mendel Feuerstein got out of Dachau on a bureaucratic error,[1] he didn't look back, but headed straight to the United States on a forged temporary visa. There he made the rounds of the various immigrant and refugee relief organizations, picking up whatever handouts he could. It wasn't much of a payday, but then, that was the story of Mendel's life. Back in Poland and Germany, he had made a living (if you could call it that) out of insurance fraud. It was the usual thing—throwing himself under a wagon's wheels, hurling himself in front of a pogromist's cudgel— and, quite frankly, he was lousy at it. His biggest payday was five million marks in 1924, which may sound like a lot, but given the state of the German economy at the time, it meant that he *owed* slightly more than fifty-seven dollars. Moreover, things didn't look like they'd get much better in the States. To top it off, his family back in Poland informed him that the local authorities were interested in having a lengthy discussion with him. One day he was feeding slugs into the pie dispenser at the Automat, when a voice behind him said in Yiddish, "You know, if you tie a string to it, you can get your slug back." He turned around, and faced a figure as worn-out and run-down as he was.

"Laszlo Gruber," said the man, extending his hand. "Why don't you join us?"

The "us" in question was a group of refugees, all of whom shared pasts and presents virtually identical with Mendel's. From all over Europe, they'd fled their pathetic, shifty, and shiftless lives,

---

1. He had been marked down for *ubersonderbehandlung* (super special handling, i.e., release), as opposed to just plain *sonderbehandlung* (transfer to the East).

only to find themselves no more successful in America. Like Mendel, they moved from Automat to Automat, never staying too long at any one.

"They tell me I didn't suffer enough back in Hungary to qualify for refugee relief," moaned Laszlo. "What do they think life with my wife was like?"

And so it went, each man with his hard-luck tale of failure and fear.

"What we need," observed Laszlo despondently, "is a way out. A way out of our old lives, and a way into a new one here."

The tales of woe continued, while Mendel pondered what he'd just heard.

"What if there was a way to wipe out our pasts and start here with not only a clean slate, but a full wallet?"

Although he had them with "full wallet," they listened further to what he had to say.

"So we fake our own deaths," sneered Baruch Ferdsgoniff, wringing the soup from his beard back into his bowl. "I've done that before. It never works."

"That's the genius of this plan," continued Mendel excitedly. "The problem with most fake death scams—and believe me, I know from what I speak—is that the insurance companies have all the re-sources and time that they need to investigate one death. But what if there are hundreds of thousands, millions of deaths? Do you think that the insurance companies are going to care about us?"

The men may not have been the world's best con men, but they still had a lifetime of shady business contacts to draw upon. They got these to send letters from Europe to major Jewish organiza-tions, declaring the horrific atrocities being committed by the Ger-mans. Back in the States, they themselves swallowed a lifetime of objections and actually got jobs at some of these organizations, where they were able to quickly process these dire warnings with little oversight. By the end of 1941, the word was out that the Ger-mans were brutal butchers, and it wasn't hard to convince the

American people that they were capable of anything, including genocide.

Now, to be sure, Auschwitz was no picnic—except, of course, for the second Sunday of each month, and Hitler's birthday, when they brought out the Ferris wheel—but *genocide* does seem to be a fairly harsh term for what was practiced there by the Germans. So while the effectiveness of wartime propaganda can be understood, the question remains as to how such a huge lie could be perpetuated through the last sixty years. The dirty little secret of historians is that such occurrences are actually fairly common. Scholars today know that as a result of a simple typographical error by an archivist at the court of Charles II, the "Great Plaque" of 1665, the epidemic of tooth decay brought about by the ready availability of cheap sugar from England's Caribbean colonies, was recorded as the "Great Plague." Closer to home, the sacking of Washington, D.C., during the War of 1812 was a little bit of spin control by then-President James Madison, who felt that convincing people that the invading British had burned down the White House would be easier than explaining that he'd fallen asleep while smoking in bed. Indeed, there is even some question today as to whether the War of 1812 happened at all, or if it was just a complicated marketing ploy to get Americans to buy "American Toast" instead of "English Muffins."

Historians are just as gullible as anybody else—show them some eyewitnesses and a few primary sources, and they'll fall for anything, hook, line, and sinker. Consequently, when the war ended, historians fell all over themselves to uncover new aspects of the genocide. Thus, even the most harmless sites became transformed into sinister cogs in the death machine. The steam coming out of the steam baths at Auschwitz was misidentified as "Zyklon B gas,"[2]

---

2. It may be that Auschwitz was chosen as the site for the steam baths as a cost-cutting move, since the name of the town itself was coincidentally a shortened form of *Auslandern Schwitzbaden*, i.e., "foreigners' steam baths," and saved the notoriously miserly SS money on signs.

even as the piles of hair at the Reichsinstitut fur Kosmetologikal Studieren located nearby were used as evidence for the hundreds of thousands of victims who were allegedly gassed there. So too were the pizza ovens at Majdanek used to provide rations for the Italian forces in Russia described as crematoria. And the harsh commands that could be heard from miles around the puppy farm at Buchenwald seemed proof positive of the cruelty of the Nazi regime.

> **Even as the piles of hair at the Reichsinstitut fur Kosmetologikal Studieren located nearby were used as evidence for the hundreds of thousands of victims who were allegedly gassed there. So too were the pizza ovens at Majdanek used to provide rations for the Italian forces in Russia described as crematoria.**

The Germans contributed to this atmosphere since they very vocally did promulgate anti-Jewish policies.[3] If Hitler was going to go on the radio and threaten to exterminate the Jews, he really can't be too surprised if people took him at his word. It is a sore point with his admirers, however, that nobody ever views as equally authoritative the numerous speeches he gave in which he referred to himself as "the ultimate Aryan love machine." And of course, the Allied governments sought to maintain the façade of German monstrosity even after the war ended. Imagine the embarrassment of going to war because a certain country presented a particular threat, and then discovering that the threat never actually existed. This motivation was particularly strong for the Soviets, since the Germans had become so highly esteemed during the war for their many charitable deeds on behalf

---

3. People searching for an explanation for Hitler's obsession with the Jews have long speculated that he was of partial Jewish descent, and that that explains his antipathy (self-hate, apparently, making more sense than anti-Semitism). This is untrue; during middle school he was, however, the only non-Jewish member of a local doo-wop group in Linz, the Oesterreich-Aires. He was dropped from the group when his father quit letting them use the garage for practice, which may have been the event that sent him off the anti-Semitic deep end.

The presence of the Ferris Wheel places this picture in later April, probably in 1943. In that year, Reichsfuhrer Heinrich Himmler ordered the Ferris Wheel replaced with a Tilt-a-Whirl after an embarrassing trip on the wheel resulted in him shrieking like a schoolgirl and vomiting.

of the people of the Ukraine. Where the Ukrainians saw the Germans as the providers of swimming pools, pony rides, and soft pretzels, the Soviets wanted them seen as tyrants and mass murderers, and what better way to demonize them in the eyes of the Poles and Ukrainians than to accuse them of exterminating the Jews, whom those people so dearly loved? Laszlo had worked a crooked tourism scam years earlier, sending suckers to "dream vacations" in run-down dumps in the Carpathians. It only cost him vodka money to get some of his former associates in the railroad industry to talk too loudly in local bars about "transports" of Jews to "resettlement camps," where they were exterminated. Money for such projects was siphoned from the organizations the conspirators were working for. Vodka, for example, could be covered up as part of a water purification program for the Pripet Marshes.

In the United States, Mendel and the others established the "Council of Survivors of the European Genocide."[4] Dozens of escapees from the camps spoke before Congress. That many of these "survivors" (most of whom were hired from Bowery flophouses for the price of a bowl of soup and a bottle of Mogen David) spoke English with Spanish, Italian, Irish, and Chinese accents only seemed to highlight the international nature of the threat. And at any rate, they were saying what Congress, and the American people, wanted to hear. International religious and human rights organizations were also conned. Back in Poland, an acquaintance of Mendel's by the name of Leibish Gloibzeller made a living before the war as a professional converter, accepting Jesus as his personal savior in a wide variety of denominations. He now put that experience to good use, reporting as a Catholic, Lutheran, Uniate, Orthodox Christian, and Southern Baptist to assorted Christian institutions on the mass murder of the Jews. Those institutions, understandably, checked with one another to ascertain the

---

4. CSEG was their little joke, since that's what they were looking for from the government. In their defense, they were recent arrivals, and their ability to both spell and pronounce *check* was limited.

veracity of these statements, and of course found almost perfect corroboration. Hearing of these accounts, the International Red Cross conducted its own investigations. Nobody really knows what those original field reports contained; they were intercepted in the IRC mailroom by a conspirator, who then replaced them with doctored reports full of atrocities. As the war was drawing to its close, the conspirators had all collected handsomely from assorted American insurance companies, having died several times under several names. Mendel thought it would be best if they parted ways and never saw one another again.

"Maybe," said Laszlo. "But maybe we should wait a little bit. There's still the question of what happens when the war is over and the world finds out that there was no genocide."

"So what?" snorted Mendel, pausing to light a cigar butt he'd picked up from the floor of the Automat. "So they'll realize the atrocities were false. The same thing happened after the last war."

"Exactly, and what else happened after the last war? The Germans paid out big."

"Yeah, but they paid out to countries, not individuals," observed Lev Petzler, who had spent several years and a couple of pages both soundless and nameless.

"Ah," crowed Laszlo triumphantly. "That's where this war is different. This time, the victims *are* individuals. All we have to do is keep the con going, and there's going to be another big payday from German restitution. Don't you want to receive payment for your expropriated factories and stolen artwork?"

He looked expectantly at the group, but surprisingly, found little approval in their eyes.

"Look," said Mendel apologetically. "It's been a good scam. But I've got enough money. I never thought I'd say that—believe me—but I do. Why risk it all now?"

Laszlo sighed. "All right, for once I'll be honest: It isn't about the money. It's about professional pride. Look at us. Think of all the petty scams and cheap cons we've pulled over our collective life-times. We almost never got paid, and we almost always got caught. But right now, we've pulled not only the biggest scam of our lives, but maybe the biggest scam in history. And you know what? *I don't want it to get found out.* Forget about getting caught. I just don't want this scam to end. We fooled the entire world. We have put to-gether this masterpiece, and if we just work a little longer, we'll have the satisfaction of knowing that not only did we make the world our pigeon, but we kept it in our coop. We'll be the greatest con men of all time."

"Just wait a minute," objected Baruch, who had shaved his beard and now wore an expensive, soup-stained tie. "Nobody's going to know but us."

"And that, my friend, is what makes us the greatest."

The men looked at one another and one by one nodded their assent.

As Germany collapsed, millions of refugees fled to the West, and the Americans and British found themselves having to care for a huge population of displaced persons. It wasn't hard for the con-spirators to secure positions in the DP camps as translators, ad-ministrators, and interrogators. It didn't take a lot of prodding for many Jews to believe themselves to have been victims of a pro-gram aimed at exterminating them, particularly when the Red Cross, the pope, and the governments of England, France, the So-viet Union, and the United States were all telling them that it was so. To be sure, many, many Jews did die; given the fact that they were living in a war zone, this is not too strange, and it did add a certain amount of vérité to the stories of mass murder. Those who survived simply presumed that they were among the lucky few who made it. Thus, when Mendel, representing the United States of America in all its authority, asked former Auschwitz inmates "How often did the Germans make selections to send people to the gas chambers?," nobody thought to question what those selections were for,[5] or whether or not the gas chambers actually existed. In other cases, they were able to convince refugees that there was nothing waiting for them back home, as their neighbors were not eager to return the lawn mowers, hedge trimmers, and houses they had borrowed during the war years. They might convince some that their families were deceased; others, that they were still very much alive. For example, when Fayge Perlmutter expressed her desire to return to Poland, Lev reminded her of what life with Herschel Perlmutter—with his never lifting a hand around the house, his picking his toes at the table, his flatulence—was really like. She headed to Palestine and never sent so much as a postcard.

As any reader of *The Star* or *National Enquirer* can tell you, wealthy, famous people really long for nothing more than the simple life. As a result, celebrities like Franz Menken, who had starred in *Golem, PI*, an enormously successful series of Czech films about a clay homunculus private eye brought to life by kabbalistic means in 1930s Prague, were convinced by "Doctor" Ferdsgoniff, the psychologist, that this was a golden opportunity to enter a life of liberating anonymity. Laszlo used his position in a refugee organization and his skills as a travel agent to channel to the American countryside traditional Jews who would have stood out because of their dark clothing, long beards, Yiddish language, and insularity. It is now known that many "Amish" communities are really made up of Hasidic Jews. Like most Hasidim, they never bought televisions, but unlike their urban peers, who were at least exposed to modern technology by virtue of living next door to it, these Hasidim who moved from primitive rural Eastern Europe to primitive rural Middle America simply never became aware that such wonders as nacho machines and The Clapper ever existed, and thus remained as technologically backward as their Amish peers.

The greatest coup of them all was pulled off by Leibish, who

---

5. Even now that remains unclear, although it seems that many were for the Auschwitz dodgeball team, which, lacking any protective gear due to wartime constraints, did have a fairly high mortality rate.

converted one more time, this time to communism. Thus ideologi-
cally purified, he secured a job in the new government. When the
first postwar census of Poland came in, he was able to convince
his fellow apparatchiks that the numbers had to be wrong.

"How can millions of Jews still be alive? Are you suggesting that
Comrade Stalin was incorrect about the crimes of the fascists?"

Faced with an irrefutable argument like that, the good people at
the Census Bureau self-deprecatingly wrote off the previous figures as resulting from "a Polish census," and changed them to better correspond to the party's estimates. Even after Leibish left
Poland in 1956, nobody wanted to admit to the error, and so suc-
cessive censuses continued to go by the original numbers. It has
only been in the last decade or so that the real numbers are starting to come out. As for the seeming invisibility of the Polish Jewish
community, many traditional Jews had become accustomed to
cheeseburgers and Saturday morning cartoons during the war (at
least in the less rigorous camps), and saw little incentive to go
back to their old ways, and over the last fifty years assimilation,
particularly in light of the communist regime's hostility to the Jews,
doubtlessly took place on a wide scale.

As is often the case, once the conspiracy was firmly and successfully launched, it took on a life of its own. Most of the major
players in the game became aware of what was going on, but from
professors to politicians, too much was invested in the Holocaust
for anybody to let it go. During the 1950s the pope was reportedly
presented evidence that the genocide never took place. His response was, "I know that and you know that, but what do you think
it's going to do to my 'infallibility' if we let *them* know that." Even
enemies of the Jews have been uncomfortable allies in perpetuat-
ing its memory. According to one highly placed official in the American Nazi Party: "Look, we've got a lot invested in Hitler—T-shirts,
action figures, grilling machines. The only thing he's got going for
him is that he's the guy who took care of the Jews. Without that,
he's just a guy with bad breath who spat when he talked and led

During the 1950s the pope was reportedly presented evidence that the genocide never took place. His response was, "I know that and you know that, but what do you think it's going to do to my 'infallibility' if we let *them* know that."

a catastrophic war in which millions of Aryans were killed and Germany was split in two for fifty years. Would you follow *that* guy's philosophy?"

As Laszlo had predicted, in the early 1950s, West Germany was eager to be readmitted into the family of nations, and was willing to pay handsomely for the ticket.

The Holocaust ultimately offered a big payday, not just to the conspirators, but to countless survivors, and the State of Israel.[6] As for Mendel and Laszlo, who would become "Mike" and "Larry," they, along with the others, had made a bigger killing than any con man could ever dream of, and lived reasonably well on the proceeds thereof.

---

6. By the mid-'90s when Germany was struggling with the costs of unification, the German finance minister asked the Israeli ambassador ever so discreetly if Germany might see some of that money returned. The ambassador responded, "Money? I don't know anything about any money..."

CHAPTER TWENTY-THREE

CLASS CLOWNS

For Raphael Krochmal, it was the final humiliation: forced to leave a hobo dinner because of his poor table manners. As soon as he'd put the wrong spoon into the hobo chili, he knew he'd made a mistake.

"We ain't bums, pal," declared the railyard's hobo potentate. "We're hobos, and we know how to mind our manners."

It should be noted that while we may see hobos as being impoverished transients, many hobos were from middle- and upper-class backgrounds. "Goin' a hoboin'" was first popularized by William Jennings Bryan during the election of 1896, and the trend was soon picked up by such cultural luminaries as Henry Adams, William Randolph Hearst, and Edith Wharton. Although it fell out of favor in the late 1940s, old money was still doing it into the '70s, as evidenced by the unauthorized leave a young George Walker Bush took from his National Guard Unit to ride the rails, as his father, grandfather, and indeed, many Skull and Bonesmen, had done before him.

Raphael flopped down in an open car and proceeded to light a cigar butt.

"Hey, Mac, I saw what those mamzers did back there. Tough break. You mind if I get a drag?" a voice called out from the darkness.

"No problem." Raphael handed over the butt to another hobo, who looked about a decade younger than his own thirty-one years. "Although I suppose there's some sort of rule about waiting until I take two drags."

"Tell me about it. Schmuel Walchinsky." He offered his hand. "I got kicked out because of this." He showed the bandana wrapped around his hobo pouch. "It's a solid. This season, hobo bandanas are supposed to be prints."

They were soon joined by William Levitt, whose hobo shanty had failed to meet the local building standards. The three men commiserated over the road their lives led them down. Schmuel and Raphael had come to the United States as young men, but despite their years in the country, they never seemed to quite understand the intricacies and complexities of American culture. Class in particular made no sense in its American form. While in many ways America was more open than Europe, that very openness made class a much more serious business for those interested in maintaining class distinctions.

In Europe, recognizing class differences was simple. The upper class was taller and fatter, a result of their having access to such luxuries as food.[1] They lived in houses as opposed to hovels, and while they often ate with their hands instead of utensils, they at least ate off dishes, as opposed to the poor, who had to use their hands as dishes as well. Even that wasn't so bad (except for soup), but using hands as cookware was pretty painful. Also unlike the poor, they were able to change their clothes periodically. In the poorest European communities, like Ireland, Galicia, and Sicily, the poorest families often only had one set of clothes for everyone, leading to considerable gender confusion, among other problems. In the United States, however, the relative material wealth of even the poor meant that the middle and upper classes had to go to considerable lengths to define themselves. Maybe the poor could afford meat, but could they afford to have the twenty or more courses that were customary at most middle- and upper-class homes? Maybe they could afford to use plates and utensils, but could they afford the dizzying array of specialized utensils and dishes, much less have the esoteric knowledge of when to use

---

1. The connection between girth and wealth began with the nobility, who, after generations of inbreeding, had lost their chins. They thus had to develop double-chins, in order to have even a single chin.

them? Dinner at the Vanderbilt mansion during the first quarter of the twentieth century regularly offered guests no fewer than twenty-seven spoons, including a spoon for clinking glasses before making an announcement, a spoon with a hole in it for when you didn't want the aspic but proper form dictated that you pretend to eat it, and two spoons for stirring after-dinner coffee—one for clockwise, one for counterclockwise. Maybe they could change their clothes several times a week, but could they do so several times a day, as necessity dictated? Would they know when to wear an ascot, when to wear a cutaway coat, when to wear an enormous strap-on phallus? (The answer is the Walpurgis Nacht cotillion, but only east of the Mississippi.) And sure, they might

Dinner at the Vanderbilt mansion during the first quarter of the twentieth century regularly offered guests no fewer than twenty-seven spoons, including a spoon for clinking glasses before making an announcement, a spoon with a hole in it for when you didn't want the aspic but proper form dictated that you pretend to eat it, and two spoons for stirring after-dinner coffee—one for clockwise, one for counterclockwise.

have four walls, but what color were they, and what sort of furnishings did they have? America truly offered a bewildering array of possibilities for the uninitiated. And it seemed that nobody was more bewildered than Raphael, Schmuel, and William, who, despite being a native-born American, still just didn't seem to get it.

Schmuel had tried his hand as a salesman, but it seemed that he was always inappropriately dressed. A big part of his problem was that he was easily influenced by his peers, but always got it a little off, or a little too late. He'd wear white after Labor Day; he'd wear stripes and checks together, because different managers wore different patterns; he'd wear one shoe, and not realize that the friend he was emulating was an amputee. Whatever it was, he got it wrong, and it cost him several jobs in the public eye. Raphael had experienced similar problems in his ill-fated career as an escort for lonely ladies of "a certain age";[2] only with him, it was meals. He'd be schmoozing a woman and everything would be going well, but then he'd use the wrong fork,[3] or the wrong glass, or he'd start picking his teeth with her pince-nez, and it would be over. This failure, in turn, led him to develop an eating disorder, as he ironically craved solace from the very thing that was the source of his misfortune. As he became pudgier and doughier, he couldn't even get dates anymore, much less ruin them. As for William, while he had worked for his father, a real estate developer, he wasn't exactly a success. He suffered from a rare disorder, claustragoraphobia, a fear of wide-open spaces enclosed in small, confining spaces. Thus, the hobo life—traveling in small rail cars under the wide, open skies—was ideal for him. As a result, he built small, confining homes in wide-open areas of Long Island, and was relieved from his position when his father declared that even if somebody wanted to live in such small homes, they wouldn't schlep all the way out to the Island to do it.

"The problem," said Schmuel glumly, "is that trying to become American is too hard. We need America to become like us."

"Exactly," echoed Raphael. "We need to have a restaurant where everything is simple, where anybody can go in, anywhere in the country, and all the food is the same, and doesn't take a college degree to figure out how to eat it."

"And we need a store," suggested Schmuel, "where anybody can walk in and buy what everybody is wearing, and know that it's the right thing. No checking the date, or the temperature—it's always in fashion."

"And we need a neighborhood," said William, "where a man can breathe freely from the narrow confines of his own home."

They all agreed that it would be a wonderful world, but that

---

2. Specifically, *old* age.
3. Such as hers.

there wasn't any way it could happen. They went their hobo ways and never imagined they'd see one another again, much less their dream fulfilled. Then as so often happens, fate stepped in and lent a helping hand, when just a few years after this conversation, the United States found itself in the Second World War, and the three conspirators found themselves in uniform. Schmuel was a supply sergeant, Raphael was a mess cook, and William was a Seabee. They ran into one another in the wake of the conquest of the island of Imo Jiwa, one of the lesser-known battles of the Pacific. The island was occupied by the Japanese at the start of the war because of the large quantity of wasabi that grew there, and was intended to supply the condiment to Japan's garrisons. A sloppy radio operator mistook it for Iwo Jima and when the assault on that island was taking place, mistakenly ordered a mixed invasion force of marines and soldiers to take the island, which was lightly held. The naval bombardment destroyed the wasabi refinery, which led to a massive spill into the lagoon. When the marines hit the beach, they felt like their skin and lungs were on fire, and it was reported that the Japanese were using chemical weapons. Although the invaders soon learned what happened, the mistake was never rectified at headquarters, and led to the Japanese commander's execution after the war. William was helping build barracks for the troops, Schmuel was issuing them new uniforms, and Raphael was serving them chow. William invited them back to his barracks.

"So what are we going to do about it?" asked William, from under his bunk.

"About what?" responded Raphael, who was known as "Kroc" to the guys in his unit. He popped a fistful of smushed sashimi into his mouth.

"About the plan to remake America."

"Are you serious?" laughed Schmuel, who had gone from "Ski," to "Alphabet," to "Walchin," to "Walton."

"Why not. Look around you. These guys are happy if they have any fork to use, if they have a pair of dry pants, and if they have a roof without Jap mortar rounds coming through it. They're living, eating, and dressing alike, in the most monotonous way. How hard could it be to get them to do it back stateside?"

They talked into the night and came up with a long-term plan. It wasn't going to be easy, and it required a lot of things falling into place, but each man promised that if he became a success, he would help the others.

The first to get started was Levitt, who went home and convinced his father to give him another chance. Using his military contacts, he got ahold of some inexpensive supplies from a buddy who requisitioned supplies for a fraudulent "Ft. Mendel Greenblatt" located on Long Island and began to build his model community, Levittown. The small, unassuming homes in the middle of an as-yet unpopulated Long Island were like a dream come true for him. Soon, veterans desperate for housing, backed by GI Bill loans and accustomed by years in the military to basic, uniform housing, were lining up to live there. More important than the four Levittowns he built,[4] however, were the precedents he set. His communities were built in the middle of nowhere, with lots of room for large-scale economic development. They were inhabited by the new middle class, former have-nots who lacked all the class pretensions of the old middle class. And most important, they were built around the car—literally, since Levitt conducted a pagan ritual when he laid the foundation of each development in which he buried a car in the center and made various offerings to it. That was particularly important as the suburban model was adopted around the country, including California.

That's where we find Raphael, who was now going by the name Ray Kroc. Although William had offered to help him out financially to get started, he didn't want to accept until he felt he had a sure thing. While he kept his eyes open, he had given up on the life of a

---

4. Most sources list only three; they are unfamiliar with "Levitt Motown," a community outside of Detroit for recently discharged jazz musicians he built to answer charges that his suburbs were racist.

low-rent gigolo, and had actually become a salesman, marketing a high-powered blender called the Multimixer. He would give demon-strations of the machine's power by processing various things through it, such as combat boots, phone books, and a 1938 DeSoto. He would then consume the result, showing how the Multimixer could make anything edible. In 1953 while on a selling trip in Southern California, he dropped in to San Diego's naval base to visit an old navy buddy of his who'd stayed in the service as a cook. With the Korean War ended, he found a considerable quantity of "carcasses, bovine, military grade," on his hands, which sounds pretty bad, but it was still a notch above Paramilitary Grade.

"You think you can do anything with this?" he asked Ray, hacking through the gristle with a cleaver.

On a whim, Ray took a hunk of carcass and ran it through the Multimixer. Then he seasoned the thick, pasty liquid and poured it onto a griddle like pancake batter. After they fried up, he took a couple of the patties, slapped them on some buns, and he and his buddy gave it a try.

"You know," said his friend, "this isn't bad."

"So," said Ray, "how much you want for these carcasses?"

Two days earlier, Ray had checked on some customers, the McDonald brothers, who had a tremendously successful restaurant, and they'd talked about setting up franchises. He was interested, but he'd done the math and wasn't sure if there was enough profit in it. With the military grade carcasses, there was. He went to William, received a loan, and began to work like a devil to create his dream restaurant. No utensils, no confusing menus, and no matter where you went, it was the same. And again, for a generation that had experienced military chow, it offered a strangely reassuring experience that was reinforced when Ray got retired General Douglas MacArthur to endorse the chain, with the slogan "I've been to McDonald's for the cheeseburger, and I shall return."

After a few years of getting his business started, Ray and William tracked down Schmuel. Indeed, it was a mark of pride for

Ray that he never forgot his old friends. The "Hamburglar" and "Mayor McCheese" were not costumed characters dreamt up by marketing executives. Hamburglar was actually a particularly depraved and derelict old hobo with whom Ray used to ride the rails and Mayor McCheese an old friend who had suffered a particularly disfiguring injury when his head got caught between passing trains. As for Schmuel, he had been stationed in Arkansas at the end of the war and had stayed there. As easily influenced as ever, he had taken a page out of Ray's book and had re-created himself as Sam Walton. He had taken another page out of Ray's book and had become something of a gigolo, eventually landing himself the daughter of a prominent local banker. Using those connections, he had tried again in the world of retail, and with his father-in-law's backing and his wife's polishing, was doing considerably better, operating franchises of the Ben Franklin discount stores. Still he itched to strike out on his own, and after a long discussion with Ray and William, both of whom offered him support, he finally decided to do so. The two also offered him a little advice that would make Sam the most successful of these three highly successful conspirators. As Ray's weight had increased over the years, he had become obsessed with making other Americans as pudgy and doughy as he was. Aside from just adding more meat to the sandwiches, he had even taken to soaking nonmeat products in suet, a practice that led the FDA to declare in 1968 that iceberg lettuce could be no more than 28 percent beef fat. That number was

> **The "Hamburglar" and "Mayor McCheese" were not costumed characters dreamt up by marketing executives. Hamburglar was actually a particularly depraved and derelict old hobo with whom Ray used to ride the rails and Mayor McCheese an old friend who had suffered a particularly disfiguring injury when his head got caught between passing trains.**

Burger King began to circulate this picture of Mayor McCheese back in his hobo days in an effort to besmirch the reputation of McDonald's. Given the source, the picture was viewed with some suspicion, but experts have since confirmed its authenticity.

raised to 49 percent in the 1980s, and in 2002, "iceberg lettuce" was redefined to include the fat in which the lettuce had soaked.

Combined with a life lived in sidewalk-less suburbs and having to drive everywhere, Americans' waistlines were expanding. Sam saw this trend crystallizing and opened Wal-Mart, a store where all the clothes were a little bigger than in other stores (but without changing the sizes), where the pants had a little more room, where the shirts were a little less snug. The legs of the chairs were a little stronger, and the seats of the chairs a little bit wider. Essentially, he made everything designed to cater to fat people, without announcing he was doing so. Did Wal-Mart offer the sort of staggering array of outfits that a Gimbel's or Macy's did? No, but then it didn't have to. Increasingly adipose Americans were more than happy to give up variety for comfort and price, and never stopped to wonder why it was that the only place where the size thirty-six pants still fit was at Wal-Mart.

Together these three men reshaped postwar America, transforming the way that we lived, shopped, and clogged our arteries. They made an America that zhlubs like themselves would be comfortable in. And if this account doesn't square with what you'll find on the official Wal-Mart or McDonald's Web site, well, if you haven't it figured out by now, you can't believe everything you read.

CHAPTER TWENTY-FOUR

CUTTING THEM DOWN TO SIZE

The unfortunately named Julian Small stepped into the shower and the abuse immediately began.

"I say, old boy, you seem to have forgotten something," said Chad.

"What's that, old chum, a mushroom?" said Brad.

"Small, your penis looks funny," said Thad, who wasn't terribly witty, but whose family was rich as Croesus (though being that Croesus was from Asia Minor or some other disreputable place, they preferred if people didn't make the association).

It was 1951, and it had been years since he had been tormented by his classmates, but those memories still drove Julian whenever he had doubts about his life's mission. Not the mission assigned to him by his parents, who had seen him as an experiment to create a perfectly assimilated American, but his own personal mission to circumcise gentile America.

Julian's upwardly mobile father, Sheldon, had changed the family name from "Klein," and made a fortune in the garment industry by patenting and marketing the low-friction zipper. Early zippers, with the rapid and high-friction movement of metal on metal, tended to get very hot, leading to burned fingers. There were also at least twenty documented cases of clothes catching on fire, and some theorize that the Triangle Shirtwaist Fire broke out when a new batch of zippers was being tried out in the overcrowded factory. He then went into real estate, ingeniously developing two communities at the same time, Chester and Westchester. Nobody actually lived in Chester, but it served as a foil for the pretensions of Westchester's Jewveau-riche migrants, most of whom had fled the Bronx, only to be driven back from the gates of Greenwich by the bayonets of the Connecticut State Militia.[1] As for the Smalls themselves, he built a palatial manor for his family in upstate Rockland County, an address that he felt would never be associated with the Jews. Although he and his wife, being modern people, didn't convert, they had no plans to raise their children with any religion, leaving them unblemished, tabulae rasa. Fate, in the form of Sheldon's Orthodox parents, Velvl and Hinda, intervened, and when little Julian was a mere eight days old, they kidnapped him and gave him a bris. His parents would later pretend that the "penisectomy," as they called it, had been performed in a hospital in response to an unspecified medical emergency. In what he considered to be the height of poetic justice, Sheldon cut off contact with his parents, and the bris was the extent of Julian's exposure to Judaism, but it was enough to mark him for life.

Growing up, Julian attended a string of WASPy institutions in which he was usually the only Jew, which at that time meant the only boy whose penis had been snipped. Despite the best efforts of his parents to make him fit in, he always felt like he didn't belong, and things only got worse when he hit puberty and was hit by the mandatory showers following lacrosse at the Prestigious Snodgrass Preparatory Academy. Like the other institutions he attended, it wasn't particularly good, and generally catered to the second-tier children of second-tier WASP families. What really attracted Sheldon to the Prestigious Snodgrass Preparatory Academy was that one: it had the word *prestigious* in the name, which

---

1. The preservation of Greenwich as a gentile preserve was actually the single victory in the several-hundred-year history of the Nutmeg State's militia. Known as "The Spice Boys," they had refused to participate in the American Revolution, claiming that they were laying a trap for the British in New Haven. During the War of 1812's invasion of Canada, they had actually boarded ships and set sail in the opposite direction, later insisting that they were planning a surprise amphibious assault on Nova Scotia and were blown off course. And during the Civil War, they had tried to expel Connecticut's black population on the grounds that they were Confederate spies, but their efforts failed when the Rhode Island militia refused to accept the eight blacks (some sources list nine, but the last was actually just an Italian organ grinder whose wagon had broken down en route from Boston to New York).

allowed him to claim his son went to a prestigious school. And two: it admitted Jews, or more appropriately, Jew, essentially in exchange for a generous donation of land. Aside from his penis looking different, it seemed to Julian that it was smaller, not necessarily because it was, but because it was clearly missing something. It was during those years that he saw what his life's purpose was; the question was how to accomplish it, to convince non-Jewish men to have the tips of their sons' petzls snipped off.

For Jews, of course, there was a theological motivation for the grisly deed. In fact, it may be argued that the bris itself is the greatest proof of the divinity of the Torah, since how likely is it that Moses would have looked down one day and said, "Oh, well, that's just too big. There's got to be some way to make that smaller. Maybe I could just take a little off the top." And you've got to figure that even if he did, when he brought it to the rest of the Jews, they'd tell him that

> **In fact, it may be argued that the bris itself is the greatest proof of the divinity of the Torah, since how likely is it that Moses would have looked down one day and said, "Oh, well, that's just too big. There's got to be some way to make that smaller. Maybe I could just take a little off the top."**

while they'd go along with funny hats and no cheeseburgers, the penis snipping was a definite deal-breaker. But while Divine Commandment might work for the Jews, it seemed unlikely that Christians would buy into the idea of cutting off their foreskins as a sign that they *aren't* God's Chosen People. Since religion was out, Julian decided on science. The teen years were hellish for Julian, but he shone far and beyond his fellow students academically,[2] focus-

---

2. There is a theory that the reputation Jews have for intellect is derived largely from the desensitizing effects of circumcision. According to this theory, since uncircumcised penii are more sensitive, when adolescent Christian males were called upon to stand up and answer questions in class, most would refuse to due to embarrassment at their almost constant state of erection. Their less-priapic Jewish classmates were less reticent, and thus got higher grades.

ing heavily on biology and anatomy. With his grades, and his father's endowments, it wasn't hard to get accepted to Harvard. His
studies would have been interrupted by the war, but his experiences had so traumatized him that he'd become positively phobic
about getting naked in front of other people, and was qualified as
4-F when it took two MPs to strip him for his physical. Due to the
shortage of medical students at the time, Julian had to perform the
studies of two men and thus was able to graduate in half the time.
While at medical school and doing his residency, he found that his
experiences were hardly unique, and that there was a whole generation of Jewish physicians whose parents had thrust them coldly
into an uncircumcised world. As they moved on to take positions at
hospitals and medical offices around the country, Julian knew that
he would have a receptive audience among his medical peers. He
studied under the nation's top experts in pediatrics and urology, as
well as ritual circumcisers, honing his knowledge, skills, and reputation. Meanwhile, having inherited the family fortune, he quietly
set up the American Pediatric Penilogical Institute. In 1948, bolstered by his research (which was reviewed and confirmed by his
friends), the institute's medical journal began publishing papers by
Julian, now billed as the nation's premier pediatric penilogical sci-
entist, arguing the numerous health benefits of circumcision. The
data were pretty good; more surprising, nobody questioned the
merits of avoiding an increased .015 percent risk of penile cancer
by accepting a 100 percent risk of having somebody put a blade to
your kid's penis. Still, these findings might have vanished into ob-
scurity along with various other medical revelations of the era (like
communism causing cancer, or cigarettes making you gay) had it
not been for Julian's ingenious use of advertising. The institute
took out ads not only in the major medical journals, but in major
mainstream media as well. The approaches varied. Some suggested that, given the health risks affiliated with foreskins, it was
somehow less than patriotic to keep it. Others evoked America's
new consumer culture, suggesting that circumcised penises were

more streamlined, efficient, and aesthetically pleasing. And the best featured a GI in a foxhole, about to be overrun by hordes of Red Chinese, desperately reaching for a belt of ammo for his .30-caliber Browning machine gun. The belt is just out of reach and the caption reads "His buddy would be there for him—if smegma hadn't put him out of action!"

The best featured a GI in a foxhole, about to be overrun by hordes of Red Chinese, desperately reaching for a belt of ammo for his .30-caliber Browning machine gun. The belt is just out of reach and the caption reads "His buddy would be there for him—if smegma hadn't put him out of action!"

What the people reading the journals and ads didn't realize was that Julian was pushing more than just traditional circumcision. The foreskin, medically speaking, had been a great unknown. Jews didn't view it in scientific terms, they just knew it had to go, and go fast. Christians didn't care one way or the other. What Julian discovered in his research was that there was another layer of superfluous tissue below the foreskin, which he called the "fiveskin." The special clamps used by mohels didn't touch it. Logic might have dictated that since you already had a group of people who were widely recognized as the world's leading authorities on the subject of foreskin removal, the medical profession might simply have followed their lead. But Julian, of course, was advocating a modern, scientific, space-age procedure that had nothing in common with any sort of tribal ritual, and that would completely remove the fiveskin as well, all without anyone being the wiser. When his top-ranked, Harvard-educated peers adopted his procedure, and inspired others to do so, parents were grateful for the preservation of their progenies' penile purity, never suspecting that the final product would look the same, but always be just a *little* smaller than those of their Jewish peers.

By the early 1960s, over 80 percent of male infants in the United States were being circumcised. Even though by the '90s,

The American Pediatric Penilogical Institute (APPI) launched a nationwide ad campaign using a number of different approaches. This ad—posted in Obstetric and Pediatric offices all across the country—did a good job of convincing Americans who were apprehensive about America's future in the Space Age to have their sons snipped. Despite offering a sizable sum, however, the APPI failed to get Chuck Yeager to undergo the procedure and become the group's spokesman.

people were questioning the validity of Julian's research, new justifications had been found, and many parents opted for the procedure solely on aesthetic grounds, or so that their son's penis would look like their own.[3] Julian remained a dedicated advocate of male circumcision. In 1959, he met and married Susan Goodfriend. Ms. Goodfriend's parents (originally, the Gutfreunds) had essentially done to her what Julian's had done to him, and her years as the only zaftig brunette among willowy blondes had given her the same negative body image that he had. They met at their therapist's office, and six months later they were married. We don't know if they ever got fully naked with one another, but in 1962, they had a son. Named William (after Julian's grandfather Velvl), he was circumcised by a mohel.

---

3. Which leaves one wondering what exactly these fathers are doing with their sons—"Okay, Timmy, let's make shadow puppets with our penises!"

CHAPTER TWENTY-FIVE

IS THAT COMMUNISM ON YOUR COLLAR?

Herman LeWine scanned the *Wall Street Journal* for encouraging signs, but found none. In category after category, it seemed that 1949 marked the end of the postwar spending boom. For a while, it had seemed that it would go on forever, and assorted economic experts pontificated on the way that the new economy had moved beyond the boom-and-bust cycle. But fate had proven them wrong. The problem was that the boom had been so effective that over the course of four years, America's consumers had bought damn near everything they could possibly use. Now that might not normally have been bad for Julian. After all, as a Madison Avenue adman (albeit a fairly minor one),[1] his job was to get people to buy more. However, the industry as a whole was in the middle of a major crisis, a result of the radical economic ups-and-downs of the previous two decades.

During the 1930s, advertising had virtually ground to a halt, since nobody had any money to buy anything. During the war years, things didn't much improve, because there was nothing to buy. In the five years since the war, however, a surplus of money, products, and the desire to make up for lost time meant that if you wanted vets to buy a house, or a car, or a razor, all you had to do was announce it was available, and the next day, they'd be waiting around the block to buy it. Consequently, admen didn't really have to try, and their work showed the lack of effort. For example, the top award-winning ad for 1948 was "IBM stands for International

---

1. It was his great shame that he still lived with his parents in the Knickerbocker Village housing complex on the Lower East Side. Every morning he would rise at five in order to schlep out to New Rochelle so that he could take the train into the city with the more successful admen.

Business Machines." It easily beat out the nearest competitor, "Ford: Buy It," which was considered too cerebral. But while that effort had been fine during the time of plenty, the lean years had begun, and the bottom lines of both corporate America and the ad companies they hired were suffering. The whole industry was hurting, but it was the little guys like Herman who would be the first to go. "What I need," he thought, "is a gimmick."

Herman was snapped out of his reverie by the sound of his next-door neighbors arguing again. As they had for so many years, the voices of Julius and Ethel Rosenberg reverberated through the small apartment. It was bad enough living with his parents; having the Rosenbergs next door added a whole new level of misery. If it wasn't the arguing, it was people coming and going at all hours of the night, and if it wasn't that, it was the personal unpleasantness

In 1948, this ad led IBM to double its sales of computers from one to two. Those numbers may not seem like much, but considering that the computers in question weighed ten tons and took up an entire floor, they were pretty impressive.

IBM
stands for
International Business Machines.

of the two. Whether it was trimming their nails in the elevator, refusing to hold the door for him in the lobby, or periodically reminding him that when the revolution comes, Madison Avenue flacks for capitalism will be hung from the tallest lampposts, the Rosenbergs presented a thoroughly distasteful spectacle.

Herman sighed and picked up *The New York Post*, New York's most reliably liberal paper, hoping to block out the noise. "Those Rosenbergs," he thought, "could single-handedly kill the Communist Party. If I were a red, I would try to be everything the Rosenbergs aren't." He turned a few more pages desultorily, and then stopped. He ran that thought through his head.

"Maybe that's it," he said, amazed at its simplicity. "The American people are content with who they are and what they have. But what if they needed to ensure that nobody thought they were something else...."

He spent the next few minutes trying to understand what it was he had just thought. After he had that sorted out, he knew what he had to do next.

The following morning, he placed a call.

"U.S. Attorney's Office, Roy Cohn speaking, may I help you?"

"Roy, this is Herman LeWine. I need to call in that favor. Can we meet?"

Herman and Roy had met Hillel five years earlier, at a Hanukkah party at the Columbia Hillel[2] that Herman had gone to with his cousin, a fellow law school classmate of Roy's. Herman was just a month back from a tour of duty in the Pacific, and it wasn't really his scene. Two days later, however, he got a call from Roy. He knew that Herman had considerable emergency medical experience as a navy corpsman. Would he be able to come over to Roy's apartment to help with a matter that required a certain amount of both skill and discretion? Herman came, and upon entering the apart-

---

2. Hillel: An organization designed to provide Jewish students with a convivial meeting place on college campuses, with a fortified basement in case things go bad.

ment found Roy bent over, something stuck in his posterior. To be specific, it was a Princeton linebacker. The specifics of how they became stuck, and separated, require a greater understanding of both anatomy and geometry than the authors of this work could ever hope to assemble.

Roy had made a wise choice, as this was the sort of thing that Herman had frequently encountered among lonely marines, and he soon had the matter resolved. Herman assured the younger man that he would never reveal the events of the night. Roy, from a prominent family that wouldn't have appreciated the scandal, was most grateful, and had promised Herman that if he ever needed help, he should call. Since then, Cohn had used his family connections to become the youngest U.S. attorney, and rose to national prominence prosecuting leaders of the Communist Party of the United States under the Smith Act. Passed in 1940, the Smith Act made it illegal to conspire seditiously against the government of the United States. (Raging impotently and fulminating drunkenly, however, were still okay.) It was an important case, but there seemed to be little future in indicting communists. Certainly, communists were viewed negatively—but then, so were jazz musicians, male cheerleaders, and Unitarians. Still, nobody really saw them as a serious threat. As late as 1948, Harry Truman was still referring to Stalin as "Uncle Joe," which by itself wasn't too bad, but it got a little creepy when Stalin would encourage Truman to sit on his lap. Some in the GOP might have criticized Truman as being soft on communism, but it was conservative Republicans who were the most eager to pull the U.S. military out of Europe. And while the House Un-American

> **As late as 1948, Harry Truman was still referring to Stalin as "Uncle Joe," which by itself wasn't too bad, but it got a little creepy when Stalin would encourage Truman to sit on his lap.**

Activities Committee might have been investigating communism in Hollywood, it was hardly to the detriment of the party that a cavalcade of celebrities paraded themselves before the committee in defense of the Hollywood Ten. In fact, screen legend Humphrey Bogart's appearance on their behalf led three branches of his teenage fan club to join the party. This, however, was something new. The Rosenbergs were a truly unseemly *couple*, and that, to the mind of Herman, made all the difference. The American people might not pay attention to the devious workings of Hollywood literati or party bigwigs; after all, what did they have in common with them? But the Rosenbergs were another matter—everyone in the country would follow the story of a family, just like their own, but traitorous. The whole thing appealed to the drama queen in Roy, who was looking to add another feather to his cap, and he agreed to set up a surveillance post in the LeWines' living room. To explain the presence of the G-men to his parents, Herman told them that he was establishing a local branch of the Jewish War Veterans.

Roy had hoped to just get enough evidence for another Smith Act indictment. What he actually found blew him away: The Rosenbergs were at the center of an espionage ring transferring atomic secrets to the Soviets. In the interests of protecting Herman (and keeping prying eyes from exploring their previous contacts), they first arrested other members of the ring, and then traced the Rosenbergs back through them. But it was the surveillance tapes from the apartment that ultimately provided the most damning evidence, like this exchange below:

Ethel: *Did you call Stalin?*
Julius: *I was busy today.*
Ethel: *You were "too busy" to call Stalin yesterday.*
Julius: *Yesterday I had to fix the air conditioner.*
Ethel: *And still it doesn't work. My husband the electrician: When it comes to giving secrets to Stalin, he's a genius technician, but in his own apartment, he can't get the air conditioner to work.*

Julius: *May be I could fix the air conditioner if you'd stop your yap-
ping for once. Is it too much to ask that I can have a glass of tea
and read my* Daily Worker?

This testimony was perhaps the single most damning evidence
at their trial. Julius's response that he was talking about giving
the secret recipe of his mother's noodle kugel to Jerry Stalin in
apartment 5G for the latter's birthday party strained the imagination of the jury, particularly after Mr. Stalin testified that he would
never have sought the recipe for such a sweet kugel. The jury
concurred—the kugel was much too sweet.

While Roy was getting his indictments ready, Herman was
making his own preparations. His agency was making a big presentation to Hathaway Shirts, and he had managed to convince
his boss to give him a crack at it. The art department wasn't sure
about his concept, but they gave him what he asked for. The day
before the presentation, as per arrangement, Roy arrested the
Rosenbergs, and their pictures were splashed all over the papers. By the time the Hathaway people showed up at the office,
the image of the Rosenbergs was etched firmly in everybody's
mind. Herman unveiled his ad—a picture that contrasted "the
Hathaway Man"—tall, well-built, handsome, one-eyed beautiful
woman on his arm—with the sort of man who doesn't wear Hathaway, a man who bore a striking resemblance to Julius Rosenberg: short, thin, four-eyed, clutching a copy of *The Daily Worker*.
Needless to say, Herman got the account and a big promotion.
While other ad agencies would also jump on the bandwagon,
Herman was the first out of the gate, and rapidly produced major
campaigns for a number of large accounts. For Sears, one woman
says to another, "Dear, that dress makes you look like Ethel
Rosenberg!" to the latter's horror.[3] For GE, the ad stated: "The

---

3. Roy was actually planning on releasing Ethel, but Herman convinced him to pursue
a conviction, since with her on the docket, he could also craft ads for the women's
market.

Rosenbergs didn't use GE appliances. Do you?" Westinghouse would flip this around a few years later, showing a picture of an electric chair with the caption: "The only Westinghouse appliance used by the Rosenbergs."

Of course, nothing lasts forever, and the Rosenbergs were no exception to the rule. Even as the Rosenbergs were being readied for execution, Roy and Herman were preparing for the next stage. In 1950, Senator Joe McCarthy from Wisconsin made an offhand reference to communist infiltrators in the State Department. It led to partisan infighting in the Senate, but probably wouldn't have gone any farther had Roy and Herman not intervened. Roy had become aware that McCarthy had a secret—and costly—vice. He only wore silk underwear. Moreover, he could only wear a pair once before discarding it. The cost was bankrupting him, so that when Roy approached him and suggested that if McCarthy were to open a wider investigation into communism in the U.S. government, to hire Roy as his legal counsel, and to make sure to mention certain products in his questioning of suspected communists, Herman would make sure that he never ran out of clean boxers.[4] Thus, in the midst of interrogating possible communists and fellow travelers about their political habits, McCarthy would periodically veer into questions about their spending habits. For example, the Senate was treated on April 14, 1953, to the following line of questioning with Mr. Sidney Felder, an English teacher from Forest Hills, Queens, who had done some work for Radio Free Europe.

> **McCarthy had a secret—and costly—vice. He only wore silk underwear. Moreover, he could only wear a pair once before discarding it.**

---

4. Roy also made a little extra on the side, since he agreed to only wear clothes provided by Herman's clients in exchange for a small consideration.

> **Sen. McCarthy:** *Mr. Felder, when you attended these [meetings of The Josef Stalin Admiration Committee, suspected of being a communist front[5]], were you clean shaven?*
>
> **Mr. Felder:** *Yes, Senator, yes I was.*
>
> **Sen. McCarthy:** *And did you use a Gillette razor?*
>
> **Mr. Felder:** *No, I don't believe that I did.*
>
> **Sen. McCarthy:** *Let the record show that Mr. Felder, suspected communist fellow traveler, does not use a Gillette razor.*

By early 1954, it was no longer necessary to push specific products as being noncommunist; the very act of purchasing had come to be seen as a patriotic act, largely through the works of McCarthy, who reserved particular scorn for those whom he felt didn't own enough things. The hearings actually had to be postponed when he became apoplectic at one man's remark that he only had three pairs of pants. As a result, corporate sponsorship for the senator dropped precipitously, while at the same time, his habit had reached two pairs a day. Against Roy's advice, he accepted an offer from the Marine Corps to defame the army. The end result, as we know now, was the senator's censure and drastic decline. He died a few years later of cirrhosis of the liver, wearing the same pair of underwear he'd worn the day before. Roy Cohn went on to become a fixture both on the New York party circuit and in the highest echelons of the Republican Party. A man of rare courage and integrity, he refused to come out of the closet just because it was fashionable, and heroically clung to the lie that he was dying of liver cancer instead of admitting to his faddish AIDS. As for Herman, he soon became a partner, then set off to establish his own agency. He never did make it to New Rochelle, but from his Upper East Side penthouse, he could see it on a clear day.

---

5. Ironically, it wasn't. What they admired about Stalin was his long-standing support for the recognition of Men's Rhythmic Gymnastics as an Olympic sport. Under two hours of intense questioning from Senator McCarthy, however, Mr. Felder did concede that the group's name could have used some work.

CHAPTER TWENTY-SIX

COMPROMISING POSITIONS

The year was 1956—America's economy was booming, Ike was on the way to another landslide victory, and the country was at peace. Yet despite all this—and the amorous ministrations of Sheila Rabinowitz, his longtime companion—Morris "Moe" Schmutter was not happy.

"Do you have any idea what it's like being a divorce lawyer in Greenwich, with all these facockte, middle-class goyim? Everybody's happy! The men think their wives are hot numbers if they let them shtup twice a week, and the women think their men are great lovers if they can get it in the hole on the first try. They don't know what they're missing."

In his own inimitable way, Moe had put his finger on the little discussed, embarrassing truth about the postwar period: For middle-class America, the sex was lousy. Of course, as Moe noted, they didn't know any better. The men had fought in WWII or Korea, got married, got good jobs, and moved to the suburbs. Aside from the occasional trip to a hurried and harried hooker, and the furtive caresses[1] of their foxhole buddies, their sexual experience was pretty much limited to their wives. As for the women, they had even less experience than the men, their familiarity with *amour* consisting largely of awkward moments in the backs of vehicles. Since very few people owned cars in the 1940s, the vehicles in question tended to be buses and trains, which meant that the

---

1. *Furtive caress,* or "FC" as it was commonly known, was WWII-era military slang for "XXX man-on-man action," as in "The MPs caught two GIs in an FC behind the PX, and sent them to give the LT at HQ a BJ ASAP." It should be remembered that due to the increased paperwork entailed by the war effort, letters were under strict wartime rationing, resulting in rigidly supervised acronymization.

awkward moments consisted primarily of smoldering looks. While this may seem fairly tame, at the time, the general consensus among the nation's leading Episcopalian physicians was that smoldering looks could cause pregnancy. In fact, *Key Largo* was almost banned until Lauren Bacall, under pressure from the film's producers, the House Un-American Activities Committee, and Ernest Hemingway himself, agreed to downgrade her looks from "smoldering" to "steamy." Consequently, no matter how small the boat, or how clumsy the motion in the ocean, there was little to dissuade America's wives from believing that sex with their husbands was like a cruise on the *QE2*.

The general consensus among the nation's leading Episcopalian physicians was that smoldering looks could cause pregnancy. In fact, *Key Largo* was almost banned until Lauren Bacall, under pressure from the film's producers, the House Un-American Activities Committee, and Ernest Hemingway himself, agreed to downgrade her looks from "smoldering" to "steamy."

"Well, Moish." Sheila purred, got down in front of him, and unzipped his fly. "You should worry more about what *you're* missing."

Moe leaned back and let Sheila go to work. "Baby, if those goyim knew what you could do, they'd be leaving their wives in a heartbeat."

Even before Sheila finished, Moe had a huge smile on his face.

Three days later, Moe met at Lou Siegel's restaurant with the two other divorce attorneys from the greater New York area. Both had the same problems as Moe, and both listened intently to what he had to say.

"Look," said Ira Mandelstam, "I want to break up marriages as much as the next guy, but if a guy wants to look at some naked broad, he can do it already. Or don't they sell *Playboy* in Greenwich?" At the time, *Playboy* was a fairly respected publication and luminaries such as Ray Bradbury, James Jones, and P. G. Wodehouse contributed stories, with the last also posing for a February pictorial.

"You don't get it, Ira. So a guy looks at *Playboy* at the barbershop, he gets all worked up, and goes back home to the little missus. Thirty seconds later, he's sound asleep. But he sees one of these films, he gets all worked up, goes home, and thirty seconds later, he's wondering why she doesn't do what the girls in the movie do. After a few months of this, he's wondering just how green the grass is on the other side of the fence and that means payday for us!"

"It's genius," said Sydney Ginsberg. "Just tell us what you want us to do."

After dessert, they all got to work. Ginsberg had a cousin who had been a photographic assistant at *National Geographic*. From him, they got equipment. Ira had a side business as a bail bondsman, which gave him a sizable pool of men willing to act as performers, and as shills for the final product. But the pièce de résistance belonged to Moe. Back before he and Sheila had settled down together, she'd had a successful career in burlesque. She gave him a list of girls who might be willing to perform with their pasties off. She also gave him a phone number of an old acquaintance she'd made while performing. Moe had recognized that it wasn't enough to simply make men feel that their sex lives were inadequate; *they* had to feel inadequate as well. Moe made the call, and the next week the three attorneys met with a young and un-

At the time, *Playboy* was a fairly respected publication and luminaries such as Ray Bradbury, James Jones, and P. G. Wodehouse contributed stories, with the last also posing for a February pictorial.

known Norman Podhoretz for a schvitz. Podhoretz was fresh out of the army and had not yet developed a reputation as a neocon intellectual. What he did have a reputation for, at least in some circles, was having the largest schlong this side of Milton Berle. Although there was no record of just how big it was, Moe had peered through the steam and re-marked to Ira, "I think that's the kid Sheila was telling me about, but I don't recognize the midget on his lap."

Moe laid out the situation for Podhoretz: The real action would be performed by Mandelstam's felons. All they wanted from him was what they referred to as "intimate close-ups." Desperate for work and considerably more bohemian than he would care to ad-mit later in life, Podhoretz agreed. Initially he had wanted to wear a prosthetic foreskin to ensure that he couldn't be recognized, but Moe was able to appeal to his sense of ethnic pride to ensure that the only cap he wore was his yarmulke. The girls, the guys, and the schlong in place, Ginsberg's cousin began shooting. The final prod-uct, *The Landlord*, starred an uncredited Norman Fell, and ran to twelve minutes, only two of which were dialogue.[2] Ira's cadre went to work, parlaying barroom conversations and winking confidences into sales of film and still photos. The target areas were Greenwich, Brooklyn Heights, and West Englewood, all chosen for their low divorce rates and high per-capita income. Within six months, the number of divorces in each area had skyrocketed, with virtually all of the increase stemming from what the litigants explained as "connubial incompatibility." Most of these came from men, but a few were from women, doubtlessly those who had come across their husbands' videos and, now that they had something to com-pare their mates to, found them wanting.

After several more productions, the three attorneys realized that they were spending a lot on marketing and getting fairly little in return. Rather than bringing the mountain to Muhammed, they would bring Muhammed—or, more to the point, thousands of Muhammeds—to the mountain. By a happy coincidence, the owner

---

2. It was in response to the line, "I'm sorry, I don't have enough money for rent; maybe there's some *other* way I can pay you?" that he first delivered the smile to the camera that he would later make famous as Mr. Roper. His success in the part of the landlord led Fell—at that point, a low-level numbers runner in East Harlem—to pursue a career in acting.

A rare still from the seminal porn film, *The Landlord*. In 1968, Norman Fell and Norman Podhoretz teamed up to locate and destroy every copy of the film they could find, and in seven months of bribing, begging, and busting heads, managed to get all but one. That copy was owned by Charlton Heston, whose prominence both in the entertainment world and the conservative movement kept it, and his sizable collection of erotica, out of their hands.

of a Times Square theater had to liquidate his assets to pay for his divorce, and they were able to pick up the location for a steal and convert it to a cinema. Soon, Times Square was packed with men in gray flannel suits, catching a quick flick between martinis. The theater soon attracted competitors, and as Moe's income rose with the divorce rate through the early 1960s, he found it increasingly difficult to put off Sheila's demands to formalize their relationship with a trip under the chuppah. Sheila soon found, however, that being an honest woman in Connecticut was not all that she'd hoped it to be. She decided to pass the time—and help pay for the inground pool that Moe claimed they couldn't afford yet—by stirring up a little discontent among her distaff neighbors. She began by regaling them with tales of her days in "theater," always converting her own sexual exploits into those of her "friends." After she got them to question their husbands' performances in the bedroom, it wasn't hard to get them to start voicing their complaints about what the breadwinners didn't do in the rest of the house as well. Soon, instead of coming home to a martini and pot roast, the men of Greenwich were arriving after a long day to find notes informing them that their wives were "out with the girls," and that there was a TV dinner in the freezer. Their wives, of course, had friends, sisters, cousins, and so forth, and soon, this wave of feminine discontent began spreading to other parts of the country, where it caught up a housewife and frustrated journalist by the name of Betty Friedan. America's feminists would never know that if it weren't for the porn they so stridently protested, their movement wouldn't even exist. As for Moe, he was making money hand over fist, but alas, would only be able to enjoy half of it: In 1971, Sheila took the rest—and the pool boy—to Florida, where she and a succession of pool boys have enjoyed a well-deserved retirement in Boca Raton.

CHAPTER TWENTY-SEVEN

BAGELS AND LOCKS

Purim[1] 1963 brought little joy to Harris Plotnick. As owner and operator of Plotnick's Doors, Windows, and Locks, he faced dire economic conditions that overshadowed the joyous commemoration of the ancient slaughter of thousands of Persians. The problem was that nobody in Harlem needed what he sold. Things had not always been that way. The '40s and '50s had been a golden era for the home security business, what with everybody concerned with Nazi spies, communist subversives, and pod people. But by the early 1960s, the Nazis were safely ensconced in Latin America and the industrial suburbs of the Midwest; the Red Menace had been quashed by McCarthy, HUAC, coeds, and the Pill; and the pod people were rapidly assimilating and pursuing the American Dream. To make things worse, Harris's shop was located in Harlem, which was perhaps the safest neighborhood in the United States; there was no great demand for new doors, window, or locks, since, given the virtual absence of crime, people had no reason to replace the old ones. This information may come as a shock to some people, buying, as they do, into stereotypes of African Americans.[2] There had been some gang violence in the

---

1. Purim, aka the Feast of Lots, is a curious celebration of intermarriage, alcoholism, and killing on a massive scale. Given its troubling origins, the Church Fathers chose not to co-opt it by locating a Christian holiday in the same week, so it remains fairly unknown to the larger gentile population. It's sort of a cross between Halloween and Mardi Gras, but with fewer razor-embedded fruits or bare breasts.

2. *African American* is a cultural, not a racial, term that is useful if used properly. It often is not, however, and does at times leave something to be desired. For example, although a white American born in South Africa would seem to be a clear-cut African American, as the term is currently used, he would not be. Consequently, some activists have advocated using the term *Blafrican American* to make the race of the subject clear. Similarly, people of mixed-race ancestry would be referred to as *Halfrican Americans*. Insofar as these terms are just silly, not to mention fictitious, we will refrain from using them.

1930s and '40s, but Duke Ellington and Count Basie had arranged for a big-band summit and gotten the factions to settle their differences through jitterbugging contests. But whatever truth those stereotypes were based on came later. In the early '60s, nobody was replacing broken windows, nobody was hocking stolen merchandise at Bistritsky's Pawn Shop, nobody was buying switchblades or brass knuckles at Goldfish Army Surplus, and so on. If only there was some way to stir things up....His morose reverie was broken by the sound of Lewis Goldfaden coming to blows with Sol Thomashefsky.

"Wallace? You like the Left so much, try mine!" shouted Goldfaden, swinging at Thomashefsky.

Plotnick sighed. *Every Purim it's the same thing*, he thought. *These two are lifelong friends, but they get some schnapps in them and the next thing you know, they're refighting the election of 1948.* He was about to down his own shot when the amber liquid caught his eye.

He had the solution to the problem, but first he had to solve the problem of the solution: How to get the famously abstemious blacks to drink? Coming from the South, often from dry counties, and being thoroughly churchgoing, the black community heavily frowned upon drinking, and in many black homes, it was almost impossible to find a liquor bottle that wasn't empty. When Plotnick was a boy, his mother used to get him to take medicine by putting it in pudding. Although the psychological associations this entailed led him to become a morbidly obese hypochondriac, it was a valuable lesson he thought he could apply to his current problem. The key was to come up with something that would not immediately incite a backlash, something unfamiliar, innocuous. Nothing came to him until he visited his brother-in-law Izzy at the latter's beverage wholesale business in Hunts Point. Walking through the stacks of crates, he came upon something he'd never noticed before.

"Hey, Iz, what's this 'malt liquor' stuff? Is it like a malted milkshake?"

"Yeah, like the H-bomb is like a slingshot."

Izzy explained to him all about malt liquor, which at the time was actually considered to be a beverage of sophisticates. Malt liquor started in France, where it became all the rage when absinthe was banned. The leading lights of the Lost Generation took to it during their expatriate days after the Great War, and popularized it among the smart set back in the States. Most of the meetings of the Algonquin Round Table were liberally fueled by malt liquor, leading Dorothy Parker, after she drunkenly called Edna Ferber a "hoochie mama" for allegedly glancing flirtatiously at Charles Macarthur, to pen the epigram: "About last night, it's all my fault, for drinking more than a single malt." With the repeal of Prohibition, malt liquor fell out of favor, but still retained a loyal following within the upper strata of society. This was precisely what Harris had been looking for: A beverage that was potent, but that wouldn't evoke an immediate negative response from the black authorities, and that had a sophisticated image. And that was really the hook that Harris would use.

The one real weakness that Harlem's blacks had was fashion. Everybody was trying to outdo one another. Black leaders tried to channel this competitive streak into something reasonably productive, like church, but were unable keep the desire to dress better and sharper than the next guy from spilling out into the street.[3] If Izzy could market malt liquor as a fashion accessory as opposed to merely a beverage, he could make it as much a "must-have" as a conk and a pair of two-tone Stacy Adams. In order to start the competition, he needed somebody to compete with, and he had just the person in mind, his nephew, Irving. Although it had been a family embarrassment when his sister Stella had married a black man, Harris felt that family was family, and

---

3. At times, literally, since Harlem's small storefront churches often couldn't contain the elaborate outfits that congregants wore, and at least on two occasions, the pressure from the mammoth headgear worn by those inside led walls to collapse.

Ernest Hemingway enjoys some *chiens de quarante* with friends in Paris in the 1920s. Although by the late 1930s, malt liquor was passé in France, Papa's enduring affection for the beverage and the subculture that surrounded it led him to entitle a novel *I Tips a Forty to Barcelona*. At his publisher's request, he changed it to *For Whom the Bell Tolls*.

had kept in contact. This wasn't always easy, since Irving was, to put it simply, a con artist. He always had some get-rich-quick scheme in the works. Among his earlier scams were "Ne-Grow," a "dietary supplement" that he had to stop selling when Bill Russell threatened a lawsuit over the unauthorized use of his likeness, and Afro-Disiac, a product the purpose of which needs no elaboration, but which ultimately led to several trips to the emergency room.

His latest scheme was the "Nation of Hinduism," a poor rip-off of the Nation of Islam. Billing himself as "Rajiv X," he stood on 125th Street exhorting blacks to discover their heritage by purchasing what he called "The Bhagavada Ghetto" and his special line of beef-free meat products. Although he did manage to acquire a small and very confused following, it was not a big moneymaker, so when his uncle offered him and his followers free clothes and some spending money, and all he had to do was stand around on the corner drinking some soft drink, how could

> **His latest scheme was the "Nation of Hinduism," a poor rip-off of the Nation of Islam. Billing himself as "Rajiv X," he stood on 125th Street exhorting blacks to discover their heritage by purchasing what he called "The Bhagavada Ghetto" and his special line of beef-free meat products.**

he say no? It took some begging and borrowing, but Harris outfitted the ersatz Hindus in the latest from Horvitz's Harlem Haberdashery on St. Nicholas, and sent them out, malt liquor in hand, to the busiest corners in Harlem. The effect was electric. The throngs of admirers who gathered around them might not have been able to get new Stacys, or a sharkskin suit, but they could sure afford what they were drinking. Informed of Harris's plan, Izzy (who had put up some of the money) had convinced some local stores to start carrying bottles of malt liquor, and they began flying off the shelves.

At first, the malt liquor didn't seem to be having much of an impact, perhaps in part because by the time the plan was under way, it was already autumn. Certainly, there was a growth in alcohol-fueled crime over the winter, but the real impact was felt the next summer, in 1964. Hot weather meant more drinking, meant more rage, meant more crime. And it was that year that Harlem exploded, in the first of the great urban riots that tore through the country in the 1960s. Sociologists, criminologists, and proctologists[4] tried to find the source of the chaos, none of them suspecting the truth. In the wake of the riots, Harris's business was booming, and it only got better. Harlem being Harlem, other black communities around the country copied their fashions, and soon the malt liquor and rioting craze spread nationwide.

America had never seen anything like the malt liquor epidemic that swept across the country in the 1960s, and was little prepared to deal with it. Sure, there had been the hula hoop epidemic, but it really wasn't the same thing. Who wanted to go to work, or get an education, or sing doo-wop songs over flaming garbage cans, when they could sit on a stoop drinking forty-dogs all day? It set off a cycle of violence, unrest, and disorder that destroyed the fabric of life in the inner cities, which is still being felt today. Indeed, many observers felt a wave of relief when the heroin epidemic hit the same neighborhoods, feeling that it would take the edge off the malt liquor violence.[5] By that point, however, Harris was no longer around to reap the rewards—Izzy, who had become a major player in the industry by becoming the

> **America had never seen anything like the malt liquor epidemic that swept across the country in the 1960s, and was little prepared to deal with it. Sure, there had been the hula hoop epidemic, but it really wasn't the same thing.**

---

4. According to proctologists, the constant sitting on the stoops led to serious hemorrhoids, which made sufferers cranky, irritable, and ready to throw down.

sole distributor of malt liquor in the Northeast, had helped arrange a late-life career shift for him as a PR man for the liquor lobby. And as for Irving, he rode the wave for another few years, and then, with his uncle's help, moved out to Oakland, where he was able to use his unique history to capitalize on two important trends that were popular in nearby Berkeley at the time: the adulation felt by many college kids for all things black, and the interest they had in Eastern spirituality. The Nation of Hinduism was reborn as the Afro-Asiatic Tantric Ashram, and on the sales of the reconfigured Afro-Disiac alone, Irving never had to worry about money again.[6]

---

5. It should be noted, of course, that the observers in question were largely dope fiends. In their defense, however, it should also be noted that the addition of but one letter would turn those same dope *fiends* into dope *friends*.

6. Irving eventually disassociated from the Ashram in the mid-'70s, which then became the Black-Oriental Temple of Love, then the Institute for Afro-Asian Affairs, then various other forms before it achieved its current incarnation, the Democratic Leadership Council.

CHAPTER TWENTY-EIGHT

NOTHING IS CERTAIN
BUT DEATH AND TEXAS

The highball glass shattered against the TV screen.

"Itche," said Rose Grunboim, looking, as always, perfectly turned out. "You need to relax."

"I can't help it," cursed Isaac Grunboim. "I just see that man's hair, and I lose control. Look at it!"

They both stared at the screen, bourbon running down President Kennedy's smiling face.

"That hair is costing me a fortune!"

Ike poured himself another highball. He surveyed his living room, content with what he saw. He had come a long way since Bobruisk, where he had first shown prodigious talent as a haberdasher. Not only did that skill save his life on more than one occasion—we dare you to find a Cossack who doesn't like a snappy new hat—it gave him the opportunity to start a new life in the land of the free. Arriving in Galveston in 1919, he soon made his way to Dallas, where a cousin had a men's clothing store. There, fate intervened, when President-Elect Warren Harding happened to be stopping by on the way to pay the traditional preinaugural visit to a Mexican whorehouse.[1] "Ike," as his non-Jewish customers called him, gave the great man a homburg he had just designed. Harding got numerous compliments and wore it to and from his swearing-in ceremony. Thus was born a new tradition, and one with considerably fewer painful consequences. Ike's fame spread, and he soon was one of the most in-demand hat designers in a country in which every adult male wore hats,

---

1. The tradition was established by Zachary Taylor and maintained until FDR's second term, when, as part of his program to ramp-up America's depressed sex industry, he visited a New Orleans bordello.

with Dallas's own Neiman-Marcus featuring his work exclusively. All that, however, ground to a crashing halt with JFK's election. Not only was he the first Catholic president, he was also the first president since Buchanan to not wear a hat.[2] Given his charisma, popularity, and, most important, his tousled good looks, it should come as no surprise that his administration saw a drastic decline in hat consumption among the American public, and Ike was not happy. As he saw, all that he'd built up in his forty-plus years in this country was in jeopardy, all because of one man. He turned off the TV.

"Just looking at that mamzer's tousled hair makes me sick."

"Calm down, Itche," soothed his wife of thirty-five years. "There's nothing you can do about it. Besides, it's January right now. Let's say he wins next year. He's only got another six years, and then Lyndon will take over, and he loves your hats."

"Oy, six more years." He sat down and drained his glass.

She brought him another drink. "Of course, if there were some way for Lyndon to take over before then…"

"Feh, Rose, look at him, with his touch football. He'll live past 120."

"Of course, what do I know?" She shrugged. "I suppose somebody would have to kill him."

"Kill the president? Are you crazy?"

"Oh, you know I don't know anything about politics. I mean, I guess you'd need to know people in the FBI, or CIA, or Secret Service to get close enough to him and get away with it. Forget I said anything. I'm going to bed, dear. Don't stay up too late."

She closed the door behind her and smiled.

A week later, Ike handed J. Edgar Hoover a brand-new gray felt snap-brim as the latter got a polish at the Hialeah Race Track's shoeshine stand.

---

2. In private, however, it was rumored that Buchanan used to wear a sunbonnet and demand to be referred to as "Mrs. Chillingworth."

"Ike, you've done it again. May I?" He replaced his old hat with the new one. "Perfect, as usual."

"And, as usual, I have an identical one for you, Clyde." He handed the matching hat to the man who was seated to Hoover's right: Clyde Tolson, J. Edgar Hoover's inseparable right-hand man. Although Tolson and Hoover were long rumored to be lovers, a growing body of evidence strongly suggests that Tolson was actually a brilliant puppeteer and Hoover was in truth not a human, but an incredibly malignant Muppet.

"May *I*?" He sat in the chair to the left of the country's top law-enforcement officer.

"Of course, Ike," said Hoover breezily. "You know I always have time for the one man who knows more about our heads of state than I do." It wasn't the first time he'd made the joke.

"Can we talk about that confidential matter I mentioned on the phone?" Ike looked nervously at the shoeshine boy.

"Pepe doesn't speak a word of English. Trust me, it's fine."

"Have you given it any thought?"

"Have I? Let me tell you something—you may be looking at the only man who hates his hair more than you do. You may not have noticed this, but…well, I've thinned a little on top."

"Nonsense, sir."

"Now, now, don't be kind. We both know it, and so does Kennedy. Well, since he took over, I can't wear my hats—*your* hats—anymore. He's always ribbing me about my hairline, calling me 'Cue ball' and 'Curly.' Ever since he started preparing for his trip to Berlin later this year, he's started calling me 'Herr von Chrome Dome.'"

"So you're unhappy with him."

By now, Hoover was off in his own world. "That damn tousled hair. Do you know who has tousled hair? Pinkos and perverts. Look at pictures of Stalin when he was a young man. His hair's tousled. And don't get me started on Liberace. And Bobby's even worse. Not only is his hair even more tousled, but…but…" He fought to regain control. "But last week, he called me in to discuss his organized crime nonsense, and he began to beat my head like a bongo drum, that lousy beatnik!" Indeed, it is not well known, but Bobby Kennedy did briefly hang out with Jack Kerouac and the other "subterraneans" in San Francisco during the mid-'50s, after Joe McCarthy chose Roy Cohn over him as his legal counsel. As attorney general, he often showed up for cabinet meetings stoned and used to constantly get on Robert McNamara's nerves by calling him "the secretary of Squaresville."

> Hoover was off in his own world. "That damn tousled hair. Do you know who has tousled hair? Pinkos and perverts. Look at pictures of Stalin when he was a young man. His hair's tousled. And don't get me started on Liberace."

"So, if something were to happen to the president, say he were killed..." Ike prompted.

Hoover returned from his reverie and said soberly, "I'd have to investigate it with complete thoroughness. That's the sort of thing a pinko or pervert would do, and I would make sure that every law enforcement agency in this country was focused *completely* on the sorts of pinkos and perverts capable of such a heinous act. Do I make myself clear?"

At that, he allowed a small smile to cross his lips.

"Crystal, Mr. Director." Ike got up to leave. "You and Clyde will have your new panamas by the middle of May."

Three hours later, Ike was in his hotel room, planning his next move, when there was a knock on the door. He opened it and a thin, somewhat seedy-looking man in his early fifties walked in and introduced himself.

"Meyer Lansky?" Ike said, taken aback and fairly impressed. "The gangster?"

"That's *Myron* Lansky, and while I have been a gangster, I currently prefer to think of myself as an entrepreneur. And I think I can solve your 'problem.'"

Myron Lansky was, to put it kindly, a bottom-feeder in the world of organized crime. Indeed, if he had been in show business, he would have been a celebrity look-alike, since his "career" depended almost entirely on the similarity between his name and appearance and that of Meyer Lansky, a real *macher* in the criminal world. Myron was always following in Meyer's footsteps, establishing rackets just close enough to the great man's without incurring his wrath. When the Bugs and Meyer Gang was hijacking beer deliveries, the Bud and Myron Gang was hijacking chewing gum deliveries. When Meyer Lansky was setting up casinos in Broward County, Myron was running cockfights in Duval County.

Most recent, Meyer had the Hotel Nacional in Havana, and Myron had the Motel Nacional located not in Havana, but in Oriente Province. Business was lousy, but in 1956, fate stepped in, in the form of Fidel Castro and his guerrillas, who needed a place to stay. Not only was the Motel Nacional reasonably clean and inexpensive, it served traditional Jewish cuisine, for which Castro had developed a taste when his roommate at the University of Havana Law School used to have him over for Friday night dinner. Castro's victory seemed to finally put Myron in a position to profit, and while other foreign-owned businesses were being nationalized, Castro left the motel alone.

But once a schmendrick, always a schmendrick, and Myron made the mistake of asking Che Guevara to pay his bar tab.[3] He was soon dubbed an "enemy of the revolution," and, like Meyer Lansky, was forced to abandon his Cuban properties and make his way to Miami. Unlike Meyer, who retained his position in the national crime syndicate, however, Myron was forced to take a position as cook at Feinlieb's Kosher Beach Kabana. For a year he'd been looking for a way to gather a stake and follow up on his new million-dollar idea: a one-horse town he'd discovered in Nevada called "Los Vegas," which he planned on marketing as a low-budget version of the real thing. The problem was that his pre-

---

3. Che was a notorious cheapskate, though in his defense, this was long before he started reeling in all that money from T-shirt licensing agreements.

vious cozy relations with Castro had ruined even what little reputation he had previously enjoyed in the criminal world, and nobody would touch him. Then he got a call from "Pepe," aka, Pedro
Rabinowitz, who had been working on a master's in English lit at
the University of Havana before the revolution, and who fed Myron
hot racing tips in exchange for free blintzes.

As Myron saw it, if he killed Kennedy, he could get Castro to pay
the bar tab, and get the Mob to give the go-ahead on Los Vegas.
Castro's antipathy to JFK needs no explanation; the Mob was upset because after becoming president, Kennedy had snubbed Frank
Sinatra and started cozying up to Andy Williams. It was widely believed that Andy Williams commanded a vast legion of undead
Confederates. Although it turned out that a lot of his Southern fans
just had really poor hygiene, at the time, the Mob thought it was
safer to take on the president than Williams. With Hoover running
interference on the investigation, all he needed was the button
man to do the hit, and a fall guy to take the rap. He had the
shooter, a guy who more than once had cried on his shoulder at
closing time at the Kabana about how JFK had done him wrong. It
was up to Ike to provide the patsy.

George Bush wouldn't normally have met with someone like
Ike Grunboim outside of a haberdashery, but when Ike explained
what he wanted, Bush was glad to oblige. His loathing of Kennedy
was both deep-rooted and complex. Old money vs. new money,
WASP vs. Irish Catholic, Yale vs. Harvard, disappointment vs. stunning success—any one of these offered a clue as to why he despised his fellow New Englander. Of course, the fact that
Kennedy had shtupped his very drunk fiancée, Barbara Pierce,
during a USO dance back when she was a sophomore at Smith
might have also played a part. When he heard about it, navy
bomber Bush went berserk and tried to sink Kennedy's PT-109.
Kennedy, ever the golden boy, shot Bush down, which only added
fuel to the fire. Furthermore, Bush was not happy with Kennedy's

plans to dismantle the Yalie-dominated CIA (which Bush, of course, denied any connection to) and replace it with one of his typical grand liberal institutions like the Peace Corps, run, doubtlessly, by Harvard-trained eggheads.[4] Thus, when Ike asked for help, Bush denied knowing anything, but gave him the number of "The Amazing Mesmero," aka Bernie Shapiro. Not only had Mesmero, a stage magi-

Of course, the fact that Kennedy had shtupped his very drunk fiancée, Barbara Pierce, during a USO dance back when she was a sophomore at Smith might have also played a part. When he heard about it, navy bomber Bush went berserk and tried to sink Kennedy's PT-109.

cian and hypnotist, assisted the Bushes with their eldest son, George W's preteen bedwetting problem, he had some contacts that might prove useful to Ike. Some years earlier, Mesmero had assisted the CIA in a mind-control program known as MK-Ultra. From that experience, he had the names of a number of people scattered around the country who, when given the right posthypnotic suggestion, would do anything they were told. One of those people was Lee Harvey Oswald, who had been unwittingly put through the program while stationed at a military base in Japan, and who had since moved to Dallas. Conspiracy theorists have often wondered how a defector married to the daughter of a KGB colonel could be let back into the country. The truth is that many alumni of MK-Ultra were used for various odd jobs by the CIA, and the CIA station chief in Dallas kept Oswald around to make sandwiches for his late-night poker games.

On November 22, 1963, shortly after noon, Ike was sitting down in front of twenty eyewitnesses, chairing a meeting of the Congregation Sharay Tefilah Hanukkah Gala Planning Committee. They

---

4. It's unclear what form the final plan would have taken, but it seems that the new spy organization would have been called "The Super Spying Action Team" and would have been led by a young Harvard psychology professor named Timothy Leary.

Unaware of the historical significance of the photo in the collection of tchotchkes his grandfather had left to him in his will, Mitch Lansky included it in a box he donated for a rummage sale at the West Beverly Hills chapter of Hadassah.

decided that the guest of honor would be Morey Amsterdam.[5] The president was riding slowly through Dealey Plaza, the sun shining down on his motorcade.[6] Lee Harvey Oswald was sitting in the window at the Book Depository, robotically making a deviled ham sandwich, his rifle propped in the window. Myron Lansky was driving through the Nevada desert, looking for the perfect spot to build his Flamenco Hotel. And Arthur Miller, the recently cuckolded husband of Marilyn Monroe, was sitting on the grassy knoll, a rifle at his shoulder, a famous head of tousled hair in his sights.

The American hat industry, of course, never fully recovered. Ike did, however, have the satisfaction of personally fitting Lyndon Baines Johnson for the hat he wore to his second inaugural. He was so happy he decided to buy Rose a new mink coat and to take her on a trip to Hawaii. Castro paid Che's bar tab and then expelled Guevara, fearing any further drain on the revolution's coffers. Arthur Miller never wrote anything good again, but could still drink for free at most bars as "the guy who shtupped Marilyn Monroe." The Warren Commission put the blame on "pinko" Oswald, and the only "serious" criminal investigation, conducted by the New Orleans District Attorney's office, placed the blame squarely on a strange coterie of perverts. Myron decided that Los Vegas was another failure waiting to happen, took his seed money a little farther west to California, and became a reasonably successful film producer in L.A.[7] Oswald, of course, was killed by Jack Ruby, aka Jacob Rubenstein, while in police custody in Dallas. It was supposedly the result of a series of coincidences, and maybe it was, but look at the picture of the shooting and ask yourself: Why is Oswald the only person in the entire scene who isn't wearing a hat?

---

5. This led to rumors that Morey Amsterdam himself was in Dallas at the time of the assassination and was somehow involved. In fact, Amsterdam was in Saigon at the time, doing a benefit for the B'nai B'rith of Indochina.

6. Somewhat ironically, several of his Secret Service men swore they couldn't see anything, since under the president's orders they couldn't wear hats and the sun was in their eyes.

7. Admittedly, that's *Las* Angeles, which is the film capital of *Baja*, California.

CHAPTER TWENTY-NINE
CRASHING THE PARTY

Reuben Finkelstone sat outside the committee room, awaiting its judgment and confident of the result. The year 1966 was a banner one for him. He was finally breaking free from the strict control of his authoritarian father, Professor Hyman Finkelstein. The day after his eighteenth birthday, he had had his name legally changed to one that he thought better reflected his new status as a future member of America's ruling class.[1] He had started at Yale, a move that enraged his father both personally and professionally. And today would be his pièce de résistance—joining the campus branch of the College Republicans.

The sergeant-at-arms stuck his head out. "You can come in now, Finkelstein," he said in his curious accent, a strange mix of Texas and Connecticut.

"That's Finkelstone," corrected Reuben, but it was too late. He entered the room and stood where the sergeant-at-arms gestured with his paddle for him to stand.

"Mr. Finkelstein," announced the chairman, his nasal voice a register not normally produced by the human larynx, forced out through a jaw clenched so tightly you'd need the jaws of life to pry them apart. "Your membership request has been denied."

Reuben was shocked.

"May—may I ask why?"

The committee members looked uncomfortably at one another. There was a long silence, punctuated at last by the sergeant-at-arms.

---

1. Granted, it wasn't much of a change, but at the time, you paid by the letter.

"Well, Finkelstein, isn't it as plain as the nose on your face?"

The silence gave way to relieved laughter.

"After all," continued the chairman, in a jovial mood now, "the College Republicans are looking for men who are a cut above, and let's face it, you're more of a cut *below*, if you catch my meaning."

Reuben was crestfallen. He looked so disheartened that even his tormentors took pity on him.

"There, there, old boy," comforted the chairman. "Don't be so glum. Now drop your pants and get ready for your rejection paddling like the good fellow you hoped yourself to be."

Disconsolate, he dropped his trousers. All the times he'd imagined himself being in this position, he never thought it would hurt so badly. Then the paddling began.

Growing up a red-diaper baby had been no great thrill.[2] For as long as he could remember, Reuben's parents had schlepped him from one protest to another. At times these protests were at cross-purposes, one day protesting to force a munitions factory to hire black workers, then a few months later, after they had been hired, protesting that it be shut down because it was part of the military-industrial complex. His childhood was one continuous demonstration. His parents banned French toast (until the French left Indochina), English Muffins (until the British left Malaya), and Spanish omelets (they gave his father gas). Like many party members, his father, a Brooklyn College professor of theoretical reality,[3] had been blacklisted in the early fifties, and for years had to resort to various subterfuges to find work, including spending two years impersonating Julia Child at a small cooking school in

---

2. Although it still sounds better than being a brown-diaper baby, until you really think about it.

3. It was a complicated interdisciplinary field that used physics, a variety of social sciences, and penmanship to explore the nexus between things and the stuff that they seem to be. He was considered both the father and the sole adherent of the discipline, and would be its leading figure until the development of realistic theory in the late '70s made him completely obsolete.

His childhood was one continuous demonstration. His parents banned French toast (until the French left Indochina), English Muffins (until the British left Malaya), and Spanish omelets (they gave his father gas).

western Delaware. While the memoirs of some red-diaper babies indicate that they reveled in the small, intimate world of the party of their youth—the summer camps, the potlucks, the busty Jewish folksingers in tight sweaters—Reuben loathed it from the start. How he wished that he could go trick-or-treating like the other children, but of course, his father insisted that Halloween was "a holiday built on the blood, sweat, and tears of fudge-packers and other confection workers." And the one time he did let him go it was even worse—imagine your reaction upon opening the door of your east Flatbush home in 1956 and finding a small boy dressed like V.I. Lenin standing there. The bottom line is that by the time he turned eighteen, he was ready to get out, and this, the College Republicans, would have been both the ultimate rebellion against his parents as well as the entrée into the American mainstream that he so craved. Looking at the confident smiles on the horse-faces of his tormentors, he wished they could understand what it was like to be on the outside. But of course, that could never happen.

They were born to it, he thought. *Those lucky bastards are the most American of Americans. They have the names, the pedigrees, the connections—they'd have to actually be found guilty of treason for anybody to question their credentials....* An idea began to germinate.

"Excuse me, sir, but may I have another, and ask a question?"

"Yes on both."

"Why aren't any of you fellows in the military?"

An uncomfortable silence followed.

"Well," said the chairman at last. "The thing is that, like one of our members said a few years back, we've got other priorities."

"Exactly," seconded the sergeant-at-arms. "We're not antimilitary, it's just that we're awful busy here."

"But see," said Reuben, trying to hook them. "Don't you think that's a problem politically? I mean, if you ever plan on running for office, you better give this some thought. Right now, there's a whole generation of Americans not just serving, but actually fighting in Vietnam."

"Sure," said the vice-chairman, "but that's hardly a problem. I mean, a bunch of kids from mill towns and ghettoes won't really be in our league, will they?"

"But what league will you be in? Think about this—in the last thirty-five years, there's been only one Republican president, and he was a war hero. Those kids from mill towns may not run, but they sure as heck vote. Why should they vote for you?"

"Because…because we represent American values?"

"Sure, you and I know that, but how will you convince the people who vote? They'll just see you as a bunch of draft dodgers."

"That's not fair! We have deferments!"

"And it's not like the Democrats are doing any better!"

The increasing tone of desperation in their voices convinced Reuben that they were ready.

"No, but the Democrats are seen as being the party of the people, while you fellows are seen as out-of-touch elitists. Your not serving will be seen as being a sign of snobbery. Unless…"

"Unless what?" they shouted, virtually in unison.

"Well, I had an idea…."

Reuben explained his plan to them and they agreed. If he could do all that he promised, they'd welcome him with open arms into the GOP. Not just him, but anybody who assisted him. Reuben was not alone in his aspirations. Most of his friends from East Flatbush were as tired and embarrassed by the whole communist thing as he was. They wanted to celebrate the Fourth of July. They wanted to watch John Wayne movies. They wanted to be able to say the word

"Rosenberg" without hearing an explosion of apoplectic invective from everyone around them.[4] Like many teens, they wanted to rebel against all that their parents raised them to believe, and that meant becoming Republicans. They were Reuben's secret weapon. After leaving the meeting, he got on the phone to friends at half a dozen college campuses around the country. All had experienced similar rejections in their efforts to join the GOP, and all listened eagerly to his plan. He laid out the basics to them, and they agreed to meet in Brooklyn during winter break to work out the details.

At that time, college kids were actually strongly behind the war effort (and really, why shouldn't they have been—it's not like they were doing any fighting). From 1965 to '67, Columbia featured a dunk tank on the quad, where students could throw grenade-shaped balls to try to dunk a frat boy dressed like Ho Chi Minh, the proceeds going to the USO's Emergency Donut Fund. At the University of Wisconsin, sororities would knit ammunition belts and barrel covers for M-60 gunners. And even at Berkeley, the championship 1966 water polo team dedicated the game ball to the Navy SEALs. All that was about to change.

Say what they would about their upbringing, a life in the party did teach Reuben and the others to be disciplined, organized, and deceptive. One of his friends, Seymour Ringelbum, was actually raised for the first six years of his life as a black Baptist, part of his parents' efforts to infiltrate and organize a neighborhood church. All those skills would be applied to the task at hand. And while you can take the boy out of the party, you can't take the party out of the boy; they felt that the pampered children of the bourgeoisie who were their classmates wouldn't know what hit them. With their background, it wasn't difficult to develop pamphlets, slogans, and even the occasional idea. They recognized perhaps more than anyone how pow-

---

4. Despite his treason and poor grooming habits, Julius Rosenberg remains a hero to many on the Left, predominantly because of the legendary floats he constructed for New York's annual May Day parades in the 1940s. Even opponents of the communists couldn't help but admire 1943's "Stalin Tears Hitler a New One."

erful a force teen rebellion was, and knew that college campuses were teeming with kids as eager to break out of the button-down, crew-cut, nine-to-five world they'd grown up in, as they themselves were eager to break into it. They went back and forth as to whether to create a front organization or simply infiltrate an existing group, and decided that given the situation, the latter made more sense. They picked the Students for a Democratic Society, which already had the advantage of being leftist and located on most of America's most important campuses. Back at school—Harvard, Yale, Columbia, University of Wisconsin, Berkeley, and Brigham Young[5]—they began to put the plan into effect. It wasn't difficult for them to infiltrate and take control of the campus SDS groups. Their skill as propagandists meant that they could usually draw crowds to their functions, and their connections in the party meant that no matter where they were, they had access to radical speakers, good grass, and busty Jewish folk-singers in tight sweaters, which was enough to keep them there. Some of the more enterprising branches even hired hookers to dress like beatniks and sleep with select attendees. This got more men to come to meetings, and inspired more coeds in the group to put out themselves, which got even more men to come to meetings. Hopped up on pot and tight sweaters, America's college students found their minds were easily swayed by the weighty dialectical materialism of the SDS. When that didn't work, there were more obvious methods to be used.

> **Their skill as propagandists meant that they could usually draw crowds to their functions, and their connections in the party meant that no matter where they were, they had access to radical speakers, good grass, and busty Jewish folksingers in tight sweaters, which was enough to keep them there.**

---

5. The conspiracy wasn't entirely successful, although the Salt Lake City branch did manage to entice a number of Latter-Day Saints to drink coffee and publicly question the wisdom of the domino theory.

At the University of Wisconsin, Seymour Ringelblum published doctored photos in *The Daily Cardinal* showing American soldiers slaughtering Vietnamese villagers who bore striking resemblances to beloved American cultural icons like Donna Reed, June Cleaver, and Betty Crocker. At Berkeley, Jerome Hilquit went one step further, and actually hired some local longshoremen to dress like marines and assault the homecoming parade.[6] And at Yale, Reuben plastered the campus with leaflets reminding students that JFK, the man who had gotten the U.S. into Vietnam in the first place, had attended Harvard. And of course, what started at the nation's most prestigious schools soon was emulated all around the country. It didn't hurt that as '67 rolled into '68, more and more students saw their college years—and with them, their deferments—drawing to a close. And of course, even if the politics didn't mean anything, there was always the sex and drugs.

Of course, not everyone on campus was joining. Most students were fairly apathetic. And the College Republicans were actively opposed to the movement. When SDS would hold an antiwar rally, the College Republicans—presuming they didn't have anything more pressing to do—would hold a prowar rally. They were often much smaller, sedate affairs, sometimes far off campus, but still the statement was made. And considering the violence that spilled over into college campuses in 1968, many College Republicans truly came to see themselves as being on the front lines. As Drudge Hannibaugh, the conservative columnist, wrote in his column of 11/11/03, "I'm No Chickenhawk": "There were many days when I would have gladly traded places with the grunts in the Mekong River Delta. They at least had some respite from the assault. But for us, it was a constant struggle, involving day-to-day

---

6. To be perfectly honest, he actually just got a bunch of longshoreman who were planning on assaulting the parade anyway to put on the uniforms.

contact with the enemy. At the end of the day, the grunt could hunker down in a secure rear area; for us, the enemy was just a dorm room away."

Nixon won in 1968, helped in part by the inability of the Democrats to control radical protestors at their convention in that year. Reuben and his friends from East Flatbush eventually gave up control of the SDS, and without their discipline, the group splintered into smaller, more radical, and even less-frequently-bathed factions. The contacts they made in college served them well, and not only were they allowed into the GOP in the 1970s, but their neoconservative clique came to be an increasingly influential faction within their new party. Reuben himself founded The Institute for Educational Integrity, which under the cover of raising standards,

Perhaps more than anything, this photo, which first appeared in a 1968 SDS leaflet, radicalized the youth of America. As Abbie Hoffman put it years later: "They could have done June Cleaver, or Harriet Nelson, or even Lucy Ricardo, and it would have been cool, man. But when these cats did Donna Reed, man, I, like, had to do something."

uses communist propaganda methods to produce Republicans.[7] As for the old conservatives who had sat out the war on the Ivy League campuses, the out-of-touch elitism of which they so frequently denounced, by the 1990s, they were ready to enter the political fray. And thanks to Reuben and his comrades, whereas once their refusal to serve their country might have been a handicap, a generation of GOP draft dodgers got the right to proudly challenge their Democratic rivals by saying things like "unlike my opponent, I wasn't out burning American flags while our boys in Vietnam were dying to defend them."

---

7. Consider this example from a fifth-grade math book produced by the institute: "Bruce is an artist. He receives a $500 grant from the NEA. With that, he donates $50 to NPR, uses $147 to purchase a crucifix, a vibrator, and ten pounds of camel dung for his art project, and spends $180 on pot for himself and his boyfriend. How much of your parents' tax dollars does he have left?"

CHAPTER THIRTY

RAISING THE STEAKS

Asher Goldberg had it all: a lovely wife, Maddie, and two sons, David and Jackie; a huge house with a swimming pool in one of the most prestigious neighborhoods in Cherry Hill, New Jersey; and perhaps the most thriving cheese-steak joint in all of Philadelphia. The year was 1967 and his two-floor, one thousand-square-foot establishment, Goldberg's Cheesesteaks, located on the corner of Broad and Cypress streets, was doing remarkable business. During lunchtime, people would stand on line for over thirty minutes to sample the best sandwiches in town.

Arthur grew up in downtown Philadelphia, one flight above the kosher restaurant owned by his parents. Dovid and Ruthie were Hungarian émigrés, who, confusing the First World War with the Second World War, had spent three years hiding in the basement of a pizzeria in Fiume. There, they picked up the culinary arts—as well as a terrible case of rickets—and after smuggling themselves to America in a giant wheel of mozzarella, set up their own restaurant.

The Goldbergs' restaurant made the best kasha varnishkes in town. The key was the schmaltz, which acted as a glue to combine kasha, noodle, and onions in a perfect platonic union.[1] Asher took the principle behind his parents' kasha varnishkes and applied it to the cheese steak. Meat and onions were left overnight to soak in schmaltz and then fried and refried in schmaltz each morning. No one knew why Goldberg's cheese steaks tasted so much better than the competition's, but the lines kept getting longer and longer.

---

1. The truth is that the noodles wanted more of a relationship, but the onions just wanted to remain friends.

Asher's status as Philadelphia's cheese steak king was confirmed when the previous king, Anthony Tattagla, divorced his wife and was forced by the pope to abdicate.

All of that came to a grinding halt on October 2, 1967, at the groundbreaking ceremonies for Veterans Stadium, which had been built just around the corner on Pattison Avenue. Asher had known about this day for years. Since 1938, Philadelphia's teams had been playing on the other side of the city in Connie Mack Stadium,[2] which held roughly thirty-three thousand fans. The Vet, which held nearly twice that many fans, was a multipurpose stadium, a state-of-the-art facility that would be the largest in the National League to date. When the community board met years earlier, Asher had supported the $52 million project, figuring that the influx of fans would only make business better. Unfortunately, that wasn't the case.

While many immigrants and their children flocked to America's pastime as a way of assimilating, Asher never really took to baseball. Thus, he had no sense of the storied relationship between baseball and food. Some even speculated that baseball's appeal to Americans had more to do with the lure of the inexpensive and hearty food that was sold at the ballpark than it did with the acts of athleticism that occurred on the field, but at times, the two went hand in hand. For example, after the 1931 season, Yankees fans went to the stadium primarily to see Babe Ruth's legendary feats of gustatory excess—during one doubleheader with the White Sox, he consumed forty-three hot dogs, a gallon of beer, and Chicago's batboy.

In terms of taste, nothing could top a Goldberg's Cheesesteak. But while Veterans Stadium frankfurters might have tasted like they were made out of a pig's butt (which, considering what really

---

2. It was long presumed that the legendary Athletics manager took the name "Connie Mack" simply to avoid the burden of his real name—Cornelius McGuilicutty. It is now known, however, that it was a stage name he used for a strangely successful off-season career as a chanteuse of light pop standards.

went into them, was a real accomplishment), there was simply no way that Asher's prices could compete. Suddenly, the neighborhood was dotted with cheap hot dog stands and pushcart Crackerjackeries, all of which ate into Asher's profits. He tried to fight fire with fire, but "Goldberg's Cheesesteak Night" at the stadium ended disastrously when fans angry at a bad call hurled their free sandwiches at the field, scalding numerous members of the Phillies in a rain of melted cheese and forcing most of their starters to miss several games. Not only were his sandwiches banned, many fans viewed him as being personally responsible for their missed games.

In less than two years, Goldberg's Cheesesteaks found itself on the verge of bankruptcy. Asher was contemplating these and other unpleasant thoughts at a table in his almost empty establishment one day in October 1969 when he noticed a wiry, young black man two tables away eating a chili cheese steak and trying to hold back tears. The man's name, Asher soon found out, was Curt Flood.

Flood was an all-star outfielder for the St. Louis Cardinals who only a day earlier had been traded to Philadelphia. Asher pulled a napkin out of the dispenser in front of him, sat down next to Flood, and asked him what was the matter. Flood explained that his entire family lived in St. Louis, that he had just invested all of his money in a dry-cleaning business there,[3] and that his current salary prevented him from moving his family to Philadelphia. Readers accustomed to professional athletes' stratospheric salaries may be unaware that in 1966 the average player made seven thousand dollars per year, which was actually less than the guys who rolled the tarp onto the field when it rained—they were Teamsters.

"So, why don't you say no?" asked Asher.

"It's not quite so simple," replied Flood. And indeed it wasn't. Labor relations in baseball were still governed by the controversial re-

---

3. The authors suspect that Norman Lear, a die-hard Cardinals fan since childhood, patterned George Jefferson on Curt Flood.

serve clause, a clause that gave ownership the right to renew a player's contract upon the expiration of a contract. This was a holdover from 1863, when in order to placate those border states afraid that the Emancipation Proclamation would apply to them, Lincoln promised the owner of the Chevy Chase Chattel that no matter what happened, he'd still be able to hold on to his best players. The length of the extension wasn't specified, but it was interpreted to last for the life of player, although some owners conceded that a player could legally be declared a free agent on his seventy-fifth birthday. The de facto result was a quasi-indentured servitude extending ad infinitum.[4]

Lincoln promised the owner of the Chevy Chase Chattel that no matter what happened, he'd still be able to hold on to his best players.

Asher came up with an idea. If the reserve clause were overturned and baseball players allowed to have their salaries determined on an open market, those salaries would skyrocket and owners would have to either close shop or come up with additional revenue to pay those salaries, revenue that most certainly would come from higher prices on concessions. Once the price of the hot dogs went up, there was no way people would choose them over his cheese steaks.

The next day Asher introduced Curt to his considerably older second cousin Arthur, a former secretary of labor, Supreme Court justice, and ambassador to the United Nations, but still referred to by his mother as "the one who didn't become a doctor." Asher's parents had sent him varnishkes throughout law school, and he was willing to listen to what Asher had to say. Asher plied him with cheese steaks, then explained the situation to him.

Arthur Goldberg was outraged by Flood's plight. "In America, a man is not a piece of property to be bought and sold irrespective of

---

4. That's three Latin terms in one sentence. Even Julius Caesar could only get through two before reverting to his native Shakespeariean English.

his wishes. If he had won him in a high-stakes pai-gow game it would be one thing, but this is obscene!"[5] And so the showdown over the century-old reserve clause began. Major League Baseball's lawyers argued that without the reserve clause, all of the rich teams would get all of the good players, and that the clause was therefore essential to the best interests of the game.[6] Flood's lawyer, Arthur Goldberg, argued that the system violated the Thirteenth Amendment, and moreover that it bordered on Bolshevism, thereby appealing to both anticommunists and abolitionists.

The case came before the Federal District Court of Manhattan in 1970. Flood lost. Then the case came before the Court of Appeals. Flood lost. Finally, the Goldbergs and Flood had nowhere to go but the Supreme Court. And on June 18, 1972, the Supreme Court ruled that Major League Baseball was exempt from antitrust laws. There are various theories about this. Some speculate that some of Goldberg's former peers on the court wanted a little payback for his habit of never chipping in for the beer; others believe that Nixon, fearing that people would blame him for losing both Vietnam and baseball, threatened to reveal the truth about how William Rehnquist got the nickname "Water Polo" unless he ruled against Flood. Whatever the reason, Flood had lost again.

The three-year battle that had been waged took its toll on Flood. He grew distant from his family, his cleaning business went bankrupt, and what's worse, he was shown no signs of solidarity among the fraternity of major league players. Superstars like Tom Seaver, Willie Mays, and Pete Rose refused to testify in his behalf, not wanting the public to view them as rabble-rousers, though Rose did place a 3-1 bet that Flood would come out victorious. Broken by his experience, Flood then moved to Denmark. And if you think that playing baseball in Japan is a step down for a major leaguer, you've

---

5. Although the devotion of Jewish women to mah-jongg is well known, the obsession that many Jewish men have with pai-gow is, up to this point, unexplored.
6. A certain shipbuilder from Cleveland paid careful note of this train of thought in the newspaper the following morning.

Superstars like Tom Seaver, Willie Mays, and Pete Rose refused to testify in his behalf, not wanting the public to view them as rabble-rousers, though Rose did place a 3-1 bet that Flood would come out victorious.

clearly never seen the Copenhagen Little Mermaids take the field.

Things only got worse for Asher Goldberg in 1972. That year, the Phillies traded a veteran pitcher to St. Louis for little-known lefty Steve Carlton, who proceeded to win twenty-seven games and post a 1.98 ERA.[7] Meanwhile, feeding off the excitement of their new ballpark, the Vet consistently held spectacular promotional events that kept the crowds coming through the turnstiles. The Vet reportedly sold over twenty-five thousand hot dogs on the afternoon in which the world-famous Karl Wallenda walked across the middle of the stadium on a high-wire far above the highest bleacher seat between games of a double-header.[8] With business at an all-time low, his wife, Maddie, tried to convince him to close Goldberg's for good. "Maybe you're right." Asher sighed. "Major League Baseball is bigger than organized crime, which is bigger than U.S. Steel, which is bigger than the Beatles, who are bigger than Jesus.

"Forget about Jesus: What these ballplayers need is Moses... Wait a second, that's it!" said Arthur, in a moment oddly reminiscent of three thousand years of Jewish conspirators.[9]

Moses Miller (better known as Marvin) had spent most of his life in the labor movement: first at the International Association of

---

7. For those of you who aren't baseball fans, that's good.

8. As soon as Wallenda finished he was arrested for sneaking in without a ticket.

9. We would like to use this occasion to note that this is hardly the only time in which Jews have conspired against the national pastime. In 1919, Arnold Rothstein's fixing of the World Series created the "Black Sox" scandal in order to launch a fashion trend after his henchmen hijacked a Fruit of the Loom shipment. In 1965, the owner of the Hebrew Publishing Company, still angry that the Dodgers had abandoned Brooklyn, changed the dates on all the Jewish calendars to ensure that Sandy Koufax couldn't pitch when game one of the World Series fell on Yom Kippur. And there was the case of Dr. Noah Sternchos, who injected Bill Buckner's ailing back with Benadryl instead of Novocain just before the sixth game of the 1986 World Series as revenge against his cheating wife, Rhoda, a die-hard Sox fan from Newton, Massachussets.

Machinists, then at the United Auto Workers, the United Steel Workers, and finally head of the Baseball Players Association. More important, in 1961 he had lost an all-night pai-gow game to Arthur, and the latter, feeling that it would be inappropriate for the secretary of labor to own an indentured servant, had set him free.

Miller agreed to take on the reserve clause in 1975. For years, he had wanted to call a strike, but felt that such an unpopular move would be doomed to failure. Flood's case, however, had created a certain wellspring of sympathy for baseball players' dire economic straits, especially after people saw the picture of the 1971 American League pennant–winning Baltimore Orioles celebrating their victory by eating fancy cat food, and of 1970 National League Rookie of the Year Carl Morton turning tricks in Times Square. The

This baseball card comes from a 1969 limited-edition series. The series also featured Carl Yastrzemski squeegying a car on Yawkey Way and Rollie Fingers panhandling on the Lower Haight while pretending to be a Vietnam vet.

strike forced the owners to binding arbitration on the matter and arbiter Peter Seitz, who, for the rest of his life, always seemed to have plenty of cheese steaks lying around, ruled in favor of the players. The reserve clause was dead.

But the shrewd Miller didn't stop there. He knew he had the owners where he wanted them and offered what appeared to be a compromise. Despite the fact that the reserve clause was no longer applicable, Miller offered to sign a deal in behalf of the players in which they would promise not to exercise their option to become free agents until they had played six years for a major-league team. Miller understood the law of supply and demand: A trickle of free agents each year was in the players' long-term interests. That way the supply of free agents would ensure a higher demand for talent each year.

The rest, as they say, is history. As players' salaries soared, owners were forced to raise the prices on stadium concessions. Today, at a Philadelphia Phillies game hot dogs ($8), peanuts ($3), and medium sodas ($5) for a family of four will cost a family $65. Not surprisingly, business soared at Goldberg's Cheesesteaks. In 1980, the same year that the Philadelphia Phillies won the World Series, Asher retired and moved to Miami with Maddy, leaving the business to his two sons. As for Curt Flood, he never did make it back into the majors, but with a little assistance from Asher, opened the best cheesesteak shop in all of Scandinavia.

CHAPTER THIRTY-ONE

LORD GYM

As usual, Addisu Solomon had drawn a crowd for his sales pitch, but as usual, not the response he'd hoped for. As he posed on the crowded Nairobi street, the onlookers jeered at his impressive physique. Addisu's problem was that while when he looked in the mirror, he saw powerful biceps, quads, triceratops, delts, and so forth, they, at least according to the things they hollered, saw a strangely bloated, grotesquely inflated caricature of a human. In the early 1980s, East African physiques tended to come in two forms: thin and emaciated. While nobody wanted to have the latter, nobody saw a problem with the former.[1] Aside from traditional abhorrence of gluttony, the dominance of East African long-distance runners and the growth of the supermodel phenomenon and anorexia only confirmed for them that their was nothing wrong with their bodies. Sighing, Addisu packed up his placard billing himself as "The Ethiopian Samson," put away his reasonably priced brochures explaining how even the sickliest of men could achieve muscular perfection, and went home, more doubtful than ever that he would fulfill his dream of opening the first Western-style gym in Kenya.

A lesser man might have given up then, but for Addisu, this was merely one more challenge to overcome. As an Ethiopian Jew growing up in poverty-stricken East Gondar, he had known prejudice, as the Christian children mocked him for his refusal to eat the

---

1. We shouldn't say nobody. The Somalis actually cultivated emaciation. This explains the hostile reaction the Americans got. The Somalis felt that we were trying to make their women hideously adipose while we were turning our own women—which they knew only from the Mogadishu editions of *Elle* and *Seventeen*—into gorgeously slender Somali-esque vixens. They responded as ferociously as American men would if the U.N. banned breast implants and began to remove them from American women.

flesh of living goats and to participate in the village Christmas Tap Dancing Extravaganza. Moreover, a sickly child, he was even picked on by the kids from the more affluent West Gondar neighborhood in the Jewish school his devoted parents scrimped to send him to, who mocked his thick "Eastie" accent and the simple homemade stew he brought for lunch every day, which, since his parents couldn't afford a container, had to be carried in his pockets. Then came the war. Not to be confused with either the American or Spanish wars of the same name, Ethiopia's civil war resulted in the collapse of the regime of Emperor Haile Selassie, who had survived nearly four decades in power, deification by the Rastafarians, conquest and exile by the Italians, and the release of a horrifyingly bad collection of easy-listening favorites in the early 1960s, "Singin' and Swingin' with Selassie."

Addisu's parents were killed and he had to fend for himself. Hiding in a basement one day, he happened upon a comic book advertisement for Charles Atlas's muscle-building course.[2] Although the comic was nearly forty years old, the address was still good, and Addisu wrote a heartfelt letter explaining his circumstances. The Sicilian-born Mr. Atlas, perhaps feeling a twinge of remorse or nostalgia, was so moved that

[2]. It was an issue #1 of *The Ro-Man*, a popular Italian series of the 1930s and 40s. Short on subtlety but heavy on the action and cheesecake, it featured a fascist cyborg who battled Italy's enemies, including the cunning Frog and the cruel Germ Man. Although Mussolini claimed that the resemblance between him and the Ro-Man was strictly coincidental, the partisans who captured and executed him reported that he went to his death trying to vaporize them with "Dest-Ro Vision."

he agreed to forgo the usual fee (which, at that time in Ethiopia, was either one young he-goat or two easy payments of one bushel of millet each) and send his muscle-building information to Addisu on the house. Say what you will about Selassie, he kept the mail coming and Addisu got his package. Working day and night, even as he, along with many other Ethiopian refugees, made his way to Kenya, the young man built himself up over the course of a decade and was ready to make his fortune teaching others the skills he had mastered. Which brought him to the point where we introduced him.

Nursing a beer through the night, he caught the news from the TV over the bar. The announcer was talking about the new disease that was sweeping through the United States. "I'm surprised they haven't blamed us for it," said the bartender. "Something bad happens, and they blame it on black people." He turned off the TV, leaving Addisu to his thoughts. The bartender was right, he thought, but he only got half of it. It's true that the Americans were quick to blame blacks for their problems, but they also had a do-gooder impulse that led them to try to help Africans, even if the results were often clumsy. Periodically American aid agencies would descend upon his refugee camp, forcing food on the residents, no matter whether they were hungry or not. As far as the Americans were concerned, a thin African was a starving African. They once pounced on a runner the day before a race, and by the time they were done stuffing him, he could barely stand up, much less run a marathon. In fact, they often made people sick by overfeeding them. Actually, the French, with their rich cream-based sauces, were the worst when it came to this. Addisu frequently heard Africans' protests that they were lactose-intolerant met with a haughty, "Non, non, you simply haven't had dairy prepared the right way before!"

The truth is that there were a lot of health problems in Africa. How hard would it be to convince the Westerners that this AIDS

After Mussolini was overthrown, the new prime minister, Field Marshal Pietro Badoglio, ordered the destruction of every issue of *Ro-Man* that could be found. Although he claimed that this was to stamp out remnants of Fascist propaganda, it later turned out that he was a collector and was hoping to drive up prices.

really was spreading in Africa? If they thought there was a problem (*especially* one that could harm *them*) they'd try to solve it. And if the Africans thought that their health was at risk... Well, that's the part that made Addisu smile.

Addisu began to spread rumors of people wasting away and dying from a mysterious ailment. This wasn't hard to do, since people wasted away and died all the time. Furthermore, Addisu's rumors suggested these people all were somehow connected—having sex, using the same toilet, sharing jujubes, and other high-risk behaviors.[3] Western doctors received these rumors with considerable alarm, even if they couldn't verify them, and preliminary reports began to filter back to the United States that not only was AIDS spreading in Africa, but that it was in a particularly dangerous (read: heterosexual) strain. As these rumors began to slowly seep down from the medical community to the larger population, Addisu decided to speed things up. Three years earlier, he had made the acquaintance of a struggling comic by the name of Andrew Silverstein. Silverstein's career had reached such a low that he was performing at Addisu's cousin's bar mitzvah at the Mombassa Marriott.[4] After the show, Addisu and Andrew spent the night drinking Manischewitz Cream Sorghum and commiserating over the unfortunate turns their lives had taken. Addisu, who had some experience in the field, convinced Silverstein that he needed to re-create himself, to make himself into a new person. Now Andrew Silverstein was a rising star known as Andrew Dice Clay, and Addisu wrote to him to ask him to return the favor. He wanted Clay to start doing routines about Africans and AIDS so that the two would become inextricably linked in Americans' minds. Andrew Dice Clay began the monologues, and other comics ripped them off, and it wasn't long before the association between AIDS and

---

3. At no point was it even rumored that the disease started when someone had sex with a monkey. It was suggested, however, that heavy petting with bonobos could be a high-risk activity.

4. Everybody knows all the top comics—and bar mitzvahs—play the Mombassa Hilton.

Andrew Dice Clay began the monologues, and other comics ripped them off, and it wasn't long before the association between AIDS and Africa became instinctive in the minds of most Americans.

Africa became instinctive in the minds of most Americans. Now all Addisu needed was to have some actual evidence and he was home free.

Wearing a suit borrowed from a friend's mortuary/photo studio, the glasses from a Groucho Marx gag nose, and bearing a variety of semi-official-looking documents and data, "Dr. Hyman Grinblatt" began to make the rounds of the various Western aid agencies. At each one, he informed them that his clinic had been detecting numerous cases of what seemed to be this "AIDS" that the Western press was discussing. The truth is, given the health conditions in a place like Nairobi, it wasn't difficult to find cases that fit the profile. Malnutrition? It's AIDS. Malaria? AIDS. Hangover? AIDS. For the Westerners, it was confirmation of their worst fears and greatest hopes: AIDS did originate in Africa, and they would have the opportunity to provide help where it was needed most.

Addisu received various grants so that he could expand his patient base for further study and research. As time went on, they felt that it was money well spent. What the Westerners really appreciated about the young doctor was his ability to relate to the people in a way that they couldn't. Where they would have posted signs discussing 'HIV' and 'AIDS' and 'T-cell counts' and other technical jargon that would have been Hutu to them,[5] Addisu could break it down in a way easy for them to understand: "Slim Disease." And his approach worked, since, judging by the data he provided them, thousands of people were coming to his "clinic." And to be sure, when the agencies visited it, it was crowded, though unbeknownst to them, more for the free s'mores than for the medical treatment.

---

5. The East African equivalent of "Greek to them." In East African slang, "Greek to them" means you want to skewer their lamb and roast it, and you don't want to know what *that* means.

As the aid agencies began reporting on the crisis, nobody questioned the truth of the accounts. And by the time of Dr. Grinblatt's tragic death in a plane crash trying to deliver lifesaving anabolic steroids to a small village on Mt. Kilimanjaro, the "AIDS epidemic" in East Africa had taken on a life of its own.

With the grant money (and the steroids), Addisu had opened a gym (the only one in Nairobi bearing the Hyman Grinblatt Seal of Approval), the promotions for which were straight to the point and borrowed heavily from the Charles Atlas ads that had captured Addisu's imagination so long ago. They featured a thin (some might say skeletal) man at a bar, watching as an attractive woman walks off with a well-built man. The caption read: "You could be *him*, if you weren't so *slim*." The man enters Addisu's gym, and then in the final panel is seen at the bar again, this time with the woman on his arm, the caption reading: "Solomon's Gym—Good Health for a Good Life." Similar ads, stressing the connection between slim physiques, ill-health, and a lousy social life, followed, and well-to-do Kenyans flocked to the gym, desperate to acquire the sort of build that told people that they were healthy. Addisu soon owned a whole chain of gyms and health clubs in Kenya. In 1991, when the Israelis airlifted most of Ethiopia's Jews to Israel, Addisu took the free flight and set up his headquarters there, eventually marrying another recent migrant, a former Miss Addis Ababa. Today, he still manages his East African health-care empire, and with his wife has established a lucrative sideline: "Solomon and Sheba Beauty Consultants," providing East African ingenues to top Western modeling agencies always on the lookout for talent with that "exotic"— and emaciated—supermodel look.

CHAPTER THIRTY-TWO

IMMATERIAL GIRLS

Fyvush Schpritzer stepped up to the velvet rope. "Freddy, Freddy Fontaine," he said to the bouncer. "I'm sure I'm on the list."

Fyvush had tried other pseudonymns including Fabrizio Fontana, Baron Fritz von Schpritz, and Charles Nelson Reilly, but he felt sure that tonight was the night. He'd met a guy, who knew somebody, whose cousin worked at this club that was supposed to be the hottest thing in the city. He was assured that his name was on the guest list.

"Here it is, Freddy Fontaine." He was about to lift up the rope when his partner checked him.

"Wait a minute," said large, bald, muscular man number two. "Is that a velour shirt you're wearing?"

"Why yes," answered Fyvush smoothly. "Yes it is."

"Then you don't get in."

Fyvush watched the cast of *Remington Steele* gliding through the VIP entrance.

"But I'm on the list!" He yelled toward the actors, "Pierce, Pierce, it's me, Freddy!" Pierce Brosnan squinted and gave a brief, perplexed nod.

"Sorry, pal, but list or not, we have a policy. You can't be too fat, too unattractive, and you can't wear velour. Now beat it, before 1974 comes around looking for that shirt."

With the sound of their laughter ringing in his ears, Fyvush slinked off, determined once again to recommit himself to a life of Torah.

Fyvush's life was marked by this constant struggle between his *yetzer hara* and *yetzer tov*[1] that traditional Jews traditionally believe are in constant conflict over control of men's souls. He grew up in Midwood, Brooklyn, the scion of two respected rabbinical families. His maternal grandfather, Rabbi Gottlieb Liebgott, was a renowned mystic and holy man, born in a small town that was at times part of Poland, the Ukraine, Romania, and Hungary, which may seem unremarkable, except that in this case, the town actually moved from place to place. By the time he was thirteen years old, he would spend his early mornings in such deep meditation that his mother couldn't wake him up for school. By the time he was twenty years old, he was reputed to have reached such an elevated level of holiness that no impure thoughts crossed his mind and no impure substances passed through his body. It was said that in order to allow him to fulfill the commandment to be fruitful and multiply, the holy one, blessed be he, performed a miracle so that the seed of Rabbi Liebgott passed through the mailman into his wife, and thus was conceived Fyvush's mother, Shanda.

Fyvush's paternal grandfather, Rabbi Velvl Schpritzer, had completely mastered and forgotten the entirety of the Talmud by the age of thirteen, to such a degree that he couldn't answer even the simplest of questions. By the age of twenty, he kept kosher to such a strict degree that he only ate animals that had undergone an Orthodox conversion. His son, Fyvush's father, wasn't so strict, but still expected the animals to commit themselves to living a Jewish life. Thus, Fyvush had inherited a family tradition not only of scholarship, but of saintly piety. It was a mantle he had trouble wearing. At the age of thirteen, he had become obsessed with celebrities. Their clothes, their homes, their cars—anything he could find. This may

---

1. The Evil Inclination and the Good Inclination, sort of the Devil and Angel perched on your shoulder telling you what to do. There's also the *yetzer kacha-kacha*, which is the A Little of This, A Little of That Inclination, which guides people to do things that are just sort of in the middle. For example, the *yetzer hara* tells you to watch porn, the *yetzer tov* tells you not to, and the *yetzer kacha-kacha* succeeds in getting you to look at the Victoria's Secret catalog.

seem an unlikely obsession for a boy of his background, but it was perhaps precisely that insularity that made celebrities so fascinating. Not only were they fabulous, they were forbidden. His obsession began when he found a hidden stash of entertainment magazines in his sister's room, and he applied the same diligence to them that his forebears had applied to Torah study.[2] More than anything, he wanted to live the celebrity lifestyle, to appear at the awards ceremonies, the talk shows, the rehab clinics. While the other students in the yeshiva were dreaming of new restrictions they could impose on their future congregants, he pictured himself in a stretch limousine, surrounded by beautiful, glamorous women, the paparazzi in eager attendance. It didn't hurt that during the '70s there were numerous "celebrities" like George Hamilton, Bianca Jagger, and Yasser Arafat, whose apparent lack of any actual function didn't prevent them from making the rounds at Studio 54, *The Dick Cavett Show*, and *Battle of the Network Stars*.[3] Thus, while Fyvush exhibited no particular talent that might warrant celebrity status, he was hardly alone. His obsession followed him to high school and into adulthood. At the age of twenty, studying in yeshiva by day and taking accounting classes by night, he couldn't take it anymore. He abandoned Judaism, dropping

---

2. Some years earlier, a similar seminal event occurred to another New York City yeshiva *bochur,* when Ralph Lifschitz found his sister's fashion magazines. Thus inspired, he fashioned himself into the trademark known as Ralph Lauren.

3. Arafat, who played for CBS as a representative of the News Division, was, of course, kicked off *Battle of the Network Stars* in 1978 when he was found using performance-enhancing drugs before competing in the one-hundred-yard dash against Hervé Villechaize.

out of yeshiva, going down to a B average in accounting, and dedicating himself to a life of hedonism and glamour.

Unfortunately, his grasp of what it took to be a modern-day Epicurus left much to be desired. Despite his best efforts he lacked the right clothes, the right connections, and the right approach. He read the gossip columns assiduously and spent many an hour outside the clubs and restaurants favored by his favorites, all with no luck. His one "success" was a brief encounter with the real Charles Nelson Reilly at a gay bar, but both men thought it best to forget the whole episode. He'd hoped for more excitement than he could handle; what he got was more rejection than he could take. After that night's humiliation, Fyvush decided not only to return to Orthodoxy, but to go to Israel. There, in Sfas, the center of Jewish mysticism, he felt that he would be able to get his soul and his life back on track. He stayed there for three years, sublimating his celebrity fixation to learning. He lived like a pietist of old, sleeping on a bench at the yeshiva, eating only when somebody thought to offer him food. He tried his best to control his urges. He fasted, he immersed himself in ice-cold ritual baths, he flagellated himself—still, he couldn't get thoughts of the lush life out of his head. One night, unable to sleep because of his desires, he pored through the decaying books in the yeshiva library, looking for something to strengthen his resolve, or at least distract him. He dropped a copy of the book of Proverbs under the table and reached down to pick it up. Instead, his hand fell on a book covered in dust, almost falling apart. He pulled it out and began to read it. What he found astonished him. It was the diary of Moshe de Leon, a thirteenth-century scholar viewed by many as the author of the Zohar, the most important kabbalistic text.

In reading the diary, Fyvush immediately recognized a kindred spirit. Most of the diary dealt with De Leon's efforts to insinuate himself into Spanish high society and the secret of his ultimate success. Like Fyvush, he fluctuated between periods of extreme piety and intense materialism. Then one day, De Leon had a revelation. Spanish society at the time was into rationalism. Everything was "Plato this" and "Descartes that."[4] So to get in with the in-crowd, he had to distinguish himself from the pack, offer them something they couldn't get anywhere else: mysticism. He claimed to discover a book revealing ancient and profound mystical truths. Like a swingin' 1960s guru, De Leon cut a swath through the squares, drawing the attention of the glitterati of all the major monotheistic faiths. His newfound irresistibility owed something to the originality of his concept, and something to the subliminal mes-sage he encoded in the text. Every sixth and ninth letter spelled out the Aramaic phrase "Obey the rabbi." It was also larded with other phrases like "Have sex with the rabbi," "Listen to the rabbi," and "Buy the rabbi's self-help tapes." The success of this work as both a marketing tool and an aphrodisiac—it led the rabbis at one Barcelona yeshiva to engage in sodomy on a biblical scale, and it is worth noting that when rabbis engage in sodomy, they do it by the book—ultimately led the rabbinical authorities to mandate that only men forty and older could study it.

Thus fortified, Fyvush decided to change all that. He returned stateside, where he assembled a group of his former yeshiva cronies, many of whom had experienced similar struggles between spirit and flesh. Some sought sex, others money, others simply popularity. Since their days of want, they had moved in a variety of directions. Some had entered the rabbinate; others had gone into business, including one who had become a highly successful podi-atrist, with numerous patients in the entertainment industry. To-gether, the former rabbinical students were able to develop a complete marketing scheme for the Kabbalah. Instead of stressing unity with God and moving beyond the physical world, they re-tooled Kabbalah to be all about the physical world, to give the practitioner greater health, wealth, and happiness. Since that was also their own goal, they developed a range of products designed

---

4. Astute—and, let's face it, nerdy—readers might have noted that Descartes wouldn't be around for a few hundred years. But the Spanish, being supremely rational, thought that he would exist.

to "maximize the Kabbalah experience" and their own bottom lines. The complete twenty-two-volume Zohar in rich pleather fetched a pretty penny, but that was only a one-time deal. More lucrative in the long run was "Kabbalah water," essentially tap water that sat in a room with a Zohar all night, absorbing its hearty kabbalistic goodness. Other products they didn't ultimately use included sports coats made out of "Zoharris tweed," "kabbalsamic vinaigrette dressing," and "Moshe de Leicious Frozen Yogurt." One clever and profitable twist was to push the sale of "bendls," little red strings that protect against the evil eye. You can buy them at the Western Wall for a few shekels, but Fyvush and his gang marketed them for $8.50 a pop. The real genius is

> **More lucrative in the long run was "Kabbalah water," essentially tap water that sat in a room with a Zohar all night, absorbing its hearty kabbalistic goodness. Other products they didn't ultimately use included sports coats made out of "Zoharris tweed," "kabbalsamic vinaigrette dressing," and "Moshe de Leicious Frozen Yogurt."**

that these were not only a way to make money, they were a way to mark potential love interests: You saw a bendl on a girl's wrist, there was a good chance she was primed and ready to go.[5] The podiatrist managed to convince some of his patients to glance at some pages of the Zohar with some of De Leon's messages encoded on them. They, in turn, brought the Zohar to the attention of their clients and associates in the entertainment world. Fyvush's plan was more successful than he could have possibly imagined, and eventually Kabbalah centers around the country drew in huge crowds of the rich and famous, and those who hoped to become rich and famous. And not only was Fyvush part of the celebrity lifestyle, he was guiding it.

---

5. Britney Spears's sales in the Hasidic Brooklyn neighborhoods of Williamsburg and Borough Park skyrocketed after she wore one in a video.

One of his great skills was providing celebrities with the things that they felt they most needed, without asking them beforehand what that was. He attributed it to the kabbalistic art of *hakaros panim* when, in reality, it was simple common sense. He would tell aging but well-preserved sex symbols like Demi Moore and Madonna that what they really need are younger men in order to regain the youthful energy they lost by devoting so much of their youth to their careers. And he would tell younger men like Ashton Kutcher and Guy Ritchie that what they really need is to be with

This is the cover of the Rosh Hashanah card sent out by Fyvush Schpritzer in 2002 to the Kabbalah Center's biggest donors. In his hand is a Kabbalosmopolitan, a drink the center was pushing at the time made up of four parts light rum, two parts white crème de menthe, and one part Kabbalah water.

the stars of their teenage fantasies or they would be trapped in a state of perpetual adolescence. Everybody's getting laid, everybody's happy, and everybody's paying their dues to the Kabbalah Center. As for his own physical needs, Fyvush never needed to press sex on his celebrity followers; that was given freely enough by the celebrity wanna-bes who wanted to explore "the great carnal metaphors of Lurianic Kabbalah's innermost teachings," a phrase that doesn't actually mean anything, but works like Spanish fly on the Kabbalah Center chicks. All he asked for was money to continue performing his good works. And his velour wardrobe helped to foster his image as a man who had moved beyond material things. Fyvush outfitted Sean Combs with a bendl during his trial for involvement in a NYC club shooting. After his acquittal, he tried to give Fyvush some clothes from his "Sean John" collection. When Fyvush declined, Combs allegedly told his attorney, Benjamin Brafman, "Yo, it's one thing to keep it real, but wearing velour? Man, that's just meshugge." Like any good spiritual leader, he had all the answers. You got the part you wanted? That's the power of Kabbalah. You didn't get the part you wanted? That's the power of Kabbalah as well, making sure you get what you *need*. And this provides a positive contrast to Scientology, since Fyvush will at times point to such gems as *Battlefield Earth* and *Vanilla Sky* and ask his listeners if they thought that getting these parts was really the best thing for celebrity Scientologists John Travolta and Tom Cruise. Some may criticize the movement as nothing but charlatanry, and they may be right. But after decades in which Jewish celebrities poured out their money to assorted swamis, gurus, and new age Svengalis, there is something a little gratifying in seeing some of that gelt headed back in the other direction.

CHAPTER THIRTY-THREE

HERRING OF TRUTH

Rabbi Chaim Schnitzelbaum surveyed his domain. After years of operating out of a decrepit tenement in Williamsburg, his window staring out at a brick wall, he had finally engineered the move of Edas Yisroel, the most prominent ultra-orthodox organization in America, into a Financial District office space befitting its prestige. Yes, Edas Yisroel had come a long way since it was founded in 1912 as a response to the crisis in communal leadership facing Polish Jewry.[1] After arriving in America, it had taken space generously donated by Itzik Pfefferkorn, the herring king of Brooklyn. Unfortunately, that space was part of the Pfefferkorn Herring Works, and even discounting the view, it was not exactly a delight for the senses. But all that was ancient history on that day in early 2000 as Rabbi Schnitzelbaum threw back the curtains and admired his view of—a wall. Not a brick wall, to be sure, but a wall nonetheless—over a hundred stories of wall, in fact, and behind it, another one-hundred-plus stories: the World Trade Center. All those years of dealing with poverty and herring meant nothing. Rabbi Schnitzelbaum knew that something had to be done.

His first stop was the Marionville Supermax Federal Penitentiary, where his brother-in-law Irving was the Jewish chaplain. Marionville was home to Aya bin Missiniu, one of the terrorists involved in the 1993 attack on the World Trade Center. Actually, he wasn't involved in the attack, per se, but he had done the catering, and

---

1. By the end of the nineteenth century, Polish Jewry had run out of impressive titles for its rabbis. Things had reached the point where there were some synagogues in which the number of officers, officers emeritus, and honorary officers outnumbered congregants, and still the rabbis kept coming. Thus it was decided that a new Orthodox organization had to be founded to create a new array of impressive positions.

that was good enough for both federal prosecutors and Rabbi Schnitzelbaum, who carried with him an attaché case full of Middle Eastern pastries. Irving was thus able to persuade Missiniu to provide some crucial information (it's amazing how vulnerable to bribery an epicurean Arab can be after a decade without baklava), and Rabbi Schnitzelbaum caught the first possible flight to the Middle East. It was a miserable experience—he was subjected to all manner of rudeness, abuse, and derision, but he soon left Israel, put on the "Deluxe Omar Sharif" outfit, which won him second prize at the 1969 Edas Yisroel Masquerade Ball,[2] and made his way to Egypt, where he caught a flight to Saudi Arabia, and from there, to Afghanistan.

To be sure, the Al-Qaeda jihadists he spoke to were a little suspicious, especially since "Omar" spoke Yiddish as opposed to Arabic. He told them this was the result of his years in the entertainment industry, and they were willing to accept this as yet more evidence of the pernicious effect the Great Satan had on the faithful. Despite their questions, he had a beard and funny hat, which certainly were points in his favor, and besides, they liked what he had to say. And let's face it—convincing Muslims to kill Americans isn't exactly like selling iceboxes to the Inuit. The 1983 truck bombing of the marine compound in Beirut was actually a response to a fairly simple question regarding whether or not that

> **Let's face it—convincing Muslims to kill Americans isn't exactly like selling iceboxes to the Inuit. The 1983 truck bombing of the marine compound in Beirut was actually a response to a fairly simple question regarding whether or not that day's official celebration of Jamie Farr's birthday meant that alternate-side parking rules were suspended.**

---

2. It was always a sore point for Rabbi Schnitzelbaum that first prize went to a rival rabbi who came dressed in full leather, gay biker finery. People thought he was dressed as a reform rabbi (at least that's how they envisioned reform rabbis); turned out he was just really secretly a gay biker.

After this picture was found on the body of a high-ranking Al Qaeda leader killed in Afghanistan, Omar Sharif was taken into custody by French Intelligence. They eventually released him after he accounted for his whereabouts at the time the photo was taken, and did an impersonation of Maurice Chevalier singing "Thank Heaven for Little Girls."

day's official celebration of Jamie Farr's birthday meant that alternate-side parking rules were suspended. Certainly, his plan seemed more audacious than their scheme for Al-Qaeda's operatives to simultaneously commandeer Kmarts across the country and turn on all the blue lights in all the aisles at the same time, thereby leading to a complete collapse of the American economy. But this business about the World Trade Center sounded good, too. Without further debate (the All-You-Can-Eat Couscous Bar at Nasrullah's Falafel Hut was only going to be open for another half hour), the plan was adopted.

Back in the States, the rabbi set up operatives in various flight schools around the country, and to keep the FBI from getting suspicious of spikes in attendance, other Al-Qaeda operatives were sent to cosmetology school and clown college. When they needed money for books, he gave it to them. When they needed tuxedos for the flight school formal, he paid for them. He did draw the line when ringleader Mohammed Atta asked for "a totally bitchin' Trans Am," but other than that, he funded and organized the whole operation. All this was paid for with funds allotted for a fictitious Bernard Manischewitz Vocational High School for the Training of Kosher Food Professionals that Rabbi Schnitzelbaum had fraudulently set up.

When they needed money for books, he gave it to them. When they needed tuxedos for the flight school formal, he paid for them. He did draw the line when ringleader Mohammed Atta asked for "a totally bitchin' Trans Am," but other than that, he funded and organized the whole operation.

When word reached him that the training was complete, the rabbi shifted his attention to the Jews who would have to be kept away from the WTC that day. He called the Mossad, telling them he was planning a big appeal drive for the Jewish National Fund, and wanted the home addresses of all the Jews in the World Trade Center. The Mossad, of course, after denying that it was the

Mossad, also denied that such a list existed, and two hours later, the rabbi found the list wrapped around an unsolicited pastrami on rye delivered by a local kosher deli. Unable to call the four thousand names on his list and tell them directly not to come, Rabbi Schnitzelbaum had to put the Omar Sharif costume back on and put to use his teenage acting experience as leading man in Camp Hiawatha's production of *Viva Zapata*.[3] During the first week of September, he visited countless Jewish communities in the greater New York area, dressed as an Arab and dropping ominous warnings to avoid the city in the week to come. On the Upper West Side, he was a cabbie, muttering angry imprecations and gesturing violently at the towers. In Borough Park, he was a customer in a grocery store thankful for being permitted to skip to the front of the line and offering his benefactor a grateful word of advice. In a Forest Hills travel agency, he was a panic-stricken, would-be traveler desperate to get a flight out of the city before Tuesday. By the end of the week, if there was a Jew who hadn't heard from *someone* that he/she should avoid Lower Manhattan, it certainly wasn't for lack of effort on the rabbi's part.

On the morning of September 11, despite a last-minute snafu when one of the Boston-area terrorists almost refused to board the plane because they told him that the special Muslim dietary meal he'd ordered wasn't available, the plan went off without a hitch. That day, the offices of Edas Yisroel were empty, the employees all at home observing "Rosh Rosh Hashanah," a new holiday that Rabbi Schnitzelbaum just decided to "try out" that Tuesday. By the time they went back to the office the next week, the WTC was down, almost all the witnesses who could connect him to the attack were dead, and Rabbi Schnitzelbaum had his breathtaking view of... New Jersey. For now.

---

3. At one point, he was actually in a Manhattan hotel at the same time as the real Omar Sharif, leading to a brief episode of Patty Duke–esque hijinks.

ACKNOWLEDGMENTS

The authors of this book would like to thank Andy McNicol and Jay Mandel at the William Morris Agency for not blinking an eye when we told them we planned to take "a humorous look at Jewish conspiracies." We would also like to acknowledge the work of our lawyer, Jaime Wolf of Pelosi, Wolf, Effron & Spates LLP, our illustrators, Allan Mietla, Jesse Brown, Cliff Mott, and Seth Olenick, and our editor, Elizabeth Beier, at St. Martin's Press, for believing in us much more than any of our Hebrew and day school teachers ever did, for understanding that there's more than one legitimate way to treat serious subjects, and for fulfilling her promise not to put a Star of David on the cover of this book. We would like to thank Jennifer Bleyer and the editors of *Heeb* magazine for revealing the myriad of Jewish identities that exist outside mainstream conceptions. Finally, we would like to thank the Jews for going through the last couple of thousand years and still being able to laugh about it all.

INDEX